Eat to Beat
Cholesterol

Nicole Senior & Veronica Cuskelly

NEW
HOLLAND

About the authors

Nicole Senior is an Accredited Practising Dietitian (APD) and nutritionist (AN) with a passion for talking about the art and science of food in language everyone understands. Nicole loves to sort through the evidence, cut through the clutter and provide effective and do-able solutions that promote wellbeing as well as honour the joy of food, cooking and eating.

Veronica Cuskelly is a freelance food consultant, home economist and an award-winning recipe writer. She has been developing and writing creative recipes for over twenty years and has written several cholesterol-lowering cookbooks. Veronica believes cooking and sharing great tasting food that is good for your heart increases the pleasure of eating.

Acknowledgements

Books just don't happen. This book would not have been possible without help from many people who were generous both with their time and their expertise. In particular, we would like to thank the following dietitians for their help with everything from sourcing research papers and photographs to providing constructive feedback: Andrea Mortenson, Barbara Eden, Bill Shrapnel, Caitlin Reid, Claire Emmanuel, Dr Susanna Holt, Jacinta Orr, Lisa Yates, Trish Griffiths, Meaghan Ramsey and Megan Cobcroft. We are very grateful to Professor Jennie Brand-Miller and Professor Sandra Capra for their invaluable assistance. We are grateful to our publisher Fiona Schultz for giving us the opportunity to write this book and for her faith in us, Lliane Clarke our editor, for bringing this book to life, Graeme Gilles for teh photography, and Amanda Biffin and Vicki Liley for their food styling and assistance in food preparation, and Amanda Biffin for her food styling. And without our colleague Philippa Sandall we wouldn't have written this book together at all. Thank you for your encouragement and editorial expertise from day one.

From Nicole: Thank you to the wonderfully talented Veronica Cuskelly, whose magic has made all the nutrition theory come alive to tempt the senses in her fabulous recipes. Your enthusiasm, positivity and expertise are so appreciated. A thousand thanks go to my husband Liam for his support and understanding during all the lost weekends buried in research and writing. Also to my family and friends for their unending faith, and to all my clients, family and friends whose high cholesterol inspired me to take action.

From Veronica: Nicole's quirky, energetic writing style made me realise from the outset that this was going to be a nutrition book with a difference. Her dedication and commitment to good nutrition being all about deliciously tasting food and expert nutritional guidelines for recipes made the journey of this book evolving a great joy. A huge thank you to my always eager and available recipe tasters, for tasting and critiquing the recipes during development and to my family and friends for always hastily accepting invitations to enjoy my culinary creations.

Contents

Part 3

Eat to beat cholesterol in your kitchen 117

Part 4

Eating plan to beat cholesterol 252

Appendices

Introduction

Heart-friendly food is good for the whole family

Food really is the best medicine, yet we live in a world where healthy food is not always the easiest choice, and the cost of drugs to lower cholesterol and reduce heart disease risk are huge. An increasing number of children are overweight and have high cholesterol, placing them at greater risk of heart disease as adults. The evidence is good for the protection afforded by heart-friendly foods and eating patterns. Physical activity and a healthy diet are as potent as any drug to promote heart health, and form part of a total package of wellness that has many other benefits for the individual and the community. Our approach will look after your whole body, not just the heart, and can help you lose a little weight as well. We wrote this book to tip the balance towards healthy food, and hopefully in a small way make a difference to the alarming and devastating statistics of heart disease. Food is nature's gift for us all to enjoy, and good food can help us be happy and well. We hope this sensible, practical and accurate information about enjoyable eating for a healthy heart will help make healthy living a reality for you and yours.

How to use this book

In Part 1: You and your heart, we set out the facts about heart disease and why it's so important to make change for the better. We explain why lowering cholesterol, managing your weight and being physically active are so important.

In Part 2: Say hello to heart-friendly foods, you will discover the truly delicious world of heart-friendly foods—what you need to know about them and how much you need to eat.

Part 3: Eat to beat cholesterol in your kitchen, is the recipe section, cooking tips, shopping lists and delicious recipes for breakfast and brunch, light meals, main meals, desserts and snacks—all with nutritional information per serve. And to make it easy we have included lots of 'Quickies'—fast and easy ideas for including these super heart foods in your daily diet.

In Part 4: Eating plan to beat cholesterol, we take a more detailed look at which cholesterol-beating foods you need to eat and how much for guaranteed cholesterol lowering results.

Most of all we hope you enjoy learning about the healing and protective powers of food, as well as the fun and satisfaction of preparing heart-healthy meals, snacks and desserts.

—Nicole Senior & Veronica Cuskelly

Part 1

You and your heart

1: Why focus on cholesterol?

By lowering your blood cholesterol, especially the bad LDL type, you can make a real difference to your long-term health and wellbeing.

High blood cholesterol increases your chances of having a heart attack. Cardiovascular disease (including heart attack and stroke) is a global problem, wiping out 17 million people every year. It remains the biggest killer in affluent nations such as Britain, Europe, Canada, the USA, Australia and New Zealand. The higher your cholesterol, the greater your cardiovascular risk.

The heart is the body's engine room, nourishing every organ, muscle, nerve and bone with oxygen and nutrient-rich blood. So, look after your heart and you can spend more time doing the things you enjoy, be able to fully participate in life with no restrictions, be around to enjoy your children and grandchildren, and live to see more great places and people. We have written this book to help you beat cholesterol by eating better and moving more.

Facing the facts

1. Cholesterol is a common and growing problem.

Rates of high cholesterol in adults

UK: 60% (total cholesterol above 5.0)

USA: 33.5% (LDL cholesterol above target for individual risk level)

Canada: 41% (total cholesterol 5.2 or above)

Australia: 50% (total cholesterol 5.5 or more)

New Zealand: 60% (total cholesterol 5.2 or above)

2. Age is no barrier.
It doesn't just affect older people. We see signs of heart disease (fatty streaks in arteries) in children and teenagers, especially if they are obese. As children learn what and how to eat from their parents, heart-healthy eating starts with family meals.

The World Health Organisation says over 60 per cent of coronary heart disease in developed countries is due to cholesterol levels in excess of 3.8mmol/L (or mg/dL, see page 16).

3. The lower your cholesterol level, the lower your risk of heart disease.

How do we know this? One of the best known, long-term scientific studies of heart disease and lifestyle is the Framingham Heart Study, based in Massachusetts, in the USA. It started in 1948 when researchers recruited 5000 people and followed them and their families over three generations, assessing their health, eating habits and activity levels every two years. From all the data collected we now know that the major risk factors for cardiovascular disease are:

- high blood cholesterol, high triglycerides and low levels of the good HDL cholesterol
- high blood pressure
- smoking
- obesity
- diabetes
- physical inactivity

as well as risk factors like your age and gender and having a family history of heart disease. Although you can't change your age or family history, you can take control of your cholesterol, especially the bad LDL type (see page 15).

Framingham risk tables predict that lowering LDL cholesterol by 20 per cent reduces cardiovascular risk by about 25 per cent over five years.

Since then, the INTERHEART study of almost 30,000 people across 52 countries estimated 45 per cent of heart attacks in western Europe are due to abnormal blood lipids (such as high cholesterol)—and people with abnormal blood lipids are three times more likely to have a heart attack than those with normal lipids.

How low do you go?

So you've had your cholesterol tested and your doctor says its fine; do you still need this book? Yes. The lower your cholesterol level, the lower your risk of heart disease—even if your total cholesterol level is within the 'acceptable range' (and we know recommendations vary between countries). Heart-friendly foods are good for everyone and can prevent cholesterol becoming a problem in the future. Research has shown that eating a diet rich in heart-friendly foods and moving a bit more can lower cholesterol without the side effects of drugs.

Heart-friendly foods are a powerful ally in the fight against cholesterol

Your supermarket and fresh produce market shelves are piled high with heart-friendly foods, so you won't find eating this way difficult to achieve, and it shouldn't add to your grocery bills. Fresh vegetables, fruits, fish, nuts, seeds, lean meats and low-fat dairy foods all the way through to wholegrain breads, high-fibre cereals, low-fat milk, and healthy oil-based spreads enriched with plant sterols. And don't forget your everyday cup of tea! Heart-friendly foods are within your reach.

2: The heart of the matter

Cardiovascular disease is still the biggest killer of both men and women. In short, the way we live is causing a large number of us to become sick, disabled or die before our time.

There is a lot we can do

So what's the solution? Is there anything we can do? The answer is a resounding yes! The majority of heart disease is preventable. The solution lies in the food on our plates, and the miles on our dials. High blood cholesterol and the risk of heart disease can be reduced by enjoying a healthy combination of heart-friendly foods and getting moving.

Prevention is better

For those who have already had a heart attack, it is possible to substantially reduce the risk of having another one by making lifestyle changes; but, of course, preventing heart attacks in the first place is the best result of all.

Having a family history of heart disease increases your risk of developing it; however, although you can't change your family or your genes, you can change your lifestyle. You can significantly reduce your risk by taking control of the way you eat and the way you live. Healthy living doesn't mean boring food and punishing gym workouts! It's about enjoying more heart-friendly foods like vegetables, wholegrains, fruits, fish, nuts and healthy oils, and being more active on a daily basis, such as walking more.

What is heart disease?

Cardiovascular disease (CVD) is the collective term for hardened arteries and blocked blood vessels that cause heart attacks and strokes. Heart attacks are a large part of the CVD problem and are the end result of blockages in the arteries nourishing the heart—called coronary heart disease (CHD). These vital blood vessels become narrowed and then eventually blocked in a process called atherosclerosis (hardening of the arteries).

How to look after your heart

The best chance of keeping your heart healthy is to work on reducing or removing the risk factors you can change. Taking control of your lifestyle can increase the length and quality of your life. And in a lucky coincidence, changing your lifestyle for the better also improves your general wellbeing and reduces your risk of other serious diseases.

1. Talk to your doctor about a CVD risk assessment.
2. If you smoke, get help to quit.
3. Keep tabs on your cholesterol levels over time.
4. Control your blood pressure.
5. Enjoy a healthy diet low in saturated fat and salt, with healthy oils and plenty of heart-friendly foods.
6. Put together at least 30 minutes of moderate physical activity every day.
7. Maintain a healthy weight and waist (lose weight sensibly if you need to).
8. If you have diabetes, maintain good blood glucose control.
9. If you drink alcohol, do so in moderation.
10. Actively manage stress.

What is atherosclerosis?

Atherosclerosis is a complex process. Put simply, the hardening of blood vessels occurs because of a build-up of fat, cholesterol and other substances inside blood vessels. It is the bad LDL form of cholesterol that is mostly to blame. What makes things worse is LDL cholesterol undergoes oxidation—a process similar to metal rusting if left out in the weather. This build-up of oxidised LDL then causes inflammation as the body tries to defend itself—similar to the redness and swelling when you get a splinter in your finger. The end result is a hardened and inflamed 'plaque', which can make the artery narrow and block it completely— especially if a blood clot gets stuck—causing a heart attack (myocardial infarction, or MI).

What are the main risk factors for heart disease?

There is no one cause of heart disease, rather factors that if present together increase the chance of atherosclerosis and heart attack. Below are the risk factors— the more you have, the higher your risk. Some you can't change, but there are many you can.

Preventable risk factors	Unavoidable risk factors
Tobacco smoking	Being older
High blood pressure	Being male
High blood cholesterol	Being from a higher risk ethnic background, eg, African-American, Hispanic, Maori or Pacific Islander, Aboriginal, South Asian or from the Indian subcontinent
Insufficient physical activity	
Overweight and obesity	
Poor nutrition	
Heavy alcohol use	
Diabetes and pre-diabetes	
Stress and depression	

Snapshot—CVD risk factors

The World Health Organisation (WHO) says:

- 8 per cent of all disease burden in developed countries is caused by high cholesterol, and over 60 per cent of coronary heart disease is due to high blood cholesterol levels.
- Over 7 per cent of all disease burden in developed countries is caused by overweight and obesity, and one-third of coronary heart disease is caused by it. Globally, there are 1 billion adults who are overweight or obese (BMI 25 or over): levels vary from 5 per cent in China to 75 per cent in Samoa but range between 50–60 per cent in affluent nations such as UK, Australia, Canada, New Zealand and USA.
- 11 per cent of the disease burden in developed countries is caused by raised blood pressure, and 50 per cent of coronary heart disease and 75 per cent of stroke is due to systolic blood pressures over 115 (systolic is the top number of a blood pressure reading).
- The total number of people with diabetes globally is described as an epidemic and projected to rise from 171 million in 2000 to 366 million in 2030.
- Lack of physical activity is increasingly common. Many of us living in affluent nations don't move our bodies enough to stay healthy. Our jobs and our leisure time pursuits are mostly sedentary.
- The INTERHEART study of almost 30,000 people over 52 countries estimated: 63 per cent of heart attacks in western Europe were due to abdominal obesity (a large waist) and those with big bellies had twice the risk of having a heart attack; and 15 per cent of heart attacks in western Europe are due to diagnosed diabetes (and many people remain undiagnosed).

Women and heart disease: the menopause connection

Heart disease is still the biggest killer of women in the Western world. Heart disease kills four times more women than breast cancer. Women share the same risky levels of blood cholesterol, blood pressure, overweight and physical activity as men, but female hormones offer some protection up until menopause. After menopause, however, all the trouble starts, and heart disease really takes hold. Research from the USA shows women don't do as well as men after a heart attack and are more likely to have a second heart attack, become disabled or die early. Because women often have the role of caring for others in the family, it is vital they take control of their own health for a long and healthy life.

Assessing your risk

After the age of 45 years (men) and 55 years (women), you must have your level of CVD risk assessed by your doctor. If you have diabetes, you already know that you have risk factors. If you're from a higher risk ethnic group, you need to start 10 years younger (ie, 35 for men and 45 for women).

High risk—what now?

The aim is to reduce your absolute risk. Your doctor will recommend you improve your lifestyle no matter what your risk level, and this means enjoying a heart-friendly diet, regular physical activity and managing stress. If you are at high risk, your doctor will recommend other forms of therapy such as medication and more regular follow-ups.

Being treated with medication to lower your CVD risk is no reason to give up on heart-healthy eating. Diet and medication work together to provide additional benefits.

For the children

Childhood obesity is considered by the World Health Organisation to be the most serious health challenge of the 21st century. Unfortunately children are likely to carry their excess weight into adulthood: so-called 'puppy fat' does not go away. It burdens children with an increased risk of chronic disease, such as cardiovascular disease and type 2 diabetes, as adults. More and more children are being diagnosed with high cholesterol, especially if they are overweight or obese. The best solution is getting the whole family into healthier eating habits and a more active lifestyle. Heart-friendly foods are good for everyone and have an important role in preventing overweight, obesity and high cholesterol as well as managing it once it occurs. The whole family can eat to beat cholesterol.

What is the metabolic syndrome?

The metabolic syndrome (also known as syndrome X) is the description given to the unlucky coincidence of having several risk factors for disease at the same time. Having metabolic syndrome dramatically increases the risk of CVD, as well as the risk of developing type 2 diabetes.

A key feature of the metabolic syndrome is having insulin (a hormone) that doesn't work effectively, a condition called insulin resistance.

You have the metabolic syndrome if you have:

- Too much fat around your middle. Waist circumference (European, East Mediterranean, Sub-Saharan African): 94cm or more for men or 80cm or more for women. Waist circumference (South Asian, Ethnic Central and South American): 90cm or more for men and 80cm or more for women.

Plus any two of the following:

- High triglycerides more than 1.7mmol/L (150mg/dL), or treatment for this.
- Low HDL (good) cholesterol less than 1.03mmol/L (40mg/dL) for men and less than 1.29mmol/L (50mg/dL) in women, or treatment for this.
- High blood pressure: Systolic BP 130 or more and Diastolic BP 85 or more, or treatment of previously diagnosed high blood pressure.
- Raised fasting blood glucose level more than 5.6mmol/L (100mg/dL), or previously diagnosed type 2 diabetes.

If you have the metabolic syndrome, you need to focus on reducing the impact by losing weight, lowering your triglyceride levels and blood pressure, and increasing your HDL levels. A heart-friendly diet and being more active will help enormously.

What is insulin resistance?

Insulin resistance is the condition where insulin does not work effectively. Insulin normally helps the body to use the glucose circulating in your bloodstream after you have eaten for energy by helping it to enter cells. In a state of insulin resistance, less glucose can get into cells and more stays in the blood. The body works harder to compensate by producing more insulin, but to no avail. Having high insulin levels significantly increases the risk of heart disease, and encourages weight gain.

High blood glucose levels increases CVD risk

In another example of the too-close-for-comfort association between blood glucose level and heart disease, researchers from the US followed over 1000 adults over 8–10 years and found those with higher long-term blood glucose levels (measured as HbA1c)—even without diabetes—had almost double the risk of heart disease. The risk of having thickened (hardened) arteries measured by ultrasound was two and a half times higher in those with the highest HbA1c than those with the lowest. The association between HbA1c and CVD risk has also been found in similar studies in Europe.

Strategies for lowering blood glucose levels, such as physical activity, losing weight and enjoying a low GI diet also reduce the risk of heart disease.

Stress is bad for your heart

Although instinctively we have known that stress is bad, scientific evidence has emerged quite recently supporting stress as a significant risk factor for heart disease. Chronic anxiety, depression and anger are widely recognised as raising the risk of heart attack. 'Stress' is a broad term, but we all instinctively know what it means. Constant work stress, social isolation, anxiety, depression and upsetting events all contribute to an increased risk of heart disease. Being a type A personality is also a risk, typified by anxiety and hostility.

Becoming aware of the signs of stress and actively managing personal triggers is an important component of good health.

The physiological response to stress was originally quite helpful. The so called fight or flight response—an adrenalin rush, faster heartbeat and the release of stored fuel into the bloodstream—allowed us to survive threats by fighting back or running away quickly. The problem is, nowadays the threats are more mental than physical but our body still reacts the same. Put simply, our body is ready to run but has nowhere to go, and so it turns in on itself and causes damage.

Stress can directly impact on the heart by increasing blood pressure and the chance of blood clots, but it can also influence our behaviour. During stressful times we tend to focus on the short term and live 'hand-to-mouth' rather than think about what we're doing. For many people this means making less healthy food choices, overeating and not making time for exercise.

Stress-busters
- Eat a variety of nutritious foods regularly through the day.
- Take time out for movement or exercise.
- Avoid too much caffeine and alcohol.
- Maintain a good sleep routine.
- Talk to others—share your thoughts and worries.
- Schedule some 'down time' to do nothing much but reflect and daydream.
- Take up yoga, or practise meditation.
- Breathe deeply and slowly into the belly.
- Build some fun into your day.
- Practise self-nurturing activities such as massage or a bath.
- Practise saying 'no' to unreasonable demands.
- Practise positive thinking.

3: The cholesterol connection

Although you can't change your age or your family history, you can take control of your cholesterol—especially the bad LDL type.

What is cholesterol?

Cholesterol is a fatty, waxy substance essential to life. It's found naturally inside our bodies, and has a number of useful purposes. It is used as a structural component in cell membranes, as a raw material to make sex hormones, vitamin D, and bile that helps digest fats. Most cholesterol is made in the liver, but we can also obtain cholesterol from food. Cholesterol and other fats in the blood are collectively known as blood lipids, and when they are high the medical term is hyperlipidaemia.

Why the bad reputation?

Cholesterol becomes a problem when there's too much of it. High levels of blood cholesterol are a risk factor for heart disease, but they also spell trouble for blood vessels elsewhere in the body, such as in the brain leading to stroke, and in the legs leading to peripheral vascular disease. High cholesterol levels are also linked with diabetes and high blood pressure. Some types of cholesterol are worse than others.

The different types of cholesterol

Cholesterol is transported around the body attached to proteins in particles called lipoproteins. Different lipoproteins have different effects on heart disease risk. The main type to worry about is Low Density Lipoprotein, or LDL cholesterol—remember 'L' for lousy. This is the bad type of cholesterol whose main purpose is to take cholesterol from the liver to be deposited in blood vessels, become oxidised, and then cause atherosclerosis (hardening of the arteries). High levels of LDL spell trouble for the heart.

There is a good type of cholesterol called High Density Lipoprotein, or HDL cholesterol—remember 'H' for happy. HDL cholesterol is good because it drags cholesterol back from the blood vessels into the liver, and out of harm's way.

There are several other lesser known types of lipoprotein being studied to more accurately predict a person's level of risk. Higher levels of Very Low Density Lipoproteins (VLDL), Intermediate Density Lipoproteins (IDL), and Lipoprotein-a (Lp(a)), and apolipoprotein-B (apoB) are known to be bad news for the heart, as is C-Reactive protein (CRP), which is a marker for inflammation.

Summary of cholesterol types

LDL cholesterol—get it down

HDL cholesterol—keep it up

Triglycerides—get it down

Why your triglycerides matter

There are other fats in the blood called triglycerides, and, as well as LDL cholesterol, these are a problem in excess. Triglycerides are usually measured along with cholesterol in blood tests, and listed as 'TG'. High levels of triglycerides are converted to bad cholesterol in the liver, and are often elevated if you are overweight or have type 2 diabetes.

Components of a lipid profile (cholesterol) blood test

- Total cholesterol
- Triglycerides
- LDL cholesterol
- HDL cholesterol
- Total cholesterol/HDL ratio

Except for HDL cholesterol, lower is better.

The total/HDL ratio gives you and your doctor an idea of the balance of power in your body between the bad cholesterol and the good HDL cholesterol. A lower ratio number is better —total/HDL ratio 4.5 or below—because this reflects higher good HDL levels.

Technical jargon explained

Cholesterol is measured in millimoles per litre of blood and abbreviated to mmol/L. A millimole is a chemical unit of measurement used in Europe, Australia and New Zealand. In the USA, cholesterol is measured in milligrams per decilitre, abbreviated as mg/dL.

What should my cholesterol be?

The lower your cholesterol level, the better. While there are some small differences in target cholesterol levels between countries, there is agreement that high cholesterol is a major risk factor and needs to be controlled.

Generally speaking, total cholesterol level should be 5.0mmol/L (200mg/dL) or less.

It is also agreed that target cholesterol levels should be lower for people already at risk of cardiovascular disease —that is, people who have other risk factors, such as obesity, diabetes or high blood pressure. What is also clear is that the LDL-cholesterol component is the most important type of cholesterol to reduce.

For those already at risk, total cholesterol level should be 4.0mmol/L (150mg/dL) or less. The LDL cholesterol should be less than 2.0 mmol/ (75mg/dL).

HDL-cholesterol is actually helpful and higher levels are beneficial. A good target to aim for is 1.0mmol/L (40mg/dL) or more. The right diet—especially eating enough healthy fats— and an active lifestyle can maintain good HDL-cholesterol levels while reducing harmful LDL-cholesterol.

More information in addition to a cholesterol level is needed to determine your absolute risk of heart disease. Talk to your doctor.

What makes cholesterol high?

There are a number of factors that can increase blood cholesterol levels. The most important factor is your family history. High cholesterol runs in families and you may be predisposed to high cholesterol because of your genes. Being male and getting older also increase the likelihood of having high cholesterol.

In terms of the factors within your control, diet is the most important. Eating too much saturated fat and not enough healthy fats increases blood cholesterol. Eating too much cholesterol-rich foods can also make things worse, but it is a relatively small effect compared with the impact of the proportion of fats in your diet. Eating unsaturated fats instead of saturated fats, and particularly polyunsaturated fats, lowers blood cholesterol.

Target total cholesterol levels around the world

	Community target	Target for those already at risk
USA	less than 5.1mmol/L (200mg/dL)	LDL less than 2.5 (100mg/dL)
UK, Europe, Canada	less than 5.0	LDL less than 2.0
Australia	less than 5.5	less than 4.0 (LDL less than 2.5)

4: Avoiding heart break

The way to a man's heart is through his stomach. In the case of cholesterol and heart health, this can be taken literally! By helping him reduce the size of his stomach — making his waist measurement smaller — his heart will be healthier. And the same goes for women.

If you're above your ideal weight, losing some weight will lower your cholesterol and reduce your risk of heart disease.

A day doesn't go by where we don't hear about the 'obesity epidemic'. We used to think that body fat just sat there and didn't do much but now we know that fat tissue (called adipose) is quite active, and in an undesirable way. Being overweight or obese:

- increases cholesterol levels
- raises blood pressure
- increases the risk of type 2 diabetes
- increases the risk of heart disease

Carrying excess weight also creates inflammation in the body and inflammation is involved in hardening of the arteries, as well as many other chronic diseases.

Am I overweight?

Overweight is defined as having a body mass index (BMI) of 25 or higher. The BMI is a reliable indicator of body fat levels for most people, but it's a good idea to talk with your doctor or dietitian for an individual assessment.

Drawbacks of the BMI

The BMI does not accurately determine body fat levels in very muscle-bound sportspeople because it cannot distinguish whether the weight is fat or muscle. It's not that great for the elderly who have lost height and muscle either.

Some ethnic groups have different BMI classifications because they are heavier in build (eg, Maori and Pacific Islanders), or they have more body fat at a lower weight (eg, South East Asians). The BMI for overweight in Maori and Pacific Islanders is 26, and 32 for obesity.

What is my BMI?

There are plenty of websites and smart phone apps that will calculate your BMI for you—all you need is your height and weight. To calculate it yourself divide your weight in kilograms by your height in metres squared. For example, 90kg divided by 1.8m squared (3.24) is a BMI of 27.8. A BMI over 25 is classified as overweight, and a BMI over 30 is classified as obese.

Waist matters

Where you store fat on your body is important for heart disease risk. Fat around the middle is bad news for the heart. This is often expressed in the simple terms 'apple-shaped' or 'pear-shaped', and apple-shaped people have the highest heart disease risk.

Measuring around your waist is a fairly reliable indicator of risky fat called central or abdominal obesity. If you have a higher waist than the targets in the table opposite, you have central obesity and it's time to take action for waist reduction. Another indicator of being apple-shaped is when your waist measurement is the same or more than your hip measurement.

In general, a healthy waistline is less than 80cm for women and 94cm for men.

How to measure your waist

It's best to have someone do this for you.

1. Take a tape measure and measure around the narrowest point, the level of your navel, or the midway point between your bottom rib and your (forward-facing) hip bone (called the iliac crest).
2. Hold the tape snugly and measure after an out breath with a relaxed posture, with the arms by your side.

There's no use in measuring your waist if your BMI is 35 or above as you are automatically at very high risk.

	Increased risk	Greatly increased risk
Men	more than 94cm (37 inches)	more than 102cm (40 inches)
Women	more than 80cm (31 inches)	more than 88cm (35 inches)

Body-fat scales

Bathroom scales are now available that can measure your percentage body fat through bio-impedance analysis. They work by passing a small electric current through your body and measuring the return current. These are not 100 per cent accurate, but close enough if you follow the instructions and weigh yourself at the same time of day each time. Although there are variations in recommended levels of body fat, acceptable levels for men are 8–25 per cent, and women 21–36 per cent.

Stop the spread!

We've all heard the expression 'middle-aged spread'—and unfortunately surveys support the idea that the battle of the bulge is slowly lost as we get older. The rates of overweight and obesity increase with age. Preventing weight gain as we age is a vital heart-protection strategy. It is much more difficult to lose weight than to prevent weight gain in the first place. Weight gain causes cholesterol and triglyceride levels to rise, and often blood glucose and insulin levels as well. It can also bring problems of low self-esteem, low motivation and can make exercising more difficult (not to mention requiring a new wardrobe).

Looks can be deceiving

It's not only people who look overweight who need to be concerned: some fat can hide out and still cause trouble. Professor Jimmy Bell coined these folk 'TOFIs': Thin Outside, Fat Inside. Sophisticated medical imaging machines have shown that thin people can still carry risky amounts of fat around their internal organs (visceral fat). A US study by the Mayo Clinic, which measured 6000 adults over a period of nine years, found 20 to 30 per cent of people fell into this thin-but-fat category. Even though they don't look overweight, people with 'metabolic obesity' are at greater risk of high cholesterol, heart disease, high blood pressure, stroke and diabetes. So how do you know if you're metabolically obese? Apart from the use of expensive imaging equipment, the easiest thing to do is to measure your waist.

What's the right diet to lose weight?

There is no one diet that's right for everyone. There are many different ways to put together a nutritionally adequate weight-loss diet. We all have different likes and dislikes, family food habits, meal routines and cooking skills—it's important that a weight loss diet suits you and your lifestyle so you can stick with it. The key thing to remember is not how many fats, carbs or proteins there are, but the number of kilojoules (calories) you are eating and whether you're getting your quota of heart-friendly foods. Extreme diets of any kind are not healthy. Let your common sense guide you towards moderation and avoid diets that eliminate or restrict whole food groups.

If you need some help to lose weight the best thing to do is make an appointment to see an Accredited Practising Dietitian (APD) or Registered Dietitian (RD) who can tailor a weight-loss eating plan to suit you and your lifestyle. Weight loss groups such as Weight Watchers can be helpful too if you need some support to stick with it.

The best way to lose weight is NOT on a low-fat or low-carb diet, but a nutritious and balanced LOW-ENERGY (low-kilojoule) diet.

Energy explained

The 'energy' in food is another word for kilojoules or calories, so a 'high-energy' food can be a good or a bad thing, depending on whether you're active enough to burn the energy during physical activity or exercise. Remember, unused food energy can be stored as body fat and can cause weight gain. To work out how many kilojoules you need, see page 252 (part 4: Eating plan to beat cholesterol).

Metabolism explained

You've probably heard people say that they can't lose weight because they have a slow metabolism. The word 'metabolism' means how much energy (kilojoules/calories) your body uses (or 'burns') each day to maintain itself. Our bodies constantly burn kilojoules to keep us going whether we are eating, sleeping, cleaning etc. Once the daily business of breathing, eating, moving and other activities are met, any unused or surplus kilojoules get stored, mostly in the form of body fat. This means that if you take in more kilojoules than you use, you will gain weight.

The speed at which your body burns those kilojoules is your metabolic rate. The higher your metabolic rate, the more food you need. The slower your metabolic rate, the greater the chance of weight gain. You can influence your metabolic rate by eating regularly, avoiding crash diets, increasing muscle and being physically active.

Weight gain is more likely to be due to an imbalance between food eaten and activity rather than a slow metabolism.

How much weight should I lose?

Just as there is no one diet to suit everyone, there is no right amount of weight to lose. For health benefits, losing just 5–10 per cent of your body weight makes a big difference to your heart disease risk factors such as cholesterol, blood pressure and blood glucose levels.

A realistic rate of weight loss is between 250g–1kg per week, with 1kg per week being more appropriate for people starting at a higher weight.

Losing 1–4cm from the waist per month in the short term with a 5 per cent reduction over a few months is a good goal.

It's perfectly normal (and in fact to be expected) to have weight loss plateaus. These occur because the body needs less energy at a lower weight. So think of the plateau as a sign post. To get off the plateau and continue to lose weight you need to do a little more (or a different type) of exercise and eat a little less food (kilojoules).

Even if you can't get down to the ideal BMI of less than 25 or your waist measurement into the target range, any weight or waist loss is beneficial. If you can't lose weight, preventing further weight gain is a good outcome for your heart.

Reassuring words

Some people are genetically programmed to be larger and the effort to slim down is unrealistic. If this is you, make the best of the cards you've been dealt and be as healthy as you can. Remember, healthy food and physical activity are protective for your heart.

You are better off being fat and enjoying a heart-healthy diet than being fat and eating badly.

The same goes for physical activity—you're better off being fat and fit, than a fat couch potato.

Thyroid alert

Having an under-active thyroid (hypothyroidism) slows the metabolism and makes weight loss very difficult, so have this checked by your doctor if you have been feeling particularly tired, lethargic, irritable, weak or if you have dry skin and hair, constipation or depression.

Forget low carb, go for low GI

We now know that being choosy about your carbohydrates (foods such as bread, rice, pasta, noodles, starchy vegetables and cereals) is just as important as being fussy about your fats. You need to choose nutritious low-GI and wholegrain sources and limit overly processed starchy foods. With carbohydrates, the key is the rate of carbohydrate digestion. And here slow is better. Foods with a low GI are slowly digested and absorbed into your bloodstream. Choosing quality carbs—the low-GI ones that produce only small fluctuations in your blood glucose and insulin levels—is the secret to long-term health, reducing your risk of heart disease and diabetes and sustainable weight loss.

What is the glycemic index (GI)?

Just as there are good fats and bad fats, we now know that not all carbohydrate foods are created equal. The GI is a tool to help you control fluctuations in your blood glucose levels by choosing the smart low-GI carbohydrates. Studies are showing that eating lots of high-GI carbohydrates tends to raise triglyceride levels. If you have high triglyceride levels, choosing low-GI foods is especially important. A low-GI diet appears to be protective against weight gain and heart disease and diabetes. The GI itself is simply a ranking of the immediate effect carbohydrates have on your blood glucose levels. Carbohydrates that break down quickly during digestion have a high GI and cause a rapid rise and decline in blood glucose. Carbohydrates that break down slowly, releasing glucose gradually into your bloodstream, have a low GI.

GI 55 or less is LOW
GI 56–69 is MEDIUM
GI 70 or more is HIGH

If you want to learn more about the glycemic index or check out the GI of your favourite carbohydrate foods, visit www.glycemicindex.com

Higher GI food	Lower GI alternatives
White bread	Multigrain bread
Orange-flavoured soft drink	Orange juice, unsweetened
Jelly beans	Dried apricots
Rice cracker	Rye crispbread
Cornflake cereal	Muesli
Puffed rice cereal	Oat porridge

Many wholegrain foods such as barley, traditional oats and grainy breads also have a low GI. This not only helps you control your blood glucose and insulin levels (vital if you have diabetes or pre-diabetes), but plays a useful role in your diet if you need to lose weight as these foods will keep you feeling fuller for longer.

Leading heart health organisations around the world encourage you to eat more heart-healthy wholegrains (see chapter 10, page 57).

Forget fat-free, go for good fats

In the case of fats, you need to ensure you're eating enough of the healthy fats to ensure you get adequate amounts of essential fatty acids (omega-3 and 6) and fat-soluble vitamins A, E and D. Healthy fats are also essential to lower cholesterol. So it's out with the fatty meats, full-cream dairy products, biscuits, cakes and pastries and in with the unsaturated vegetable oils and spreads, oily fish, nuts, seeds and avocado. You need at least 1½ tablespoons of healthy oils and spreads each day to get your quota and this amount is fine in a weight loss diet (see Eating plan to beat cholesterol on page 252).

A consensus from the world's most eminent nutrition researchers in the field of diet and cardiovascular disease, including Arne Astrup, Walt Willet and Frank Hu, published in the American Journal of Clinical Nutrition concluded that replacing saturated fat with polyunsaturated fat reduces LDL cholesterol and the risk of cardiovascular disease but the effect of replacing saturated fat with carbohydrate shows no benefit. In other words, eat fat but make sure it's the right type.

Downsize portions

Portion sizes have increased dramatically over the years and this has added to our weight woes. We must get used to smaller portions (except for vegetables which we should eat more). In short, we must get used to eating less. You will find this difficult at first—however, you will get used to being satisfied without needing to be stuffed full. Try using smaller sized plates, order an starter-sized meal at a restaurant, share a dessert or skip the bread basket.

Filling foods can help here as well, either through providing protein, low-GI carbohydrates or bulk (as in high-fibre foods such as vegetables and legumes). Get your protein satisfaction from lean meat, chicken or fish in your meals, and ensure you get your fill by ensuring you have plenty of vegetables or salad on your plate.

Retrain your appetite

To eat less and lose weight, some appetite re-training may be helpful. Many of us have tuned out from our natural hunger and satisfaction signals. This may be because we were taught as children to finish whatever is on our plate, we may be eating for emotional reasons, we may be in the habit of eating too quickly, or we're just generally stressed out and not fully 'present' when we eat. Being thirsty can masquerade as hunger as well, so ensure you drink around 2 litres (4 pints) of fluid a day (that doesn't mean sweetened drinks). Water is the best drink.

A good way to tune back in to your natural signals is to keep a food and hunger diary. Remember, it's okay to overeat occasionally, just not regularly. It's ideal to be mostly 3s and 4s on the hunger and appetite scale. Wait ten minutes after finishing food before rating how you feel.

Hunger and appetite scale
1 = uncomfortably full
2 = very full
3 = satisfied
4 = hungry
5 = very hungry
6 = extremely hungry

Fitting more into less

Cutting back on kilojoules to lose weight means you need to focus on nutritious foods to ensure your nutritional needs are met. This means eating more nutrient dense foods rather than energy dense and nutrient poor foods.

To do this you need to 'trim' extras from your diet and focus on heart-friendly foods such as vegetables, wholegrains, legumes, fruits, lean meats, low-fat dairy foods, healthy oils, nuts and seeds. Of course, being physically active is also important. You may find you can eat a little more once you are active on a regular basis.

Examples of nutrient dense foods and energy dense, nutrient poor foods

Nutrient dense foods EAT MORE	Energy dense, nutrient poor foods EAT LESS
Vegetables and legumes	Soft drinks
Wholegrains	Cakes and biscuits
Fruits	Confectionery
Lean meats	Cream
Fish	Pastry
Nuts and seeds	Savoury packet snacks

What about treats?

Treats are fine, but remember, that's what they are—treats. That means occasional. In fact, in order to stick with a weight loss diet and not create cravings that may lead to binges, it is important to allow yourself to enjoy some treat foods. The trick is to limit the quantity and frequency to still allow you to lose weight. See the eating plan on page 255 for an idea of how many treat foods (and the serving size) you can fit into a reduced-kilojoule eating plan. Of course, there are some people who stay right away from any treats, at least in the beginning stages of their weight loss diet.

Can I snack?

Choosing healthy snacks can be helpful for weight loss provided you're not eating more food than you need overall. Eating the same sized meals and adding snacks in—especially snacks high in kilojoules—and not being more active could actually result in weight gain. Having smaller meals and including nutritious foods between times can help control hunger and maintain more even blood glucose and energy levels.

Good snack choices are vegetables, fruit, wholegrain bread/crispbread, low-fat milk and yoghurt, nuts and seeds. Some people benefit from snacks while others do best on three meals a day. Listen to your body to determine how you function better.

Diet traps

Being overweight or obese can make you vulnerable to quick-fix diets, pills and potions but if something sounds too good to be true, it usually is. You owe it to yourself to enjoy good health and a variety of nutritious foods without breaking the bank or going to extreme measures. If you have tried many diets before without longterm results, then these diets have failed you and a fresh approach is needed.

5: Two steps to beat cholesterol

It's your turn to take control of your cholesterol. In this chapter we set out the steps to lowering your cholesterol and protecting your heart.

Step 1: Enjoy a heart-friendly diet

A heart-friendly diet harnesses the cholesterol-lowering abilities of heart-friendly foods. All these foods work in synergy to lower cholesterol, improve your heart health and optimise your wellbeing. In part 4 starting on page 252 we show you how you can put them together in an eating plan to beat cholesterol.

Food versus drugs to treat high cholesterol

A heart-healthy diet can produce similar cholesterol lowering results to statin medications without side effects and it provides added heart-health benefits. For example, statins can't lower blood pressure, cause weight and waist loss, lower blood glucose levels or reduce inflammation—all factors that can be influenced by diet. If medication is prescribed, a heart-healthy diet is still essential for the best health outcome. Our approach is optimal dietary therapy for lowering cholesterol levels and complements drug therapy if it is required.

Step 2: Move more

Increase your incidental activity by being active every day in as many ways as you can, such as taking the stairs rather than the lift or parking farther away from the shops. We know you've heard it all before, but you really have to do it. Find at least 30 minutes a day of moderate intensity physical activity such as walking or swimming. Doing more is even better. If your doctor says it's okay, also do some vigorous activity such as running or aerobics. In the chapter 'Move more' (page 29) we show you why being physically active can boost your health and wellbeing.

Top cholesterol beaters

- **Enjoy at least 6–8 teaspoons—30–45g (1–1½oz) a day—of added healthy fats, such as vegetable oils and margarines, both polyunsaturated and monounsaturated.**

  Getting your fats right is the first step of a cholesterol-lowering eating pattern. The golden rule is to get rid of saturated fats and replace them with healthy unsaturated fats—both monounsaturated and polyunsaturated—ensuring you include the essential omega-3 and omega-6 polyunsaturates that the body cannot make and must get from food. You can obtain healthy unsaturated fats in nuts, seeds, fish and even wholegrains, but the best sources are the oils you use in cooking and the spread you use on your bread. Good oils include canola, olive, mustard seed, macadamia nut, peanut, rice bran, safflower, sesame, sunflower, soybean and walnut oils and spreads made from these. See page 89 for further information on healthy fats and oils.

- **In these 6–8 teaspoons of healthy oils, include 5 teaspoons (25g/¾oz) a day of plant cholesterol-lowering margarine—that is, sufficient to provide 2g plant sterols.**

  Plant sterols are naturally occurring substances found in vegetable oils, nuts, seeds and grains that reduce cholesterol absorption from the gut and lower bad LDL cholesterol. Plant sterol-enriched spreads have been convincingly shown to lower blood cholesterol in scientific studies. Aim to use around 25g (¾oz) a day on bread, on sandwiches, on toast, in baking, or melted into vegetables. The result? You can lower your cholesterol by an average of 10 per cent! See page 89 for more information on healthy fats and oils.

- **Enjoy 1–2 handfuls (30–60g/1–2oz) of unsalted nuts.**

  Forget every bad thing you've heard about nuts! They're highly nutritious and packed full of heart-friendly nutrients such as unsaturated fats, plant protein, minerals, fibre and antioxidants. Enjoying 1–2 small handfuls of nuts a day has been shown to reduce the risk of heart disease and lower cholesterol—eat them either on their own or as part of a meal. Seeds are the nutrition powerhouse to grow a whole new plant and are great for you too. Nuts and seeds add flavour and texture and really dress up a stir-fry, salad, breakfast or dessert. See page 70 for more information.

- **Include foods rich in soluble (or viscous) fibre daily, such as oats, barley or psyllium-enriched cereals, eggplant (aubergine) and okra—or a soluble fibre supplement based on psyllium (isphagula), guar gum, inulin, wheat dextrin or methylcellulose.**

  Soluble fibre helps to lower cholesterol absorption from the digestive system and, as a result, reduces the cholesterol in the blood. It also slows down the absorption of glucose (sugar) into the bloodstream, which is another bonus for health. Aim for 10g soluble fibre a day or more. See page 46 and discover the fibre benefits in fruit.

- **Include foods containing soy protein daily (optimal target 25g/¾oz soy protein). Examples are tofu, soy milk, soy burgers, soy bread and breakfast cereal.**

  Soy protein has been shown in scientific studies to lower cholesterol, reduce cholesterol oxidation, lower triglycerides and blood pressure, increase (good) HDL cholesterol. The active ingredient is thought to be a type of phytochemicals they contain called isoflavones. Of course, they are also high in fibre and contain healthy unsaturated fats. Lean more about soy foods on page 67.

Top heart-friendly foods

- **Enjoy fish in at least two meals every week, preferably oily fish such as salmon, sardines, mackerel and tuna.**

  Fish, particularly oily fish, are true heart-friendly foods and this has been shown time and time again in scientific studies. The protective component is long-chain omega-3 polyunsaturated fats, among others. These biologically active fats have the ability to dramatically reduce the risk of death from heart attack by thinning the blood and preventing clots, as well as ensuring a smooth and regular heart beat. As well as eating fish, keep an eye out for foods with added omega-3. See page 77.

- **Include legumes (pulses), such as dried beans (eg, soy beans, kidney beans), chickpeas and lentils, in at least two meals a week (more is better).**

  Legumes are a cornerstone of the famously healthy Mediterranean diet. They are super-healthy with stacks of plant protein, cholesterol-lowering soluble fibre, vitamins, minerals and antioxidants. And they have a low GI and are cheap and highly versatile. Don't forget, the canned varieties save time in the kitchen—convenience plus! See page 64 to learn more about legumes.

- **Eat at least five serves (5 handfuls) of vegetables daily—a variety of colours and types, including green, red/purple/orange and white AND at least two serves (two average-sized pieces) of fruit daily (a variety of types, including citrus, berries and other fruits such as apples and pears).**

  Study after study has found vegetables are indeed nature's gifts for our health and longevity. The biggest vegetable eaters in the world also happen to be the healthiest.

Vegetables are rich sources of valuable and heart-friendly nutrients, such as vitamins, minerals, antioxidants and fibre, and all of this with few kilojoules (calories) attached. Enjoy at least five serves a day of a variety of colours and types to obtain your full quota of protection—and don't forget to enjoy them with a little healthy oil for great taste and to extract all their goodness. See page 36 for more information about vegetables.

A tenet of the famously healthy Mediterranean diet is 'no day without fruit' and this is great advice to really live by. Besides being deliciously sweet, refreshing and satisfying, fruit is packed full of protective vitamins and antioxidants as well as soluble fibre that lowers cholesterol. How can something that tastes so good be so good for you? Because this is the sweet treat nature intended for us to provide long-lasting energy to burn. See page 46.

- **Ensure half of your grain foods are wholegrain (at least 2 serves wholegrains daily): a serve is equal to two thin slices of bread, a bowl of wholegrain cereal or 1 cup cooked wholewheat pasta.**

  Wholegrains are a classic case of 'what is old is new again'. We've now realised that processing our grains makes them less nutritious and if we process them less they can deliver a hefty dose of heart protection. Wholegrains are those with the bran and germ present, such as wholemeal bread or rolled oats, whereas refined grains have the bran polished away (eg, white rice and white flour). We need to 'bring back the brown' in the form of wholegrain breads and cereals. Enjoy at least half your daily grain foods as wholegrain versions (two serves a day, such as ½ cup of brown rice and ½ cup of porridge) to lower cholesterol and keep heart attacks at bay. See page 57 for much more about wholegrains.

- **Include low-GI foods at most meals. Examples include dense grainy breads, pasta, barley, oats, sweetcorn, muesli, porridge, most fruits, legumes, milk, yoghurt.**

  Low-GI carbohydrate foods help you control your blood glucose levels throughout the day, which means more stable energy levels, happy and relaxed blood vessels and a healthy heart. GI values are simply a numerical ranking compared with glucose, which has a GI of 100. Carbohydrates that break down quickly during digestion have high GI values; those that break down slowly releasing glucose gradually into the bloodstream have low GI values. There are plenty of wholesome heart-friendly low-GI foods to choose from, such as multigrain bread, pasta, barley, sweetcorn, high-fibre breakfast cereals, muesli, porridge, most fruits, legumes, soy milk, low-fat milk and yoghurt. Lower GI recipes are highlighted in part 4 on page 252. You can check the GI of a food using the database at www.glycemicindex.com, and refresh your memory about the glycemic index on page 22.

Flavour without salt

- **Boost natural food flavours by using herbs and spices and reducing the amount of sodium (salt) that you eat.**

  Herbs and spices are proof that healthy eating really is meant to be enjoyable. Not only do these kitchen essentials add flavour without salt, but research is continually amazing us with their health benefits. Herbs and spices are where the natural flavours are, and flavour means fun to eat. Have them on hand to turn basic heart-friendly ingredients into gastronomic experiences that taste good and are good for you. You can find out much more about herbs and spices on page 54.

Choosing the right optional extras

- **If you choose to drink alcohol, limit your consumption to one or two drinks per day.**

  Alcohol in moderation appears to be protective for the heart, especially if you're middle aged or older. This is not to say you should take up drinking if you don't drink currently, but if you do enjoy a tipple you can feel good about enjoying one or two drinks a day. The other good news? It doesn't matter what type of alcohol: wine, beer or spirits, just so long as you don't have too much. We have more information about alcohol on page 103.

- **If you drink tea and coffee, enjoy them in moderation: up to 3-4 cups of tea AND 1 strong coffee (filter, plunger or espresso) or 2–3 instant coffees daily.**

  These reviving beverages are a source of essential fluids as well as protective antioxidants that help look after the heart and blood vessels. Tea and coffee are social drinks that help bring us together and help us to take time-out for ourselves. Enjoyed in moderation and without the addition of full-cream milk and too much sugar, tea and coffee can be part of a heart-healthy eating pattern. See page 110 for more information.

6: Move more

There's no getting around it, if you want to say goodbye to cholesterol you've got to get active. Your body was made to move. Today most of us have to make a conscious effort to set aside special times to be active, whether it's taking a walk or working out in the gym or playing sports.

What's so good about physical activity?

Being active reduces your risk of developing heart disease, as well as other diseases such as type 2 diabetes, osteoporosis, obesity, depression and cancer. Even moderate improvements in your fitness levels can deliver substantial health benefits. If you already have heart disease, being physically active can:

- decrease bad cholesterol levels
- increase good cholesterol levels
- improve blood flow
- increase your heart's ability to do its job—pumping the blood around your body.

It is NEVER too late to fit physical activity into your lifestyle.

What is resistance training and why is it important to our health?

Doing some low to moderate resistance (strength) training improves muscular strength and endurance. Being physically stronger helps you to walk tall and get things done. Resistance training is a method of conditioning muscles, joints and bones, which involves the progressive use of resistance to increase your ability to exert force. Lifting weights is an example, but body weight can also be used such as when doing a push-up.

Regular physical activity produces a number of favourable changes to your heart and blood vessels. The heart's ability to pump blood around your body is improved (better functional capacity). Being more active boosts mood, reduces the risk of blood clots (thrombosis), keeps the heart beating smoothly and regularly (reduces risk of arrhythmia), increases the amount of oxygen transported throughout the body and reduces the risk of atherosclerosis (hardening of the arteries).

What's the difference between exercise and physical activity?

Whether it's physical activity or exercise you do, any way you get moving is worthwhile. Including more movement in your day adds up and is beneficial. Structured exercise provides you with additional health benefits.

Physical activity is any bodily movement produced by your muscles which results in expending energy beyond a resting level. For instance, doing the ironing or washing your car are both classified as physical activity.

Exercise is physical activity that you plan to include in your day for leisure, recreation or fitness. It has a planned purpose such as improving fitness, performance, health or as a social activity. For example, swimming or going for your daily 'constitutional' walk.

Different types of physical activity

Incidental physical activity

Incidental activity is the kind you do as a by-product of daily activities and, unfortunately, it has gone backwards as technology has moved forwards. Nowadays we drive rather than walk, and push buttons rather than do things by hand. To increase your incidental activity, be active every day in as many ways as you can.

Incidental activity includes:
- taking the stairs instead of the lift
- ironing
- gardening
- doing housework
- parking farther away from the shops and walking
- walking to the train station
- getting off your bus or train a stop early
- getting up to change the television channel instead of using the remote control
- getting up, stretching and walking around at work
- walking or playing with pets
- playing with children in an active way.

Tip

Get yourself a pedometer—a little gadget you wear on your belt to keep track of how many steps you take each day. Establish your usual number (baseline), and then set small increases week by week. A good target is 10,000 steps a day—but you may want to start with 7500.

Moderate-intensity physical activity

Remember that structured exercise provides you with additional health benefits, so set aside 30 minutes each day to give your body a workout.

For example:
- aquarobics (water aerobics)
- brisk walking
- cycling
- yoga
- swimming
- golf
- line dancing
- resistance training.

Vigorous physical activity

If you are able to, vigorous activity has even more benefits. However, vigorous activity is not routinely recommended for people with existing heart disease (for example, if you suffer from angina). Check with your doctor first.

For example:
- running
- netball or basketball
- football
- tennis or squash
- uphill walking
- aerobics
- circuit training
- rowing.

How much should you do?

The widely accepted recommendation for general physical activity for adults is 30 minutes or more of moderate-intensity physical activity on all, or most, days of the week. If you have high cholesterol levels, these guidelines are even more important for you. For children, the recommendation is at least 60 minutes a day of moderate activity, and some vigorous activity is recommended.

The 30 minutes is a minimum amount. You get even more health benefits from longer periods. Thankfully for busy people and the very unfit, these 30 minutes don't have to be continuous. You can put together the 30 minutes in short bouts. For example, you could go for a 15-minute walk in the morning and then a 15-minute swim in the afternoon, or do three 10-minute walks a day.

The benefits of being active outweigh the risks

The most common risk associated with physical activity in general is hurting yourself (musculoskeletal injury), but this risk can be reduced if you increase your physical activity gradually over time. If you enjoy walking, gardening or cycling, the chance of injury is low.

Special care is needed if you have heart disease. Vigorous activity is not usually recommended and the risk of sudden death is increased. If you're still keen, you need to have medical screening and assessment first. Moderate activity is much safer.

If you're doing little or nothing now, the thought of starting might seem daunting. A change of thinking can help. Rather than thinking of physical activity as a punishment or inconvenience, think of it as an opportunity to feel better. Remember, your body was made to move. Start off slowly and realistically. Simple choices such as walking to pick up the morning paper rather than driving can make a big difference over the long term.

Tip 1: Build up gradually

Although the risks from physical activity are low, if you already have cardiovascular disease, this physical activity should be built up gradually over a period of time. The word 'gradually' should be taken seriously. Changing from a couch potato to a fitness fanatic overnight could be heart attack material, and the discomfort and muscle soreness could put you right off.

Tip 2: Before you start, see your doctor

If you are sedentary, you need to consult your doctor for a pre-activity evaluation. This evaluation should include medications review, medical review, physical examination and a history of your physical activity. Once you receive the all clear from your doctor, it is recommended that you gradually build up your activity levels from that of low intensity to the recommended level (30 minutes moderate) of physical activity.

Tip 3: Get expert advice

It's best that the level of physical activity you do is tailored to meet your needs and capacity, and takes into account any disease process, reduced function or poor balance. The best people to do this are exercise physiologists or physiotherapists.

Tip 4: Warm up and warm down to reduce the risk of muscle soreness

To reduce the risk of developing muscle soreness or injuries, remember to always warm up before and cool down after your exercise session. This means you need to start off slowly before increasing the pace, and then slow down gradually at the end rather than start off racing and come to an abrupt halt. Your muscles will thank you.

Warm up

Five to ten minutes in duration:
Begin with gentle stretches focusing on warming up the muscles that you plan to use in the exercise session—eg, if you're going to ride your bike, stretch your legs and then cycle at a slower pace than normal for a few minutes.

Cool-down

Five to ten minutes in duration: Gradually slow down your exercise pace and then stretch the muscles you used.

Tip 5: Be SMART. Set goals

In order to be more active and improve your health and wellbeing, it's important that you set goals. Personal goals will help motivate you to change and give you something to work towards. Your goals should be clear and achievable, because unrealistic goals set you up for disappointment. Ensure your goals are SMART.

SMART Goals
S—Specific
M—Measurable
A—Achievable
R—Realistic
T—Time-bound

A SMART goal example
'We will attend three afternoon aquarobic sessions each week for the next month.'

Being active is something you want to keep doing for the rest of your life, so there's no need to rush into things. By setting yourself a monthly goal, you are making the small steps needed to build larger, longer term goals. The success of achieving goals is a great motivator.

Tip 6: Keep a Workout Diary

A good way to keep track of physical activity is to keep a Workout Diary. By recording the duration, type and intensity of activity each day, you can easily see how far you have come. The Workout Diary will help you to monitor whether you are achieving your goals, and will also assist you in re-establishing any goals that may be unrealistic. Remember if your goal was to walk for 30 minutes on five days a week for the next month and you have done this easily for the last 2 months, you've definitely achieved your goal and probably need to develop another one. Remember the more you do the better, and variety of physical activity keeps your body working in different ways and prevents boredom.

You've made a great start, but how do you stay motivated to continue it for the long term?

- Don't rush into things. Set realistic goals that you know are achievable.
- Listen to your body to decide if it's time to step up your amount of activity or if it's time to rest.
- Schedule physical activities in your diary like other appointments.
- Ask your friends, family or work colleagues to get active with you.

Part 2

Say hello
to heart-friendly foods

7: Vegetables

Vegetables are low in kilojoules but high in filling power and nutritional goodness, making them great to eat when you're watching your weight and getting your cholesterol down. Eating vegetables reduces the risk of cardiovascular disease and reduces your chances of becoming overweight and developing some forms of cancer.

Vegetables are nature's very own functional foods—full of essential nutrients such as vitamins, minerals and fibre, as well as protective phytochemicals such as antioxidants. And it's never too late to start getting the veggie benefit. So pile them on your plate.

When it comes to vegetables, it's not just 'your greens' you need to eat. Let colour be your guide and aim to serve at least three different coloured veggies on the dinner plate each day. It looks good. And it is good. Colour is a useful indicator of a vegetable's protective phytochemical content. Carrots, for example, are orange because they are high in betacarotene—a powerful antioxidant—as are sweet potatoes and pumpkin.

Are you getting enough?

The more the better! It's impossible to overdose on veggies. However, most health experts recommend five servings a day as a good target to aim for. A serving is around a handful, so try to get five handfuls of vegetables into your day.

What is a serve?

- ½ cup cooked vegetables or legumes (about) 75g/2½oz)
- a medium sized potato (about 150g/5oz)
- a cup of salad vegetables (enough to fill a small dessert bowl)
- a medium sized tomato (about 100g/3½oz)
- a small carrot (about 100g/3½oz)
- ½ cup sweet potato chunks (about 70g/2½oz)
- ¾ cup (180ml/6fl oz) vegetable juice
- a cup (250 ml/9fl oz) vegetable soup.

What are phytochemicals?

'Phyto' means plant, so phytochemicals are plant chemicals. They're naturally occurring defenders of your health, rather like your body's security guards keeping out troublemakers like free radicals. Antioxidants are phytochemicals but there are literally an army of different types in the food we eat, particularly in plant foods such as vegetables, fruits, wholegrains, nuts and seeds.

What are antioxidants?

Antioxidants protect your body from damage caused by free radicals. Free radicals promote oxidation—a process similar to metal rusting. Oxidative damage by free radicals is thought to contribute to diseases like heart disease and even the ageing process. Although free radicals are formed in your body's normal biochemical processes, their formation increases during inflammation, exposure to sun, pollution like smog and cigarette smoke (your own or someone else's). Eating foods rich in protective antioxidants can reduce the damage caused by free radicals. So if you want to stay protected, 'rust-proof' your body with plenty of antioxidant-rich plant foods.

Is fresh best?

Raw or cooked? Whole or juiced? Fresh or frozen?

What's the best way to get the goodness of vegetables? Any way you can! However you enjoy your veggies—raw, cooked or juiced—it will contribute to your five servings a day. There's no need to embark on a raw food diet. While cooking reduces some nutrients and phytochemicals a little, it makes others easier to absorb. So enjoy a combination of both raw and cooked vegetables, depending on what you feel like. The fresh crunch of a crisp and cool salad is perfect for a hot summer evening by the barbecue, but nothing beats baked vegetables with a roast dinner on a chilly winter's night. Veggie soups are great, too. Cool down with a chilled soup like gazpacho; or warm up with a satisfying minestrone.

To preserve the nutritional goodness of vegetables, the best cooking methods are baking, microwaving, steaming and stir-frying. Avoid boiling as you will be pouring the vitamins down the drain with the cooking water.

There's nothing wrong with opting for convenience when it comes to buying vegetables. Choosing frozen and canned vegetables occasionally enables you to enjoy a wide variety of vegetables year round.

Frozen vegetables are picked and snap frozen at their peak which makes them a nutritious option. In fact frozen peas retain more of their vitamins than shelled pre-packed peas on the greengrocer's shelf.

Canned vegetables such as tomatoes, legumes and corn help you to prepare nutritious meals in minutes. Choose salt-reduced options where possible, or drain well—most salt is in the liquid.

Vegetable juices such as tomato, carrot and mixed juices help you achieve your five servings of veggies a day and provide a healthy alternative to soft drinks and cordials. The downside is the fibre lost during the juicing process.

Stressed out? Tired? Run down? Boost your vitality with a phyto-power pick-me-up of freshly squeezed carrot, celery and ginger juice.

How to get your 'five vegetables a day'

Breakfast

- Make a hearty beginning with wholegrain toast, grilled tomatoes, sauteed mushrooms and a poached egg on a bed of sauteed spinach or silverbeet (swiss chard).
- Start the day with zing with tomato juice and a dash of Tabasco sauce.
- Fill a small omelette with sauteed onion, capsicum, mushrooms, sprouts and baby spinach leaves.
- Use leftover rice to make an Asian rice porridge, or congee, with salt-reduced vegetable stock and Asian greens such as bok choy, pak choy or tai soi.

Lunch

- Take a salad to work. What about baby spinach leaves, cherry tomatoes, cucumber slices, blanched green beans, walnuts and avocado with a citrus and olive oil dressing.
- Have leftovers for lunch, heated up, or transformed into a soup with salt-reduced stock or some pureed canned tomatoes, or a vegetable frittata with beaten egg and a little low-fat ricotta.

Dinner

- Warm up to your main meal with a vegetable soup.
- Complement main meals with salad.
- Pile up your dinner plate with vegetables—with at least three different-coloured veggies.
- Make over your favourite recipes by adding some extra vegetables.
- With take-outs, stretch the meal and boost nutrition with extra vegetables. For example, serve barbecue chicken with baby potatoes, a cob of corn and an endive, tomato and zucchini (courgette) salad; partner pizza with a garden salad: accompany curries with extra vegetables such as cucumber or carrot raitas.

Snacks

- Crunch on a sweet and juicy cob of corn.
- Nibble on juicy cherry tomatoes.
- Dunk crisp vegetable sticks of carrot, celery, capsicum (pepper) and snowpeas (mangetout) into hummus or cucumber dips.
- Dip spicy homemade pita crisps into low-fat eggplant (aubergine) dip or peppers and corn or tomato salsa.

Why vegetables are good for you

Green vegetables are rich in antioxidants and folate. The darker their green colour, the more they contain, which is why broccoli and Asian greens are so good for you. Greens are also packed with fibre, potassium, magnesium, calcium and a little iron. Vegetables from the cabbage (cruciferous) family such as broccoli, cabbage, cauliflower and Brussels sprouts also contain special kinds of phytochemicals called indoles and isothiocyanates. Aim for a minimum of three cups of green vegetables a week for good health.

One of the reasons that vegetables and fruit 'rot' in your fridge is because they emit ethylene gas. You can now buy special storage bags and cartridges (Keepfresh) for the crisper that absorb ethylene and slow down the ageing and ripening process.

What about fresh herbs?

Give salads and sandwiches a flavour boost with basil, parsley, mint, chives or coriander. Green leafy herbs are similar in nutritional content to green vegetables. They also add fantastic flavour, but it is more delicate than dried herbs so add at the end of cooking time. To store, wrap them in paper towel and place in a plastic bag in the fridge so they last longer, or stand them up in a jar of water in the refrigerator with a plastic bag over the top.

Green vegetables

What are they?

Look for leafy greens or green skinned vegetables (that you eat the skin of) such as:

Artichoke
Asparagus
Beans
Broccoli
Broccolini
Brussels sprouts
Bok choy or baby bok choy
Cabbage
Capsicum
Celery
Chicory (curly endive)
Chilli, green
Choy sum, baby choy sum
Cress
Endive, curly endive
English spinach, baby English spinach
Gai lan (Chinese broccoli)
Gai choy
Kale
Kang kong
Lamb's lettuce (mâche)
Lettuce including crisphead (iceberg),
   cos (romaine), butterhead, and loose leaf
   (mignonette, oak, coral and salad mixes such
   as mesclun)
Lebanese cucumber
Mizuna
Mustard greens (dai gai choi)

Okra
Pak choy (or baby pak choy)
Peas
Rocket (arugula)
Silverbeet (Swiss chard)
Snowpeas (mangetout)
Spring onions
Spinach
Spring onions (scallions)
Sprouts including alfalfa, mung beans and wheatgrass
Sugar snap peas
Tai soi
Watercress
Witlof (Belgian endive)
Zucchini (courgette)

TIPS FOR GREENS
- Always have one green vegetable on your dinner plate.
- Choose darker coloured lettuces for their higher levels of antioxidants.
- Cook greens quickly (steaming or stir frying), or add at the end of cooking time to preserve their nutrient content.
- Eat greens in season and they'll be at their nutritional peak, and cheaper.
- Eat green vegetables the day you buy them if possible or store in a plastic bag in the fridge crisper to keep them fresher for longer.

TIPS FOR COOKING GREENS
Cooked cruciferous vegetables such as Asian greens, Brussels sprouts and cabbage don't taste as good the next day because their bitter flavours become more pronounced. Cook just enough for the meal, and cook lightly to keep the flavour just right.

How to get more

- Pile coloured lettuce, rocket or baby spinach onto a chicken or tuna and tomato sandwich.
- Add Asian greens such as bok choy, gai choy or gai lan to beef, seafood and chicken stir-fries, noodle soups and broths.
- Make a complete meal salad with a variety of lettuces and witlof, shredded chicken and salad vegetables.
- Add steamed and then cooled broccoli or broccolini to a green salad with radishes and serve with steamed white fish, a drizzle of extra virgin olive oil and toasted flaked almonds.
- Saute lean pork strips and cabbage, brussels sprouts or kale in some canola oil with finely sliced onion and a little sugar, dress with vinegar and serve with mashed potato and carrots.
- Make coleslaw with shredded green (and red) cabbage or wombok (Chinese cabbage), carrot, kohlrabi, coriander (cilantro) and peanuts. Stir in some shaved (or chopped) low-fat deli ham and roll in wholemeal flat bread.
- Use frozen spinach in lean beef or vegetable lasagna, filo, ham and ricotta pastries, beef and chicken soups, vegetable omelettes and frittatas.
- Broccoli, beans and snowpeas (mangetout) or sugar snap peas are delicious served cold in a red kidney bean and onion salad.
- Add some fresh or frozen peas to tuna pasta, chicken, rice or roasted vegetable couscous dishes and chicken noodle soups.

Red and purple vegetables

What are they?

Look for leafy red/purple vegetables or red/purple-skinned vegetables (which you eat the skin of) such as:

Basil, purple
Beetroot
Cabbage, red
Capsicum (pepper), red
Cauliflower, purple
Chilli, red
Eggplant (aubergine)
Endive, purple
Lettuce, red including oak leaf and mignonette
Radicchio
Radishes
Red onion (Spanish)
Rhubarb
Sweet potato, red (kumara)
Tomatoes

Why they are good for you

Red and purple vegetables are rich in antioxidants such as anthocyanins, phenolics and carotenoids. Tomatoes contain a particular carotenoid antioxidant called lycopene. Like all vegetables, they also contain vitamins such as C, and minerals such as potassium.

How to get more

- Grill halved roma tomatoes with a drop of olive oil and balsamic vinegar. Enjoy them hot with a cooked breakfast, or cool them down and add to salads or sandwiches.
- Roast capsicum (peppers) in a hot oven until the skin blackens. Place immediately into a plastic bag until cool and then remove the skin (which should slide off easily). Slice or dice and enjoy as a side dish with grilled meat or seafood and salad, in a warm beef, oak leaf lettuce and Asian herb salad, or added to pasta or sandwiches.
- Add thin red onion rings to Asian-style salads, or chop finely and add to a salmon sandwich with mignonette lettuce and tomato, or sardines on toast with baby greens tossed in lemon juice.
- Add purple basil to meat and vegetable stir-fries, or add to a green salad of cos lettuce, asparagus and mangetout (snowpeas) for flavour and colour.
- Quick-roast slices, chunks or pieces of capsicum (pepper), red onion, red sweet potato (kumara) and beetroot by microwaving first until tender.
- Make a quick beetroot dip with chopped canned (drained) beetroot and low-fat natural yoghurt and a clove of crushed garlic. Great with vegetable sticks and wholemeal pita bread triangles.
- Lightly steam or microwave purple asparagus, drizzle with extra virgin olive oil and lemon juice and zest and add to a chicken, avocado and watercress salad.
- Brush eggplant (aubergine) slices with olive oil, grill on the barbecue until tender and serve as part of a mezze platter or an antipasto plate.
- Stew rhubarb and apple until tender, add sugar and lemon juice to taste and serve as a condiment with white meats.
- Blanch cauliflower, purple or white, florets and toss through salads.
- Serve a small dish of sliced red chilli on the side of any Asian-style dishes.

Did you know?

The antioxidants in tomatoes are better absorbed when they are cooked with a little oil—enter pasta sauce! Homemade or ready-prepared, pasta sauce is a nutritious way to enjoy not only pasta but vegetables and lean meats as well. Traditional Italian cooks serve thick and rich tomato sauces with meat, fish, vegetables and legumes to add flavour.

Orange and yellow vegetables

What are they?
Look for orange-fleshed or yellow-fleshed vegetables or with orange/yellow skin (which you eat the skin of) such as:

Beans, yellow

Butternut squash

Capsicum (pepper), yellow

Carrots

Pumpkin

Sweet corn, baby corn

Sweet potato (kumara)

Tomatoes, yellow

Yellow squash

Yellow zucchini (courgette)

Why they are good for you
Yellow and orange vegetables contain antioxidants called carotenoids (e, betacarotene) and flavonoids, as well as the usual vegetable nutrient goodies like vitamin C and fibre. The orange coloured betacarotene is converted to vitamin A in the body. Vitamin A is important for healthy vision.

How to get more
- Microwave chunks of pumpkin until tender. Lightly spray with olive oil before baking until cooked and golden. Use in roasted pumpkin and tomato soup or roasted pumpkin, coriander and cumin rice with an Indian spiced beef stew.
- Snack on sweet baby carrots or cooked and cooled baby corn.
- Add grated carrot to sandwiches, mince and egg dishes or try a grated carrot, grated daikon (white radish) and grated green apple for a crunchy garnish to any Asian-style meal.
- Serve creamed corn on toast for a healthy hot breakfast.
- Barbecue or microwave corn on the cob in its husk and enjoy a delicious starter.
- Thread cubes of yellow, green and orange capsicum and quartered baby yellow squash onto skewers with cubes of lean meat or chicken and grill or barbecue for colourful kebabs.
- Make a peanut butter, grated carrot and raisin sandwich on multigrain bread.
- Halved yellow tomatoes and sliced yellow zucchinis make a colourful addition to a tuna, beetroot, cos lettuce and walnut salad.
- Butternut squash mash is a great alternative to potato mash and great with grilled fish.

White vegetables

What are they?

Look for white-skinned or creamy skinned or fleshed vegetables such as:

Avocado

Cauliflower

Celeriac

Daikon

Fennel

Garlic

Ginger

Kohlrabi

Leeks

Mushrooms

Onions

Parsnips

Potatoes

Shallots

Swedes

Taro

Turnip

Yams

Why they are good for you

Onions, leeks and garlic contain a phytochemical called allicin, as well as flavonols and sulfur compounds thought to have cancer-protective effects. Swedes and turnips are rich in a group of phytochemical called glucosinolates. Root vegetables all contain vitamin C and are a good source of fibre.

The humble spud

Potato has a high satiety index. This means they're very filling—a little bit of spud can fill a big hole.

What to do with leftover potato:

- Make a potato salad with a canola, sunflower or soybean oil, mayonnaise, chopped chives and drained canned four bean mix.
- 'Smash' them and sprinkle with dried rosemary and a drizzle of virgin olive oil (not mashed smooth, just crushed).
- Slice thinly and combine with evaporated skim milk, nutmeg and spring onions, top with a sprinkling of grated parmesan cheese and finish under the grill (broiler).

How to get more

- Try different styles of mash such as parsnip and potato with chopped onion; swede, potato and roasted garlic; potato and celeriac or yam with chopped chives. Serve with a juicy lean steak and a green leaf, tomato, shallot and mushroom salad.
- Cook cauliflower and broccoli florets and carrot sticks in the microwave until tender, then sauté briefly in olive oil and crushed garlic. Sprinkle with toasted sesame seeds and serve warm mixed with pan-fried lean beef strips.
- Cut slivers of taro and parsnip with a vegetable peeler, then deep-fry in canola oil until crisp and golden. Add them to a chicken Caesar salad to replace the croutons.
- Slice a whole head of unpeeled garlic across the centre and roast or barbecue. Serve as is—scoop out the soft, sweet flesh and eat with grilled or barbecue meats or seafood.

• Sauté leeks and mushrooms in olive oil with a little smoked paprika and serve as a toast topping.
• Add chopped ginger and thinly sliced kohlrabi to tofu and vegetable stir-fry, or add crushed ginger to boiling water with a little honey for ginger tea.

A note on mushrooms

Mushrooms are sold alongside vegetables but they're really fungi. These nutrition powerhouses are low in kilojoules (calories) but high in flavour. They contain fibre, iron, potassium, B-vitamins, copper and selenium as well as small amounts of vitamins D and B12.

Did you know?

Studies have shown garlic can reduce cholesterol, improve antioxidant levels in the blood and enhance flexibility of blood vessels, although more research is needed.

8: Fruit

Enjoying fruit every day can help to control cholesterol and protect your heart. Studies looking at links between diet and disease patterns show people who eat the most fruit and vegetables have the lowest risk of cardiovascular disease. They also have less chance of having risk factors for CVD such as high blood pressure, obesity and type 2 diabetes. How does fruit do it?

There's no clear-cut answer to this one yet. However, the protection is probably due to a combination of factors. Substances sharing the limelight are soluble fibre, vitamin C, an array of phytochemicals including carotenoids (such as betacarotene), folate and potassium. It may also be because fruits are relatively low in kilojoules (calories), are satisfying due to their high water and fibre content and have gentle effects on blood glucose levels.

Fruit is one of the sweet things in life, and a great example of naturally delicious foods that are good to eat and good for you. In many cases fruit meets the need for speed and convenience—after all, it comes in its own packaging, which is ideal for eating on the go! Enjoy fruit every day in every way you can. But remember to wash unpeeled whole fruit before eating to remove dirt, bacteria and any farming chemical residues.

No single fruit contains all of the heart-healthy nutrients and phytochemicals. The best advice is to enjoy a variety of different fruits to ensure you're getting a broad spectrum of health benefits, and make the most of what's in season. Some fruits, however, do appear to have 'star' quality, and are worth eating as often as you can. Berry fruits, citrus fruits and apples have emerged as being particularly protective, and are known to be packed with heart-friendly nutrients and phytochemicals.

As with vegetables, the clues to phytochemical and nutrient content are in the colour. In some cases the bright colours are in the skin. So don't peel away the goodness and fibre. Wash the fruit and eat the skin where possible.

Did you know?
Olives, avocados and tomatoes are technically fruits. Olives and avocados are exceptions to the rule that fruits are virtually fat-free—fortunately, the fat is mostly the healthy monounsaturated type and good for the heart.

Are you getting enough?

Most health authorities recommend at least two servings of fruit a day. A serving is an average-sized piece, such as a medium-sized apple, pear or orange, or two smaller pieces, such as plums or kiwi fruit.

What is a serve?

- 1 medium piece of fruit (about 180g/6½oz) such as an apple, pear, peach or orange
- 1 cup of fruit pieces such as sliced strawberries or melon
- 2 small pieces of fruit (about 80g/2¾oz each) such as plums or apricots
- ⅔ cup (160ml/5¼fl oz) of fruit juice.

Is fresh best?

Although fresh is usually best, there are lots of great ways to enjoy fruit—canned, juiced, dried, puréed, stewed, baked, frozen—and they all provide valuable nutrients and phytochemicals.

However, there are some vitamin losses with processing. For example, high temperatures involved in cooking, canning and drying fruit reduces the vitamin C and B-vitamin content. As with vegetables, cooking fruit in little or no water is best to prevent leaching of vitamins into the cooking water.

Freezing fruit quickly after picking preserves nutrients well. Juicing can actually increase the availability of phytochemicals because the cells are split open. Drinking fruit juices as close to the time of juicing is a good idea as some losses do occur during storage. Supermarket fruit juices are generally pasteurised (heat treated to make them safe), which causes some vitamin C (ascorbic acid) to be lost, but it is generally added back and is a natural preservative.

Watch what you drink

A freshly squeezed fruit juice is certainly a delicious and nutritious option, however beware of large serving sizes that may contain the juice from 5–6 pieces of fruit and the kilojoules to match. The kilojoules in fruit juice are similar to those in soft drink (soda)! Ask for the smallest size you can.

How to get your 'two fruits a day'

Breakfast

- Blend fruit such as banana, berries or mango with low fat milk and yoghurt for a breakfast smoothie.
- Cut up a selection of stone fruits; peaches, nectarines and plums and top with low-fat yoghurt.
- Top wholegrain breakfast cereal with sliced fruit such as strawberries, banana or canned fruits such as peaches, apricots, pears or prunes.
- Enjoy a small serve of fresh juice (top up with cool water for maximum refreshment and less sugars).

Lunch

- Combine sliced apple with some reduced-fat cheese on a wholemeal bread salad sandwich.
- Segment an orange and serve with a tuna and wholemeal pasta salad.
- Combine dried fruit like raisins, apricots and dates with grated carrot and cottage cheese to fill a multigrain roll or flat bread wrap.

Snack

- Include a piece of fresh fruit in your lunchbox, such as a crisp apple, juicy orange or mandarin, or satisfying banana ready for that snack attack.
- A small handful of dried fruit such as apricots, apple, dates or sultanas/raisins or tropical dried fruits such as paw paw, pineapple and mango with currants.

Dinner

- Add fresh mango slices to a prawn or chicken vermicelli and vegetable salad with chilli and lime dressing.
- Add dried fruit such as sultanas to spicy sauces and casseroles (eg, Moroccan tagine or Indian curry) or stir into the rice or couscous to accompany these dishes.
- Add sliced fresh pear to a green salad with walnuts.
- Microwave some pear pieces with pumpkin, onion and salt-reduced stock and purée. Top with shredded cooked lean chicken, natural (plain) yoghurt and coriander (cilantro) for a quick winter soup.

Dessert

- Finish with stewed fruit with low-fat custard (use the microwave to save time).
- Bake a fruit crumble.
- Serve a refreshing fruit salad and low-fat ice cream.
- Prepare a warm spiced fruit compote.
- A bunch of chilled grapes will add a delicious touch of sweetness to complete a meal.
- Try fresh figs served with low-fat ricotta and a drizzle of honey.

Citrus fruit

What are they?

Clementine

Cumquat

Grapefruit

Lemon

Lime

Mandarin

Orange

Pomello

Satsuma

Tangelo

Tangerine

Why they are good for you

Limes were the lifesaver of choice for early explorers to prevent scurvy on long sea voyages, and their lifesaving continues to this day along with their other citrus fruit cousins. Citrus fruits are very nutritious and rich in vitamins such as vitamins C and B-group (including folate), minerals such as calcium, potassium, phosphorous and magnesium, and fibre. Citrus fruits are also loaded with more than 170 different phytochemicals such as carotenoids, flavonoids, coumarins, terpenes, hydroxycinnamic acid and phytosterols. These phytochemicals contain both antioxidant and anti-inflammatory effects.

A typical orange contains 60mg of vitamin C, which is enough to meet the entire day's Recommended Dietary Intake (RDI). Population studies show that high vitamin C intakes are protective against heart disease.

Try adding citrus zest to desserts, juices, stir-fries and cakes and muffins for a real flavour boost. Citrus zest can be removed using a grater or special zester that cuts small curls. Take care not to take too much of the pith as this can be bitter. Citrus peel can also be dried in a sunny spot—keep in a sealed jar after it hardens and add to meat dishes.

A word of warning

Some prescription medications, including heart drugs, interact with natural phytochemicals in grapefruit. Check with your doctor.

How to get more

- Squeeze fresh orange juice for breakfast or try a juiced tangelo.
- Try lime juice with a dash of iced tea on ice for a pre-dinner (non-alcoholic) mocktail.
- Start the day with ½ grapefruit sprinkled with a little sugar.
- Pack an orange, clementine, satsuma or mandarin in the lunch box.
- Use citrus juices and zest for sauces, stir-fries and salad dressings.
- Add orange juice to carrot soup.
- Make a salad with sliced orange, legumes, finely sliced radish, torn fresh basil and lemon juice vinaigrette.
- Add sweetened chopped citrus pulp to cakes, pancakes and muffins.
- Add grapefruit, pomello or orange slices to mixed salad leaves and sliced avocado in a vinaigrette dressing to serve with chicken or seafood.
- Add chopped orange, ginger and fresh coriander (cilantro) to coleslaw.
- Prepare a creamy salad dressing with lemon or lime juice, low-fat natural (plain) yoghurt and mustard.

- Stir together a quick lemon or lime mayonnaise with juice, zest, chopped dill and prepared mayonnaise (great with heart-healthy seafood).
- Create tempting refreshments by adding sliced lemon, tangerine or lime to cool water.
- Combine slices of pink (ruby) grapefruit, beetroot and red onion with radicchio and vinaigrette dressing for an 'in the pink' salad—complements all hot and cold lean white meats.
- Dollop cumquat marmalade on steamed white fish, chicken or asparagus for a great taste.

To extract the most juice, try microwaving oranges, limes and lemons for around 15 seconds before juicing. Alternatively, roll them under your hand using firm pressure on a flat surface.

Berries

What are they?
Berries are juicy, fleshy fruits that contain one or many seeds. They look gorgeous, taste divine and add beautiful colours as well as nutrients to many dishes. There are many berries, but some of the most popular and readily available are:

Blackberry

Blackcurrant

Blueberry

Boysenberry

Cranberry

Gooseberry

Cape gooseberry (physalis)

Juniper berry

Loganberry

Mulberry

Raspberry

Redcurrant

Strawberry

Youngberry

Did you know?

Botanically, grapes, tomatoes, papaya, pomegranates, durians, lychees and persimmons are berry fruits. Cherries share the rich colours and high phytochemical content of berries, but are actually a stone fruit like apricots and plums.

Why they are good for you
Berries are leaders of the pack when it comes to phytochemical content, being packed full of antioxidants. They contain a variety of phenolic antioxidants (such as ellagic acid and quercitin), which help reduce oxidation of cholesterol in the body. Rich blue-purple colour indicates the presence of anthocyanins and proanthocyanins.

The darker the colour, the higher the anthocyanin content. Anthocyanins actually become more available with juicing. Anthocyanin is used as a natural food colouring. Berries are also rich in vitamin C.

Keep berries in the fridge to retain their nutrient and phytochemical content. Store on some absorbent paper in a single layer to keep them dry and prevent squashing.

Berries are rich in pectin, a type of soluble fibre. Pectin is essential in jam making because it helps the fruit and sugar thicken. This is why berry fruits make good jams and conserves. Look for 'pure fruit' and 'low sugar' jams and preserves for more fruit and less sugar.

How to get more

Berries are delicious and most nutritious eaten raw, but they are highly seasonal so supplement your berry cravings with frozen, dried and canned berries. Phytochemical losses are small after cooking, but heat-sensitive vitamin C content does decline. Luckily this is not a worry as vitamin C levels are high to start with.

- Add a handful of berries to your wholegrain breakfast cereal, such as muesli.
- Blend some fresh, frozen or canned berries, such as blackberry, raspberry or mixed berries, into a smoothie with low-fat milk.
- Add some fresh or frozen berries to wholemeal) pancake batter and serve with berry conserve and low-fat ricotta.
- Sprinkle some fresh or frozen blackberries, raspberries or loganberries onto low-fat ice cream.
- Stir through fresh, canned or frozen berries through some vanilla-flavoured low-fat yoghurt.
- Mix some berries into fruit crumble: try raspberry/ mulberry and apple; strawberry/boysenberry and rhubarb; blueberry/youngberry and pear.
- Add berries to wholemeal (bran) muffins.
- Scatter red berries such as blueberries, strawberries and raspberries over cut watermelon.
- Garnish roasted meats with fresh or frozen redcurrants, blackcurrants or cranberries.
- Add crushed juniper berries to cabbage or mix with wholegrain breadcrumbs, onion, dried currants and herbs for meat stuffings.
- Enjoy the versatility of gooseberries by tossing through salads or making quick desserts.
- Chomp on fresh strawberries or cape gooseberries for a low-kilojoule (calorie) snack any time.

Apples

What are they?

There's some truth behind the saying, 'an apple a day keeps the doctor away'! Apples are one of the most popular fruits and they're also a 'star' fruit for helping to lower cholesterol and keep the heart healthy. Red, green or somewhere in between, eat apples for enjoyment and for their many health benefits.

Why they are good for you

Apples are rich in soluble fibre, vitamin C and phytochemicals. They also contain potassium and vitamins K and B6. Apples are one of the richest sources of flavonoids (a group of antioxidants) in typical Western diets. The special combination of phytochemicals in apples has been shown to reduce the oxidation of cholesterol, the process that contributes to 'hardening of the arteries'.

There are more than 6000 named varieties of apple! The phytochemical composition of apples can vary, so eat different kinds to ensure you get your full quota of protection.

Apples are known as a 'pome' fruit along with pears, nashi and quince. Apples and other pome fruits have a low GI (glycemic index), which means their natural sugars have a gentle effect on blood glucose levels, and their energy is longer lasting. Low GI foods play a helpful role in reducing the risk of diabetes and cardiovascular disease. Apples also have relatively low energy density, or kilojoules (calories) per gram. In effect they fill you up without being 'fattening'.

In a study of 5133 healthy middle aged adults in Finland followed up over 20 years, those who ate the most apples had a 43 per cent lower risk (women) or 19 per cent lower risk (men) of dying from heart disease compared to those who ate the least amount of apples.

How to get more

Fresh is best to maximise nutrients and phytochemicals; however, variety is the spice of life and apples are delicious baked, dried, canned and juiced. Heating does reduce nutrient content, so cook for as little time as possible, and without water so as to reduce leaching of the water-soluble vitamins such as vitamin C. Eating apples with the skin means you will obtain more vitamin C, flavonoids and antioxidants. Apple juice usually has the goodness of the fibre removed, so eat whole apples more than juice.

- Add chopped apple to porridge with a little cinnamon and honey.
- Soak grated apple and apple juice with rolled oats and nutmeg overnight for Bircher muesli.
- Top hot fruit toast with unsaturated margarine spread, cinnamon, sugar and sliced fresh apple.
- Add quartered green apple to a platter with low-fat ricotta dip, oven-baked pita chips, dates and dried apricots.
- Snack on fresh or dried apple and almonds.
- Serve apple sauce with lean roast pork.
- Sauté sliced apple with cabbage as a side dish—serve with hot and cold white meats.
- Make a fruit frappé by blending together whole apple with skin, ice, lemon juice, mint and ginger.
- Add chopped apple to curries, such as beef, lamb, vegetable or chickpea curry.

Apples go brown due to enzyme activity. You can reduce browning by brushing the cut surface with lemon juice, and reducing exposure to the air by slicing as close to the time of eating as possible. To keep your apples fresh and crisp for longer, store them in your refrigerator in the crisper section or in a plastic bag on the shelf.

9: Herbs and spices

Herbs and spices add flavour and enjoyment to food in lots of interesting and exotic ways. Herbs are the fresh edible leaves and stalks of culinary plants, while spices are the fruit, seeds, buds, flowers, roots or bark and are usually in a dried form. Cooking with spices is a central feature of cuisines from around the globe and lucky for us, a myriad of herbs and spices are readily available for us to experiment with.

Why they are good for you

Herbs and spices make healthy eating a joy. They add fantastic flavour without the use of excessive fat or salt. A grilled chicken breast is not very exciting on its own, but dry-marinated in smoked paprika, pepper, chilli and garlic takes your taste-buds away on a wonderful journey! Being plant foods, they also contain an array of natural phytochemicals.

Can they lower cholesterol?

Herbs and spices have been used as food and for medicinal purposes for centuries. Traditionally, using herbs and spices in cooking was thought to protect from disease. Although modern research is in its infancy, results so far indicate some fact behind the folklore. Herbs and spices that have been shown in animal and human studies to lower cholesterol or reduce cholesterol oxidation include turmeric, chilli, garlic, fenugreek, cumin, curry leaf and mustard seed. Phytochemicals such as curcumin, capsaicin, and essential oils are thought to be the active ingredients. Herbs and spices also have other heart-friendly effects such as lowering blood sugar levels and triglycerides, increasing the flexibility of blood vessels and reducing oxidation of cholesterol.

The research evidence just isn't strong enough to recommend certain spices over others, but they all add interest, variety and great taste so eat them for pure enjoyment and let your imagination run wild.

A word of warning

Eating herbs and spices in food is safe; however, taking herbs in tablet form carries some risk. Just because herbal supplements are natural doesn't mean they are harmless. For example, garlic tablets can reduce the ability of your blood to clot and can cause bleeding. Talk to your doctor before taking any supplements.

How do we eat them?

- Toast fruit bread and top with honey, low-fat ricotta and cinnamon for a delicious breakfast.
- Add a dash of powdered nutmeg and cardamom to skim milk, a banana and a spoonful of wheatgerm for a spicy smoothie.
- Add a couple of bay leaves and paprika, or bouquet garni, to a vegetable soup and serve with a multigrain roll.
- Add tagine spice mix or Ras el hanout to meat/legume and vegetable casseroles to transform them into exotic Moroccan inspired delights—serve with couscous or rice.
- Mix lots of chopped curly or flat leaf parsley through vegetable soups, stews and casseroles or sprinkle over any pasta or rice dish.
- For bread with a Middle Eastern flavour, brush low fat wholemeal pita bread with canola or olive oil and sprinkle with Za'atar before warming under the grill (broiler). Serve as an accompaniment to chickpea and vegetable tagine.
- Add a vanilla bean to skim milk when making a custard and serve with stewed peaches.
- Use fresh or dried herbs such as oregano, marjoram, parsley and basil to make pasta sauces more authentic. Serve with wholemeal pasta and a crisp green lettuce and fresh basil leaf salad.
- Toss torn Vietnamese mint leaves, Thai basil leaves, finely shredded kaffir lime leaves and finely sliced chilli through hot and cold noodle dishes.
- Make a rich and hearty chilli con carne (lean mince and kidney beans) with Mexican chilli powder. Serve with steamed brown rice and a green salad.
- Dry marinate strips of lean chicken or pork in star anise or Chinese five spice before stir frying with fresh garlic and ginger and combining with vegetables—serve with steamed (brown) rice or (soba) noodles.

- Make a delicious spiced dip by puréeing cooked or canned lentils with ground cumin, pepper, coriander seeds and caraway seeds—serve with carrot and pepper (capsicum) sticks, wholemeal pita bread crisps or microwaved pappadums.
- Stir-fry par-cooked potato cubes in a non-stick pan with a little canola oil and panch phoran for a north Indian twist to the humble potato. Also great served cold as a salad with low-fat yoghurt and crushed garlic dressing.

Spice it up

A grilled chicken breast, lamb cutlet, steak or fish fillet is not very exciting on its own, but dry-marinating before cooking can transform it into something wonderful and take your tastebuds on a culinary journey. Try the range of spice blends now available, such as Moroccan or Cajun, or the many Middle Eastern blends.

TIPS FOR HERBS AND SPICES
- Dried herbs and spices will lose flavour over time. Buy them in small quantities.
- Fresh herbs have a milder flavour that is very fragile. Add these at the last minute to hot dishes and just heat through in order to keep their flavour and colour. Fresh herbs are perfect served in salads.
- Prepared curry pastes are mixtures of herbs and spices mixed with a little oil. They are a great way to transform basic meat and vegetable ingredients into authentic Indian and Thai dishes.
- Fry curry pastes in a little canola or peanut oil to release maximum flavour.

10: Wholegrains

There's no question about it. Wholegrain foods deserve star billing when it comes to good nutrition for the heart. Eating these foods made from the entire grain (the starchy endosperm, fibrous bran and the vitamin-rich germ) regularly is associated with reduced risk of many chronic diseases, including heart disease, stroke, type 2 diabetes and some cancers. How do they do it?

Wholegrain foods contain more fibre, vitamins, minerals, essential unsaturated fats, trace elements and phytochemicals such as antioxidants, phytoestrogens and plant sterols than their processed counterparts because many of the protective components in grains are contained in the outer layers that are lost in the milling process. Many wholegrain foods (but not all) also have a low GI (glycemic index), which means they are slowly digested. This not only helps you control your blood glucose and insulin levels, but plays a useful role in your diet if you need to lose weight as these foods will keep you feeling fuller for longer.

Eating a diet rich in wholegrains can reduce your risk of heart disease. In a study of 27,000 men aged 40–75 followed for 14 years, those who ate the most wholegrains had a 20 per cent lower risk of heart disease.

From the traditional to the trendy, carbohydrate-rich wholegrains are bursting with energy, providing us with protein, dietary fibre, vitamins and minerals. A staple in many parts of the world, they are ideal as the basis for satisfying meals and snacks for everybody. They also play a part with weight control. Did you know that people who eat more wholegrain foods tend to maintain a healthy weight?

Wholegrain foods are made from cereal grains such as wheat, corn, oats, rye, rice and barley with the endosperm, germ and bran layer present in the same proportion as the original grain. For example, mixed grain bread or wholemeal bread.

Are you getting enough?

Scientific reviews have found a significant association between wholegrain intake and a lower risk of cardiovascular disease. The USA food guide MyPyramid and Canada's Food Guide recommend eating half of all grain food servings as wholegrains, the British government recommends choosing wholegrain where possible, and Australia's National Heart Foundation recommends at least 6g of fibre from wholegrains daily (equivalent to 3–4 slices of wholegrain bread, or a serve of wholegrain cereal and 2 slices of wholegrain bread).

What is a serve?

2 regular slices wholegrain bread
1 thick slice wholegrain bread
1 wholemeal crumpet
1 wholegrain English muffin
1 small pita pocket bread
1 wholemeal thin flat bread/mountain bread/lavash
1 small wholegrain bread roll
4 rye crispbreads
4 wholegrain wheat crispbreads
3 brown rice cakes (thick)
6 rice/corn thins
2 wholewheat breakfast biscuits
1 cup wholewheat flake-style cereal
½ cup muesli (granola)
⅔ cup cooked oats (⅓ cup dry)
1 muesli bar
1 cup cooked wholemeal pasta or spaghetti (40g/1½oz raw)
1 cup cooked buckwheat noodles
½ cup cooked brown rice (2 heaped tablespoons/ 40g/1½oz raw)
½ cup cooked, bulgar/burghul Grano, Kamut®
⅔ cup cooked amaranth, quinoa

⅔ cup cooked barley, buckwheat, millet, teff
⅔ cup cooked, Freekeh™ (2 heaped tablespoons dry)
1 cob corn (corn or maize is a grain although often classified as a vegetable)

* Uncooked/dry wholegrains swell to 2–3 times their size with cooking. Check the pack to calculate how much to prepare to equal the servings above.

* Serving sizes may vary between countries, and may be different to the manufacturer's serving sizes given on the pack.

What wholegrain is that?

Check out our star billing grains to look for on the shelves of your supermarket, health or organic food store.

Amaranth is a gluten-free, protein-rich grain which is of high quality. Use it to make porridge, add it to soups, stews and stuffings or to grain-based salads.

Barley is rich in soluble fibre—great for lowering cholesterol and slowing down the release of energy (glucose) into the blood after eating it. Pearl barley is used in cooking to make lemon barley water, pilafs and stuffings or add to soups, stews, salads and desserts.

Buckwheat is related to rhubarb and has a high level of rutin, an antioxidant that can lower blood fats and reduce LDL cholesterol oxidation. You can buy the whole buckwheat grains, toasted groats or buckwheat flour for cooking. Or enjoy products made with buckwheat flour like soba noodles.

Bulgar/burghul is precooked and dried wheat grains. It's quick cooking and convenient to use in side dishes, pilafs or salads such as tabbouleh.

Emmer (called farro/grano faro in Italy) is an ancient strain of wheat that's making a comeback as a specialty food such as in semolina flour made from emmer used for pasta.

Farro is the dried wholegrain form of certain species of wheat, including spelt. It looks similar to bulgar and needs cooking or soaking before being added to soups or salads.

Freekeh™ is roasted green wheat, harvested young and thus rich in nutrients. It is high in fibre and has a low glycemic index (GI). Can be served as a side dish, added to soups, salads and burgers, or the flour can be used to make breads, loaves and muffins.

Kamut® is another heirloom grain making a comeback. Kamut grain can be used making hot and cold breakfast cereals, muesli, bread, biscuits and pancakes or served as a side dish.

Maize (corn) isn't officially a vegetable at all, it's a grain. Cooking corn actually increases the levels of antioxidants. Enjoy it on the cob, adding kernels to soups and stews, popping corn or any way you wish.

Millet is often used to make porridge or flat breads or mixed with other grains or toasted before cooking.

Oats contain a type of soluble fibre called beta-glucan that has cholesterol-lowering effects. They are a favourite for breakfast cereals from porridge to muesli (granola) and muesli bars.

Quinoa isn't a true grain. It is related botanically to Swiss chard and beets. It cooks in about 10–12 minutes, making it ideal as a carb accompaniment for a main meal or for a breakfast porridge. You can also add it to soups and salads and to your baking.

Rice Brown rice retains the bran that surrounds the kernel so it is slower to tenderise and cook than white rice, but it is chewier and nuttier, and more valuable nutritionally. White rice has had the bran and germ removed and is more tender to the bite and delicate in flavour.

Rye is unusual among grains for the high level of fibre in its endosperm—not just in its bran. Rye products generally have a lower glycemic index.

Sorghum also called milo, is a gluten-free grain.

Spelt (old wheat variety) can be used in place of common wheat in most recipes.

Teff is the smallest cereal grain in the world. Today it is getting more attention for its sweet, molasses-like flavour and its versatility; it can be cooked as porridge, added to baked goods, or even made into 'teff polenta'.

Triticale is a hybrid of durum wheat and rye and can be used as a substitute for wheat flour in baking.

Wheat Make the most of wheat in many different forms. Bulgar and grano make excellent side dishes. Wheat berries (whole wheat kernels) can also be cooked as a side dish or breakfast cereal, but must be boiled for about an hour, preferably after soaking overnight. Cracked wheat cooks faster, as the wheat berries have been split open, allowing water to penetrate more quickly.

Wild rice actually isn't rice but the seed of an unrelated American aquatic grass. It takes longer to cook than white rice and is relatively expensive to buy. It is often sold as a white rice–wild rice mix with a shorter cooking time because it has been precooked and dried.

What about bread, pasta and breakfast cereals?

If you like to sit down to toast made from white bread for breakfast, and enjoy steamed white rice with your takeaway, keep in mind that, delicious though they can be, these foods have something missing—they have been refined and some of their nutritional goodness is gone. For example, white bread and flour have no bran or germ and are less nutritious as a result. They also have a high glycemic index (GI) so they release their energy very quickly and require a greater insulin response, which is not ideal.

However, if you're not enthused by bread with intact grains, you'll be pleased to know that wholemeal bread can still be a wholegrain food—provided it is made from whole grains. Rolling, crushing, cracking and extruding whole grains just changes the texture and wholegrains processed in this way still contain more nutrients than their refined counterparts. However this processing makes the starch they contain more rapidly absorbed and increases the GI. It's best to eat whole grains in a form as close to their natural state as possible.

Here are some wholegrain processed foods to look for:
- Breakfast cereals labelled 'wholegrain'
- Wholemeal bread (dense grainy bread has a lower GI)
- Wholemeal pasta
- Crispbreads labelled 'wholegrain'.

Sodium alert

Some packaged wholegrain foods such as breads, crispbreads and even some breakfast cereals are higher in sodium than is ideal for a heart-healthy eating plan. In particular, buy bread with the lowest sodium level you can find. Less than 400mg per 100g/3½oz is good, but lower is better.

What about bran?

Grain foods with bran added are higher in fibre and that's good, but they're not always made with wholegrains and therefore not as healthy as wholegrain foods.

Wholegrains have been found to contain equal amounts, or even higher, of antioxidants than vegetables and fruits. Aim to eat at least half your daily grain foods as wholegrains.

How to get more

- Start your day with wholegrain breakfast cereal with low-fat milk, topped with seasonal fruits.
- Add interest to porridge with stewed rhubarb or quinces or kiwi fruit and mandarin or dried fruit, nuts, seeds and a little honey.
- Choose wholemeal bread made with whole wheat or whole rye for toast and sandwiches.
- Swap to wholemeal pasta and brown rice or start with half white and half brown.
- Substitute some or all the white flour with wholewheat flour, triticale or sorghum in baking berry muffins, nutty biscuits or cookies and fruit or vegetable breads/loaves and cakes.
- Adapt basic risotto and pilaf recipes by adding brown rice, wild rice, grano or millet.

- Snack on popcorn (skip the salt and sugar) or wholegrain muesli (granola) bars.
- Add wholewheat flour, buckwheat flour, or amaranth to pancake or pikelet batter.
- Experiment with tabouli (cracked wheat) salad by trying other wholegrains such as quinoa, buckwheat or millet. Add herbs like basil, coriander (cilantro) or mint or even try adding a touch of a favourite spice.
- Add millet, freekeh or buckwheat to vegetable and meat curries.
- Prepare a savoury tart base using cooked wholegrains (eg, teff) pressed into the base of a greased pie dish.

Grain porridge

You can make porridge with any wholegrain. Follow the cooking directions on the pack, or, add one part whole grains (eg, oats, cracked wheat, spelt, kamut, millet, barley, amaranth, quinoa) to four parts boiling water and a pinch of salt and simmer for around 20 minutes, or until tender. Add sugar, honey or maple syrup and your favourite dried fruits such as raisins or mixed dried fruit. Top with a little low-fat milk, yoghurt or soy milk.

Oats

What are they?

Oat flour

Oatmeal

Rolled oats

Scottish/Irish oats

Steel cut oats

Whole oats (groats)

Why they are good for you

Oats contain a type of soluble fibre called beta-glucan that has cholesterol-lowering effects. They do this by increasing the excretion of cholesterol out of the body, and reducing cholesterol made by the liver. Eating oats has also been shown to benefit people with diabetes. This is probably due to the low GI of oats.

All oats are good for you; however, oat porridge made the old-fashioned way with whole oats (traditional rolled oats) has a lower glycemic index (GI) than instant or quick oats. This is because quick oats have been milled to a finer texture for faster cooking time, but this makes them more quickly digested and absorbed too.

How to get more

Try these delicious ideas with oat porridge (oatmeal) for a hearty breakfast:

* Cook with mixed dried fruit.
* Swirl through some warmed poached dried figs, apricots and peaches.
* Cook with sliced banana and a dash of nutmeg.
* Cook with chopped apple and cinnamon.
* Top with natural (plain) low-fat yoghurt and a drizzle of honey.
* Top with brown sugar or maple syrup.
* Top with a spoon of unsaturated margarine spread for a savoury flavour.
* Try muesli boosted with oven-roasted macadamias or hazelnuts for variety at breakfast, or as a topping for low-fat yoghurt or ice cream.
* Choose a wholegrain breakfast cereal with oats.
* Select wholegrain bread with oats for sandwiches.
* Add oats to dried fruit and nut mixes for snacking.
* Try oat flour in orange or berry cup cakes, healthy slices, biscuits, pancakes and cookie recipes.
* Use oats as a filler for meat loaf, meatballs, patties and burgers.

Barley

What is it?
Barley flour
Breads and breakfast cereals made with barley
Hulled barley
Pearled barley
Rolled barley

Why it is good for you
Barley is rich in a soluble fibre—fantastic for lowering cholesterol and slowing down the release of energy (glucose) into the body.

How to get more
- Make rolled barley porridge for breakfast. Cook 1 part barley in 3 parts water, and allow around ³/₄ cup raw barley per person. Cook in large batches and freeze leftovers.
- Combine barley with steamed rice (or on its own) to serve with stir-fries, curries, tagines and other wet sauces.
- Add barley to soups and stews, such as minestrone.
- Choose wholegrain breads and crispbreads that contain barley.
- Cook barley ahead and have in the fridge ready to add to salads, such as rice, mixed bean or leafy garden salads.
- Combine rice and barley for a healthy risotto.

11: Legumes

Eating legumes regularly is one of the components of the Mediterranean diet that is associated with lower risk of heart disease. They are champion foods when it comes to health benefits. They are known to lower cholesterol. They may also help to lower high blood pressure. They're also great for those watching their weight. How do they do it?

Legumes are naturally high in protein, fibre, vitamins, minerals and phytochemicals. Their cholesterol lowering ability is due mostly to their soluble fibre content, but also because of the protein and phytochemicals they contain. A low GI makes them satisfying and long lasting foods that are particularly helpful for those with diabetes, or those at risk of diabetes. Legumes are the edible seeds of plants with special nodules on their roots that help them obtain nitrogen. This ability increases the protein content of their fruit (seed) that we enjoy eating.

- Dried peas—green split, yellow split, chickpeas, black-eye, soup mix.
- Dried beans—borlotti, butter, cannellini, haricot, kidney, lima, mung, navy, soy.
- Lentils—green, brown, red, puy, split lentils (Indian dahls).

The peanut is botanically a legume, but is nutritionally similar to nuts and thus usually grouped with them.

Did you know?

Falafels are made from ground legumes. Hummus is made from chickpeas. TVP stands for Texture Vegetable Protein and is made from soy and wheat protein.

Finger on the pulse

You may have heard the term 'pulses and legumes' to describe these foods. 'Pulse' is used interchangeably with legumes.

The vegetarian advantage

Because legumes are so high in protein and other valuable vitamins and minerals, they have long been enjoyed as a meat alternative. Studies on vegetarians have shown much lower risk of chronic diseases such as heart disease, diabetes and cancer, and enhanced longevity. Their high plant food intake—including legumes—is thought to be a significant protective factor.

Are you getting enough?

Healthy eating guidelines around the world recommend including legumes in the diet, either as a meat alternative or as part of your vegetable servings—vegetables should make up half your dinner plate. National Heart Foundation (Australia) recommends eating legumes in two meals a week, but this is an absolute minimum because legumes add so many important nutrients to your diet. Aim to include them as often as you can.

What is a serve?

$\frac{1}{2}$ cup cooked beans or peas or lentils (canned, drained)
120g (4$\frac{1}{4}$oz) tofu (soy bean curd)
80g (2$\frac{3}{4}$oz) tempeh (fermented soy bean cake)
1 large bean/vege burger (120g/4$\frac{1}{4}$oz)

Home cooked or canned?

All legumes must be cooked to make them digestible. With the exception of lentils, legumes must be soaked for at least 4 hours (preferably overnight) before boiling to reduce the cooking time. You can freeze cooked legumes in meal size batches and defrost as needed. The advantages of soaking and cooking legumes yourself are they maintain a firmer texture, contain less salt, cost much less and require much less packaging than the canned versions.

Canned legumes are a nutritious and quick alternative—just drain, rinse and use. Canned legumes contain more sodium than home-cooked legumes prepared with no added salt.

How can you enjoy more legumes?

Legumes have a mild, slightly nutty taste and will take on the flavour of whatever you add them to. Their chewy texture adds interest and their protein and fibre content give a dish filling power.

Breakfast

- Baked beans on wholegrain toast.
- Fill an omelette with a mixture of red lentils, tomatoes, mushrooms and green onions.

Lunch

- Combine canned, drained three or four bean mix, cherry tomatoes, finely chopped onion and some parsley with a vinaigrette dressing for delicious bean salad.
- Include brown lentils or soup mix (eg, a combination of legumes) to soups and casseroles.
- Add cannellini beans to a tuna salad.
- Add mung bean sprouts to sandwiches, salads and stir-fries.
- Make warming winter soups with vegetables such as carrot, celery, onion, parsnip, split peas, water and a little salt-reduced stock and serve with oven baked wholemeal rolls, topped with a little reduced-fat cheese.

Dinner

- Substitute half the mince for cooked red lentils for a Bolognese pasta sauce.
- Combine soaked or canned lentils with mince for meat loaf and serve sliced on wholemeal buns, topped with a chopped tomato, onion and green capsicum salsa and with lots of salad for an open burger.
- Add butter beans to a low salt, tomato-based pasta sauce to make a wholemeal vegetable lasagna.
- Cook Puy (French green) lentils in salt-reduced vegetable stock until tender and serve as a side dish for lean steak or chicken with sweet potato wedges and salad.
- Add red kidney beans to chilli minced beef for chilli con carne and serve with mashed avocado and a lettuce, capsicum and red onion salad.
- Substitute meat or chicken with chickpeas or beans in curries and casseroles.
- Cook brown rice with red lentils for two-colour rice and serve with spicy Indian dishes.
- Cook and lightly mash brown lentils with chopped herbs— try served under cooked chicken breast or fish with a salad.
- Add borlotti or kidney beans to a potato salad and serve with barbecued or grilled (broiled) fish steaks with green salad.
- Include a serving of dahl with naan bread when dining in or taking out Indian food.
- Top a baked potato with chilli beans and serve with a fresh green salad.

Snacks

- Dip into hummus with carrot or celery sticks.
- Enjoy a bean-topped bruschetta.
- Nibble on a few roasted chick peas (available in packets and in bulk from nut-sellers).
- Microwave a few pappadums on a sheet of absorbent paper—they are made with lentil flour—and enjoy them alone or with a low-fat yoghurt dip such as tzatziki.

Wind warning

If you're not used to eating legumes, introduce them gradually to avoid problems with wind (gas) caused by the presence of indigestible sugars (oligosaccharides). Discard the water they have been soaked or canned in. Wind generally becomes less of a problem over time as the digestive system gets used to legumes, however many people with Irritable Bowel Syndrome are especially sensitive to wind-forming foods including legumes. Sprouted legumes (eg, mung bean sprouts) contain less oligosaccharides and are less 'windy'.

Soy foods

What are they?

Breads and breakfast cereals containing soy such as soy and linseed breads

Miso (fermented soybean paste)

Soy cheese

Soy custard

Soy grits

Soy milk

Soy pasta

Soy yoghurt

Soybeans

Tempeh (fermented soybeans)

Tofu (soybean curd)

TVP (textured vegetable protein)

Vegetarian meat alternative products such as burgers, patties and sausages

Why they are good for you

Soybeans are the highest in protein of all legumes, and the protein is of the highest quality—similar to animal protein. Soybeans are also high in fibre, vitamins, minerals such as calcium, zinc and iron, and trace elements. Diets high in soy protein have been shown to lower cholesterol, reduce cholesterol oxidation, reduce triglycerides and blood pressure, increase good HDL cholesterol and help keep blood vessels more flexible.

Although soy beans are low in fat, the type of fat is the healthy polyunsaturated type—including some omega-3. Soybeans are also rich in bioactive peptides and isoflavones—a type of phytochemical. Isoflavones are also called phytoestrogens (plant oestrogens) and have a number of health benefits including reduced risk of hormone-related cancers (eg, breast and prostate). The phytochemicals in soy have also been found to have antioxidant and anti-inflammatory effects.

A diet with a combination of heart-friendly foods (soy protein, plant sterols, nuts and foods rich in soluble fibre like oats, barley and psyllium) has been shown to equal the effects of statin drugs in people with high cholesterol.

How much soy protein?

The optimal amount of soy protein for cholesterol appears to be around 25g/¾oz a day, but every little bit counts—especially when combined with other cholesterol-lowering dietary components in a diet low in saturated fat. It is also good to eat soy foods several times a day rather than all at once for best effects. Uncooked soy foods such as milk, yoghurt, tofu and tempeh may be better than baked goods such as protein bars and muffins because the bioactive peptides stay intact.

In the USA, soy foods may carry a health claim that says, "25g/¾oz of soy protein daily, as part of a diet low in saturated fat and cholesterol, may reduce the risk of heart disease."

Is it OK for men to eat phytoestrogens?

The answer is yes; soy foods are good for everyone. Women and men in Asian societies have consumed soy foods for thousands of years. In fact, these societies have much lower risk of chronic diseases and soy foods have been identified as an important part of their protective diet.

Can women with breast cancer eat soy?

There are some kinds of breast cancer that are hormone-sensitive, and treatment includes oestrogen-blocking medications. While women with breast cancer (or women who have had breast cancer in the past) are advised against taking isoflavone supplements, the scientific evidence suggests eating soy foods in moderation as part of a healthy balanced diet does not increase risk.

Soy protein content of soy foods	
½ cup (100g) soy flour	18g
Tempeh (100g)	18g
Soy beans (boiled, 100g)	15g
Tofu (100g)	15g
Soy beans (canned, 100g)	10g
1 cup (250ml) soy milk	8.8g
Soy burger (60g)	7.8g
2 slices soy & linseed bread	7.7g
1 tub soy yoghurt (200g)	6.6g
TVP vege-mince, prepared (125g)	5.3g
45g soy breakfast cereal	5g
NB These are approximate and may vary, check food labels	

How to get more

- Tofu and tempeh are ready to eat and don't require cooking; however, they are delicious fried in healthy oil until golden brown, or just heated through in soups and stir-fries.
- Choose breads and breakfast cereals that contain soy (eg, soy-linseed bread) for toast and sandwiches.
- Make your own breakfast cereal using soy flakes, traditional rolled oats, dried fruits and nuts.
- Try soy milk on your breakfast cereal.
- Vary sandwich fillings with tempeh or soy cheese as a protein option.
- Enjoy soy yoghurt as a healthy snack with a swirl of puréed fruit or berries.
- Add tofu or tempeh to your Asian vegetable stir-fries.
- Sprinkle diced tofu or tempeh over soups or salads.
- Substitute soy-containing flour (eg, gluten-free flour) for wheat flour in baking.
- Include a vegetarian meat alternative such as soy burgers, soy patties or soy sausages.
- Make a soy smoothie with soy milk and fresh fruit.
- Add drained and rinsed canned soybeans to salads, soups and stews.
- Grill marinated (hard) tofu and vegetable kebabs on the barbecue.
- Use miso to create soups, stocks, marinades.
- Substitute standard pasta with soy pasta.
- Order the edamame starter (steamed young soy beans in their pod) in Japanese restaurants.
- Use TVP instead of mince in pasta sauce, 'meat' loaf and lasagna.
- Serve hot fruit puddings or seasonal fruit with soy custard for dessert.

TOFU TIP

Ensure you choose the right tofu for the dish. You need 'hard' or 'firm' tofu that can be sliced to add to stir-fries and soups. Silken tofu is best to blend/purée for desserts or dressings.

12: Nuts and seeds

Nuts and seeds are super-healthy plant foods associated with reduced risk of diseases such as heart disease and cancer. Heart health associations around the world agree that eating nuts regularly is a good idea to keep the heart healthy. How do they do it?

Nuts and seeds are nutrition powerhouses packed with protein, fibre, unsaturated (healthy) fats, vitamins, minerals, trace elements and phytochemicals. They are rich in substances considered protective for the heart: an amino acid (building block of protein) called arginine; vitamin E, folate, copper (a trace element) and plant sterols. Eating a healthy diet that includes nuts can lower cholesterol. This is probably due to their unsaturated fat content; however, research suggests there are other components that also contribute to their cholesterol-lowering effect.

Eating nuts can reduce your risk of heart disease

Studies of populations show eating nuts regularly significantly reduces the risk of heart disease—eating a small handful of nuts (30g/1oz) five days a week or more is associated with a 35–50 per cent lower risk of having a (non-fatal) heart attack, and a 40–50 per cent lower risk of dying from a heart attack.

Care with nuts around children

Whole nuts and nut pieces are a choking risk for babies and toddlers and should be avoided. Nut butters are OK. Take care with serving nuts around children you don't know in case they are allergic.

What are they?

Nuts are the seeds of plants that are covered with a hard shell—seeds don't have a hard shell. The seeds of plants contain a storehouse of nutrients to grow a new plant, as well as to nourish healthy human beans!

Nuts: almonds, Brazil nuts, peanuts, cashews, chestnuts, hazelnuts, macadamias, pecans, pine nuts, pistachios, walnuts.

Seeds: linseeds, pumpkin, sesame, sesame seed paste (tahini), sunflower, chia, poppy.

Are you getting enough?

Studies suggest that to keep your heart healthy you need to eat a handful or two of nuts (30–60g/1–2oz)—or some nut butter—most days. Using nuts in cooking is a great way to keep them interesting. Whole seeds are a great way to include healthy fats and fibre in your everyday meals and snacks, and are also available in foods such as breads and breakfast cereals.

Choose unsalted nuts whenever possible. Enjoy nuts raw or dry roasted and unsalted. Nut butters such as peanut, almond and cashew butter are delicious and versatile—look for those with the lowest salt and sugar content.

Stop at a handful or two

Ever wanted to eat 'just a few nuts' and then couldn't stop yourself eating the whole packet? Nuts and seeds are deliciously more-ish, but they are high in kilojoules (calories). Portion control is key. Divide nuts and seeds into individual small handful-sized bags or containers to resist overindulgence. If you're on a kilojoule-controlled eating plan to lose weight, have smaller portions, and eat them instead of less nutritious treats like lollies and biscuits (cookies).

What is a serve?

Heart protection comes from eating small amounts of nuts (30–60g/1–2oz) most days.

The following amounts are 30g/1oz:
- 10 whole walnuts/20 halves
- 30 pistachio kernels
- 2 tablespoons pine nuts
- 15 pecans
- 2 tablespoons peanuts
- 2 tablespoons mixed nuts
- 15 macadamia nuts
- 20 hazelnuts
- 15 cashews
- 10 brazil nuts
- 20 almonds
- 4 chestnuts
- 1 tablespoon nut butter

What about coconut?

A coconut isn't a nut at all, but a fleshy fruit called a drupe, botanically similar to peaches and cherries. Coconut flesh does not contain the same heart-healthy nutritional profile of other nuts. Heart health organisations around the world agree the fat in coconut is highly saturated and cholesterol raising and should be limited.

How to get your 'handful' a day

Breakfast

- Sprinkle pecans and linseeds on your breakfast cereal.
- Spread nut butter (peanut or almond) or seed paste (tahini) on your wholegrain toast or crispbread.
- Stir nuts and seeds into natural (plain) low-fat yoghurt with a little honey.
- Chop up fruits in season, stir through some berry low-fat yoghurt and roasted nuts.

Lunch

- Combine chopped nuts (peanuts) and seeds (sunflower) with dried fruit and low-fat cottage cheese and carrot as a sandwich filling.
- Combine nut butter (macadamia or hazelnut) with banana or apple in a toasted wholegrain sandwich.

Keep coated, fried, flavoured and chocolate-smothered nuts as a treat for very special occasions, because of the extra cholesterol raising saturated fat and kilojoules (calories) they contain.

Dinner and desserts

- Make a satay sauce for seafood, lean meat or chicken using nut butter, onion, garlic, chilli and lite coconut milk.
- Add roasted cashews or sesame seeds to Asian beef salads and beef or chicken stir-fries.
- Add chopped walnuts or hazelnuts to salad dressings and serve with lean barbecued meats.
- Add roasted nuts such as pine nuts to pasta dishes.
- Top grilled fish with a pesto made with pine nuts or pistachios with fresh leafy herbs, garlic and olive oil and serve with vegetables or salad.
- Add roasted pistachios or chestnuts to poultry stuffing.
- Add chopped nuts to sliced banana and low-fat ice cream (banana split).
- Top pancakes with chopped nuts and seeds and a berry sauce.

Snacks

- Enjoy a small handful of almonds or brazil nuts as a satisfying snack.
- Mix nuts and pumpkin seeds with dried fruit for healthy pick-me-up.
- Add nuts and seeds to breads, crumbles, cakes, slices and biscuits.

What is nut meat?

Nuts and seeds are important foods for vegetarians because of the protein and minerals such as iron and zinc they provide. 'Nut meats' are a combination of diced nuts and seeds held together in a loaf with herbs and spices that can be sliced and enjoyed as a meat alternative—available in supermarkets.

NUTS AND SEEDS TIP

Because of their unsaturated (healthy) fat content, nuts and seeds must be stored correctly to prevent them going stale (rancid). Store nuts and seeds in an air tight container away from light and heat, and eat soon after purchase. To keep them longer, store in the fridge or freezer.

Almonds

What are they?

Almond meal

Blanched almonds

Flaked almonds

Raw almonds

Roasted almonds

Slivered almonds

Why they are good for you

Almonds are high in protein, calcium, vitamin E and arginine (a heart-protective amino acid). They also contain good amounts of fibre, iron and zinc. A study looking at the effects of adding almonds to the usual diet found they contributed significant amounts of monounsaturated (healthy) fats, fibre, vitamin E, magnesium and copper—all positive nutrients for heart health. Eating more almonds also had the effect of reducing undesirable nutrients—trans (bad) fats, sodium, cholesterol and sugars.

In a statistical analysis of the best dietary combination to reduce the risk of heart disease, almonds were included along with wine, fish, dark chocolate, fruits, vegetables and garlic. Researchers concluded this combination of foods consumed regularly could reduce cardiovascular disease events by 76 per cent, could increase life expectancy of men by 6.6 years, and 4.8 years for women.

How to get more

Raw or roasted almonds, and (puréed) almond butter are just as good for you and will equally help get your cholesterol down—even salted almonds have benefit, but unsalted are best in order to limit sodium which may increase blood pressure.

- Add slivered or chopped almonds to muesli (granola).
- Top fruit and yoghurt with slivered almonds.
- Enjoy almond butter on wholegrain or fruit toast.
- Snack on raw almonds with skin.
- Substitute some flour with almond meal in baking.
- Add roasted almonds to a chicken and vegetable stir-fry.
- Toss slivered almonds through steamed or microwaved carrots or broccoli.
- Combine raw almonds with dried apricots for a tasty snack.
- Add chopped roasted almonds to rice, noodle and couscous dishes.
- Stir whole raw almonds into a four bean mix, herb, tomato and asparagus salad.
- Toast flaked almonds and sprinkle on baked fish.
- Add almond meal to meat loaf, meat balls, burger patties and fish cakes.
- Coat lean meat such as pork or chicken in crushed almonds and bake.
- Top fruit puddings and parfaits with roasted slivered almonds.
- Bake apples or pears with a filling of chopped almonds and mixed dried fruit.
- Top healthy fruit cakes with blanched almonds for a decorative finish.

Walnuts

What are they?

Raw walnuts
Walnut halves
Walnut pieces
Roasted walnuts

Why they are good for you

Walnuts are the highest in polyunsaturated (healthy) fats—including omega-6 and omega-3 type—of all nuts. They are rich in fibre and protein, and also contain vitamin E, folate, manganese (a trace element) and arginine (an amino acid), tannins and polyphenols (phytochemicals).

Omega-3

30g (1oz) of walnuts (approx. 20 walnut halves) contains around 2g of plant omega-3 fat (alpha linolenic acid)—meeting the suggested daily amount for adults.

Eating walnuts can lower your cholesterol.

An Australian study of people with type 2 diabetes compared the effects of low-fat diets with and without walnuts. The cholesterol level of the subjects who just followed a low-fat diet did not change, whereas the subjects who ate walnuts reduced their LDL (bad) cholesterol by 10 per cent and increased their HDL (good) cholesterol by 30 per cent.

How to get more

- Top oat porridge with sliced banana, nutmeg and chopped walnuts.
- Sprinkle chopped walnuts over stewed apple and cinnamon.
- Present a platter of whole walnuts in their shell after dinner.
- Enjoy walnut halves with raisins or dates as a snack.
- Add walnuts along with dried fruit to scones, cakes and biscuits (cookies).
- Add chopped walnuts and sultanas or raisins to coleslaw.
- Create a wonderful pasta dish by adding steamed vegetables, chopped walnuts, olive oil, cracked black pepper and the juice and zest of a lemon to hot wholemeal pasta.
- Combine salad greens, walnuts, fresh sliced pear and thinly sliced goats cheese and serve on the side with lean chicken or beef.
- Add walnuts to couscous seasoned with salt-reduced stock, lemon juice, capers and green olives—great served with fish.
- Scatter roasted walnuts on a plate of cut vegetables and dips.
- Crush walnut pieces and sprinkle on the top of smoothies.

Linseeds

What are they?

Linseeds (also known as flax seeds)

LSA mix (contains linseeds, sunflower seeds and almond meal)

Breads, breakfast cereals and crispbreads with linseeds

What about flaxseed oil?

There have been very few clinical studies on the effects of flaxseed oil on cholesterol and heart health. Flaxseed oil is highly unstable and thus unsuitable for cooking. It goes 'off' quickly and must be kept in the refrigerator. Go for whole or ground flaxseeds (linseeds) instead.

Soy and linseed: a great combination

Foods containing soy protein and linseeds are good for you. A study found daily consumption of soy and linseed-containing foods over 3 weeks resulted in a 10 per cent decrease in total cholesterol and a 12.5 per cent decrease in LDL (bad) cholesterol.

Why they are good for you

Linseeds are rich in three protective nutrients for the heart: omega-3 polyunsaturated fat called alpha-linolenic acid; lignans—a type of phytoestrogen phytochemical; and soluble fibre that helps to lower cholesterol.

How to get more

- Add linseeds or LSA mix to breakfast cereals.
- Cook linseeds with oats for porridge.
- Buy breakfast cereals, breads and crispbreads with linseeds.
- Add linseed meal or LSA mix to fruit smoothies.
- Add ground linseeds towards the end of cooking pasta sauce, soups or stews.
- Add ground linseeds to meatloaf or meatballs.
- Add whole linseeds to muffins and biscuits (cookies).
- Toast linseeds and add to rice dishes to have with stews, curries and casseroles.
- Add linseeds to homemade bread.

Whole or ground?

Because linseeds have a tough outer shell, the nutrients are more accessible to the body from ground or crushed linseeds. Chewing whole linseeds well has a similar effect—the inner nutrients are released once the shell is broken.

The omega-3 story

Alpha-linolenic acid is one of the two essential fats required by human beings to stay healthy. Alpha-linolenic acid is plant type omega-3 polyunsaturated fat that is strongly linked to reduced risk of death from heart attack. The richest sources of alpha-linolenic acid are linseeds, walnuts, green leafy vegetables and canola oil and margarine.

13: Fish

Fish and seafood offer a bounty of nutritional goodness. There is clear evidence that eating fish and seafood regularly protects the heart. In addition, scientists have found that people who eat a lot of fish can have lower rates of depression. How does fish do it?

Fish is rich in protein, a good source of heart-friendly omega-3 fats, contains vitamins A and D, and provides helpful minerals and trace elements such as magnesium, zinc, iron, fluorine and selenium. Fish and shellfish harvested from salt water are the best source of dietary iodine—an essential trace element important for thyroid function and metabolism.

Eating fish is one of the pillars of the healthful Mediterranean diet.

How much fish?

Heart health associations around the world agree that eating fish regularly—fresh, frozen or canned—is a good idea to keep your heart healthy. Aim to eat fish twice a week, and include some oily fish such as salmon, sardines or mackerel.

What is a serve?

1 fish fillet 120g/4oz cooked
Tuna or salmon, canned 85g/3oz drained
Sardines, kippers, canned 75g/2½ oz drained
Oysters, 12 large/18 small
Prawn/shrimp, 15 medium

All fresh fish and seafood is good for you (unless it's coated in batter and deep-fried in unhealthy fat).

Make the most of the convenience of frozen fish products if it suits your busy lifestyle, but keep an eye out for saturated fat and sodium (salt) content. Battered and crumbed fish fillets, fish fingers, and fish in creamy sauces may be high— check the label and choose products with the lowest levels.

Canned fish (eg, tuna, salmon, mackerel, herring, sardines, oysters, mussels) are nutritious options. Opt for fish canned in springwater rather than brine to avoid too much salt. Tuna flavoured with herbs, garlic, onion, etc is a tasty option—they can be a little higher in sodium, but you're better off having the fish than not. Sardines in tomato sauce are another enjoyable option if you don't like them plain.

What about cholesterol in shellfish?

While shellfish such as prawns contain dietary cholesterol, they are not significant contributors to blood cholesterol levels. The biggest influence on blood cholesterol is saturated fat in the diet, and shellfish are low in total and saturated fat. Besides, most people don't consume shellfish often or in large amounts.

Are you getting enough?

People living in Western countries generally fall short of eating the recommended amounts of fish and omega-3 fats for optimum health. Scientific research shows that eating some fish is better than having none.

Cooking fish

People often say the reason they don't eat more fish is they don't know how to cook it. Your fishmonger will be a great help—just tell them what you want to make and they'll suggest a suitable type of fish.

How to get your 'two serves a week'

Breakfast

- Enjoy smoked salmon or trout with a poached egg for breakfast—try a side of steamed spinach and wholegrain toast.
- Arrange canned herring or kippers on a soy-linseed muffin spread with plant sterol spread, and top with fresh rocket (arugula) leaves and a poached egg.
- Brunch on sardines atop wholegrain toast—with cherry tomatoes on the side.

Lunch

- Combine smoked salmon or trout with avocado and salad greens on wholegrain sandwiches.
- Fill sandwiches with tuna or salmon, coloured lettuce or rocket (arugula), tomato and cucumber.
- Top a cos lettuce, corn and beetroot salad with flavoured canned tuna and a wholegrain roll.
- Enjoy some sushi with salmon, tuna or prawn filling.
- Combine cooked prawns with canola or soy mayonnaise and dill for sandwich filling.
- Mash canned mackerel with lemon zest, chopped chives and a little low-fat natural (plain) yoghurt for a wholemeal pocket bread or wrap filler.
- Make a fish and lentil soup—cook boneless white fish with no-added-salt canned tomatoes, canned lentils, salt-reduced stock and water—stir in lots of freshly chopped parsley just before serving.
- Herrings in tomato sauce make a good topper for toasted grain muffins.

Dinner

- Barbecue or pan fry fish steaks or cutlets—serve with stir-fried rice noodles with snow peas, capsicums and spring onions (scallions) or crisp green salad and wholegrain roll.
- Bake a whole fish stuffed with herbs, onion and lemon wedges—serve with roast potatoes, steamed broccoli and yellow squash.
- Bake fish fillets in foil with fresh coriander (cilantro), canola oil and lemon or lime slices—serve with a cumin and carrot couscous and steamed green beans.
- Make a fish and pumpkin yellow curry with boneless cubed fish fillets—serve with steamed brown rice and wilted Chinese greens such as gai lan, choy sum or pak choy.
- Stir-fry baby octopus with garlic and sweet chilli sauce —stir through wholemeal pasta or soba noodles and serve with a watercress, mint and snow pea sprout salad on the side.
- Cook marinara mix (mixed chopped seafood; mussels, prawns, fish, squid), in lots of garlic and canned diced no-added-salt tomatoes and toss through cooked penne pasta—serve with an endive, fennel and olive side salad.
- Brush fresh tuna or salmon and long slices of yellow and green zucchinis (courgettes) with oil and grill (broil) or cook on a griddle pan—serve the tuna topped with the zucchini, baby rocket and drizzled with a citrus dressing.
- Add clams to a brown rice risotto or pilaf—serve with steamed green beans, carrots and cauliflower or a leafy red and green salad of radicchio and mustard greens.

Snacks

- Snack on small cans of tuna or salmon—with wholegrain toast or crispbread.
- Dip prawns (shrimp) into natural (plain) low-fat yoghurt combined with canola mayonnaise, lemon zest and chopped dill.
- Offer a platter of freshly shucked oysters with fresh squeezed lemon or lime juice and fresh ground black pepper.
- Snack on smoked oysters or mussels on brown rice crackers.
- Enjoy an antipasto plate with marinated baby octopus.
- Start a meal with a selection of sashimi served with salt-reduced soy sauce, pickled ginger and wasabi (horseradish mustard).

The magic of omega-3 fats

Omega-3 fats reduce the risk of having a heart attack (primary prevention), but also reduce the risk of having another heart attack in people who have already had one (secondary prevention).

The two omega-3 fats in fish are called DHA and EPA (docosahexanoic acid and eicosapentanoic acid). Their protection is not from lowering cholesterol, but through a variety of other important effects: they keep the heart beating regularly (prevent arrhythmias), lower blood triglyceride (diacylglycerol) levels, 'thin' the blood and prevent clots, help to calm inflammation, lower blood pressure and keep the walls of blood vessels (endothelium) flexible.

Omega-3 fats are highest in oily fish such as salmon, tuna, mackerel, sardines and herring, however, other fish and seafood provide useful amounts of omega-3 too. There is also a plant type of omega-3 fat called alpha linolenic acid (ALA) found in canola oil, linseeds, nuts and green leafy vegetables and it's also good for the heart (see page 90).

How much omega-3?

Aim for around 500mg a day of omega-3 fats (EPA and DHA) which can significantly reduce the risk of cardiovascular disease. You can get this amount from around half a serve of fish (60g/2oz) from the 'excellent' list on the right. More omega-3 fats (around 1000mg a day) may be required to prevent a second heart attack if you've already had one—the American Heart Association suggests one serve of oily fish daily (from the 'excellent' list on the right) or a fish oil supplement. Talk to your doctor before taking supplements.

Omega-3 polyunsaturated fat content of fresh and canned seafood (per 100g/3½oz)		
Excellent (more than 900mg)	Great (250–900mg)	Good (less than 250mg)
Fresh	**Fresh**	**Fresh**
Swordfish	Sand flathead	Barracouta
Silver perch	Southern sea garfish	Barramundi
Mackerel	Gemfish	Black bream
Queensland mullet	Blue grenadier	Blue groper
Blue mackerel	Blue eye	Chinaman
Sea mullet	Red gurnard	leatherjacket
Atlantic salmon	Jackass morwong	Golden bream
Smoked salmon	Red mullet	John Dory
Yellowtail scad	Nannygai	Ling
Tailor	Golden perch	Rock & tiger flathead
Tarwhine	Australian salmon	Tiger flathead
Trevally	Scallop (bay)	Greenback flounder
Southern bluefin	Snapper	Garfish
tuna	Spiky oreo	Perch gernard
	Rainbow trout	Pike
Canned	King George whiting	Scaber leatherjacket
Red/pink salmon	Sand whiting	Orange roughy
Sardines	Oyster	School whiting
Mackerel	Pilchard	Tiger prawn
Herring	School shark	Baby octopus
Pilchards	Spanish mackerel	Rock lobster
Kippers (herring)	Silver warehou	King prawn
Smoked oysters	Blue swimmer crab	Yabby
Smoked mussels	Squid, calamari	Mud crab
	Blue mussel	
		Canned
		Canned tuna

* Fish varieties are Australian. Similar fish may be known by other names in different regions. Check with your local fishing authority.

* Content is for 100g/3½oz raw weight, unless canned.

* Omega-3 fat content can vary between brands of canned seafood, and can vary within the same species of fresh seafood depending on the season and harvest location and conditions.

14: Eggs

Don't be surprised to see eggs as heart-friendly foods. While they don't have the protective effects of foods such as fish, nuts, legumes and wholegrains, they are a highly nutritious and versatile food that can be included in cholesterol-lowering eating plans. How do they do it?

Eggs contain perfect protein—just the right balance of amino acids the body needs. As well as containing cholesterol, egg yolk contains mostly unsaturated fats and 10 vitamins and 8 minerals, including good amounts of riboflavin, vitamin B12 and phosphorus. Egg yolks also contain antioxidants lutein and zeaxanthin. Egg whites are protein and have no fat or cholesterol.

A group of nutrition experts in Australia (Egg Nutrition Advisory Group, ENAG) concluded that for those with high cholesterol '3–4 eggs per week in the context of a diet low in saturated fat and containing known cardio-protective foods is not associated with increased risk'.

In population studies, eating eggs is not associated with higher cholesterol levels, and research does not support the idea that egg consumption is a risk factor for coronary disease. Heart health organisations around the world no longer say eggs should be avoided, and focus more on having a balanced heart-healthy diet overall.

You can eat whole eggs, omega-3 enriched eggs and egg yolks if you have high cholesterol, but moderation is key. While opinions vary about how many eggs are okay, they don't need to be avoided altogether.

The eggs and cholesterol story

There are individual differences in blood cholesterol response to eating eggs. It is estimated around one third of the population over-react to eating more eggs and will experience an increase in cholesterol (hyper-responders), however the all-important LDL:HDL ratio is not changed and the LDL particle size is smaller and less harmful. If you already have high cholesterol and possibly a hyper-responder, there's no need to avoid eggs. Just limit eggs to no more than 3-4 a week and include plenty of heart-friendly foods.

Cholesterol in eggs
Large 60g egg—225mg
Medium 55g egg—200mg
Small 50g egg—190mg

* The US Heart Association suggests people with high cholesterol limit dietary cholesterol to 200mg per day

Eggs and plant sterol enriched foods—a helpful partnership

If you eat whole eggs that contain cholesterol, it makes sense to include plant sterol-enriched foods daily, such as cholesterol lowering margarines. Plant sterols are naturally occurring substances that reduce cholesterol absorption from the intestines (see page 93).

Omega-3 enriched eggs

These eggs are produced by providing hens with linseed (flaxseed) enriched feed—naturally rich in alpha-linolenic acid (omega-3 fat). Studies on the effects of high omega-3 eggs have shown positive effects on blood fats—higher HDL (good) cholesterol and lower triglyceride (triacylglycerol) levels. Omega-3 enriched eggs are one of the few foods that contain long chain omega-3 DHA and EPA normally obtained from fish, and so are great for those who can't eat fish.

How to enjoy eggs in moderation

Breakfast

- Serve a boiled egg with wholegrain toast and cholesterol-lowering margarine (eg, pro-activ, Benecol).
- Whisk an egg and a little milk for an omelette and serve with wholegrain toast with cholesterol-lowering margarine and grilled tomatoes.
- Top some wholegrain toast and cholesterol-lowering margarine with a slice of smoked salmon and a poached egg and garnish with fresh dill.
- Scramble an egg with evaporated skim milk and chopped parsley and serve on top of wholegrain rye toast with cholesterol-lowering margarine.

Lunch

- Pack a boiled egg for a workday lunch and enjoy with vegetable sticks, wholemeal pita bread and a dollop of mayonnaise.
- Swirl a lightly beaten egg into simmering chicken and corn soup just before serving for a Chinese style soup.
- Combine mashed boiled egg, low-fat cottage cheese and curry powder and use as a filling for wholemeal bread or flat bread wraps with watercress and black pepper.

- Fill a wholegrain roll (spread with cholesterol lowering margarine) with a sliced boiled egg, a thin slice of lean ham, wholegrain mustard and baby spinach leaves.

Dinner

- Combine sautéed onions, garlic, dill, mixed steamed vegetables, beaten eggs and low-fat ricotta and bake in a non-stick oven dish. Slice and serve with a tossed green salad and wholegrain bread.
- Make a thin plain omelette, cut into long thin strips and add to vegetable and noodle stir-fries.
- Add quartered boiled egg to a main meal salad of mixed greens, cherry tomatoes, cucumber, roasted capsicum, butter beans and tuna canned in springwater. Drizzle with olive oil vinaigrette and serve with crusty wholegrain bread with cholesterol lowering margarine.
- Stir-fry mixed Asian-style vegetables and cooked brown rice in a little peanut oil. Fry an egg in a non-stick pan sprayed with oil and serve on top of the vegetables. Garnish with chopped spring onions (scallions).
- Boil wholemeal pasta and drain. Stir through sliced boiled egg, pesto, steamed broccoli and asparagus.
- Simmer sliced green beans, capsicum and zucchini (courgettes) strips in fresh tomato puree (or no-added-salt canned diced tomatoes) with canned, drained lentils. Crack one egg per person into the mixture and cook until set. Serve with a scoop of mashed potato and a green salad.

15: Meat, poultry and game

Good news! There's no need to give up eating meat or chicken just because your cholesterol is high. As long as you keep it lean (and that means trimming off all visible fat and removing the skin from poultry) and cook it appropriately, meats can be a nutritious, delicious and satisfying part of a cholesterol-lowering eating plan. How does meat do it?

Choosing lean meats rather than fatty meats will remove a significant amount of saturated fat from the diet, which helps lower cholesterol levels. Lean meats are an excellent source of protein needed for building and repairing body tissues. They also provide iron for healthy blood and energy, zinc for immunity and vitamin B12 for a healthy nervous system. Lean meats also provide some healthy unsaturated fats, including omega-3 similar to those in fish.

Which meats?

All meats with the fat removed are fine. Buy your meat lean to begin with, or trim any remaining fat. Many supermarkets now sell a range of lean meats (perhaps called 'trim', 'lean' or 'heart-smart'). Meats to eat only occasionally due to their high saturated fat and/or sodium content are deli meats like bacon, ham, salami, cabanossi, mortadella, devon, hamburger mince and sausages.

Keep an eye out for lower fat versions of ham, bacon and sausages, but keep in mind the sodium is still high.

Lean choices include:

Chicken: skinned chicken breast (lowest in fat), chicken thighs skinned and trimmed, takeaway barbecue chicken, skin removed.

Beef: Lean steak, fat-trimmed roasts (eg, topside roast and silverside roast), lean stir-fry strips, lean beef mince, diced lean beef.

Veal: (naturally lean) steak, stir-fry, cutlet.

Kangaroo: (naturally lean) eg, steaks, mini-roasts.

Lamb: lean leg steaks, trim lamb strips, diced trim lamb, trim lamb mini-roast, trim lamb butterfly steak, trim lamb eye of loin, Frenched cutlet (bone left), lean lamb mince, fat-trimmed leg roast (easy carve).

Pork: lean leg steaks, loin steaks, scotch fillet.

Turkey: breast, no skin.

Venison (deer): (naturally lean), steaks, chops, roasts, mince (trim all visible fat if present).

TIPS WITH MEAT

- Enjoy lean red meat in 3–4 meals per week for the iron and zinc it contains.
- Enjoy chicken and white meats such as pork in 3–4 meals per week to leave room for other heart-friendly sources of protein like fish (at least 2 meals) and legumes (at least 2 meals).
- Vegetarians need to replace these with other suitable alternatives, such as legumes, nuts and seeds, taking care to ensure they get enough vitamin B12: iron and zinc-fortified foods and supplements may be needed.
- Everyone's nutritional needs are different, so the number of recommended serves of meat will vary, but generally adult women and men need at least one serve a day, and larger men and more active women need two.

Red or white meat—which is best?

Variety is a great strategy; enjoy them all! Check out the following table—you may be surprised how different lean meats compare.

Fat comparison of meats per 100g (3½oz) (raw)

Type of meat	Total fat (grams)	Saturated fat (grams)	Polyunsaturated fat (grams)	Cholesterol (mg)
Lean lamb	6.2	2.4	0.7	68
Lean beef	3.9	1.6	0.4	57
Veal steak	1.8	0.6	0.4	57
Kangaroo	1.8	0.3	0.3	51
Chicken breast	5.5	1.7	0.7	66
Turkey breast	1.6	0.5	0.42	60
Lean pork	4.2	1.6	0.7	59
Duck breast	2.5	0.6	0.4	143
Venison	2	0.8	0.4	68

What is a serve?

100g (3½oz) lean steak, chicken, raw
85g (3oz) lean steak, chicken, cooked (½ chicken breast)
½ cup lean mince, cooked (70g/2½oz)

How do I cook it?

- Pan-fry lean meat in a non-stick pan on low heat with a little spray oil to prevent sticking and serve with rice, noodles or pasta dishes.
- To ensure tenderness, cuts such as beef blade, skirt or chuck, or lamb forequarter chops are best cooked in liquid over a longer time, such as casseroles, tagines, curries and stews.
- Make soups with meats such as chuck, shin, round, brisket of beef or diced lamb forequarter.

How can I enjoy lean meats?

A healthy meal with meat is one that is balanced with plenty of vegetables or salad and some legumes or wholegrains like wholemeal pasta, brown rice, multigrain bread or corn.

Lunch

- Fill a wholemeal roll (reduced-salt) with lean roast beef, mustard, canola mayonnaise, rocket (arugula) and thickly sliced tomato.
- Turkey breast with reduced-fat cream cheese, cranberry sauce, watercress and roast zucchini (courgette) makes a perfect topping for whole-rye bread.
- Roll up chopped chicken breast and sliced mango with mayonnaise, celery slices and mesclun leaves in a lite flat corn bread wrap.
- Make a lean beef pattie and top with salt-reduced tomato ketchup, lettuce, tomato, grated carrot and pineapple on a wholegrain muffin for a great burger.
- Try an open mixed grain bread sandwich with sliced avocado, mignonette lettuce, pastrami and red currant jelly.
- Mix some cooked lean lamb though tabouli and serve in a small wholemeal lite pita pocket with sliced cucumber and a dollop of reduced-fat yoghurt.

Dinners

- Serve roasted lean beef with fresh chilli and tomato salsa, roasted sweet potato, roasted beetroot, steamed broccoli.
- Enjoy chilli con carne with lean mince, kidney bean and corn salsa on brown rice, accompanied by a green salad.
- Stir-fry lean pork and vegetables with hokkien noodles in plum sauce and toss through some roasted cashews or peanuts.
- Barbecue lean kangaroo or beef, red and green capsicum skewers, eggplant (aubergine) slices and potatoes in their jackets.
- Roast lean turkey breast filled with herbed wholegrain bread stuffing and enjoy with salt-reduced gravy, sweet corn and green peas.
- Char-grill chicken, zucchinis (courgettes), mushrooms and red capsicum and serve with a side salad of lettuce, corn kernels and tomato.
- Pan-fry veal steak, onion and tomato, mash some potatoes with crushed garlic and accompany with microwaved carrots and green beans.

Meat and weight loss

Protein-rich foods like lean meats satisfy the appetite, and help us feel full. Research has shown that low-fat, kilojoule-controlled diets with slightly larger serves of lean meat (and smaller serves of starchy foods like bread and potatoes) have helped people successfully lose weight without going hungry, and are nutritionally balanced. See part 4 starting on page 252 for an eating plan to help lose weight.

16: Healthy fats and oils

Fat has been given a bad wrap for too long. Instead of cutting out fat to lower cholesterol, more of the right fats are needed to obtain the correct balance. Healthy oils are heart-friendly foods, so go ahead and make the healthy and tasty choice. How do they do it?

Healthy oils help lower cholesterol. Polyunsaturated fats are essential and both polyunsaturated and monounsaturated fats should replace saturated fats to lower cholesterol. Healthy oils also add flavour and enjoyment to other heart-healthy foods.

Fat-free diets are not recommended in general, and especially not for people with high cholesterol. Some fats are essential—just like vitamins.

The 3-step action plan to get your fats right
- Cut right back on saturated fats found in butter, fatty meat, cheese, ice cream, fried fast food, biscuits, pies and pastries.
- Eat 30–45g (1–1½oz) a day—6–8 teaspoons—of added healthy fats like vegetable oils and margarines, both polyunsaturated and monounsaturated.
- Of this amount, include 25g (5 teaspoons) a day of plant cholesterol-lowering margarine daily—enough to provide 2g plant sterols.

What are healthy oils?
The healthy oils are the unsaturated types and they fall into two main groups—polyunsaturated and monounsaturated. These terms describe the chemical structure of the main kinds of fatty acids present. The terms omega-3 and omega-6 describe the chemical structure of different kinds of polyunsaturated fats.

Remember:
- Saturated is bad and unsaturated is good. Polyunsaturated fats provide essential omega-3 and -6 fatty acids and are needed for optimal cholesterol lowering and heart health.
- Enjoy a combination of both polyunsaturated and monounsaturated fats.

Food sources of polyunsaturated fats omega-6
Brazil nuts

Corn oil

Cottonseed

Grape seed oil

Pine nuts

Safflower

Sesame seeds and sesame oil

Soybean oil and spread

Sunflower oil and spread

Walnuts and walnut oil

Foods containing plant type omega-3 polyunsaturated fat
Canola oil

Linseeds and linseed (flaxseed) oil (see page 75)

Mustard seed oil

Omega-3 enriched eggs

Soy bean oil

Walnuts and walnut oil

Wheatgerm and wheatgerm oil

Foods containing marine type long chain omega-3 polyunsaturated fat
Rich sources are oily fish and seafood (see page 80). Smaller amounts are found in: omega-3 enriched eggs, fortified foods with added long chain omega-3 such as spreads, milk and bread.

Food sources of monounsaturated fats

Almonds

Avocado

Camellia (tea) oil

Canola oil and spread

Macadamia nuts and macadamia nut oil

Olive oil and spread

Peanuts and peanut oil

Pecan nuts

Pistachio nuts

Rice bran oil

Essential nutrients

All fats and oils are made up of fatty acids. There are two fatty acids that the body cannot make for itself and must obtain from food. These are termed essential fatty acids: linoleic acid (LA) from the omega-6 family and alpha linolenic acid (ALA) from the omega-3 family.

There are some essential vitamins that are only found in foods that contain fat. These are called fat-soluble vitamins: vitamins A, D, E and K. For example, vegetable oils are one of the richest sources of vitamin E.

Which healthy oils are best?

It's best to enjoy a combination of both polyunsaturated and monounsaturated oils. A polyunsaturated oil based margarine (for example, sunflower) balances well with olive and canola oils used for cooking. Or, a monounsaturated oil-based spread (such as olive or canola) balances well with sunflower oil or soybean oil used for cooking. Margarine (soft, trans-free) is a great substitute for butter when baking. Keep a variety of oils on hand and use the oil that best suits the dish.

Am I getting enough healthy oils?

The amount of healthy oils and spread you should eat will depend on your individual needs (see part 4 on page 252 for an eating plan), however there are general guides. For a healthy diet the Canadian Food Guide suggests 30–45ml (6–8 teaspoons) of oils and spreads daily, and the US MyPyramid suggests 5–7 teaspoons, depending on age and sex. The National Heart Foundation of Australia suggests eating 30ml per day (6 teaspoons) of added healthy fats like oils and spreads for good heart health.

What is extra virgin olive oil?

The term 'extra virgin' refers to the oil from the first mechanical pressing of the olives and is low in natural acidity and rich in phytochemical antioxidants and flavour. Normal olive oil is usually a mixture of virgin oil and refined oil. 'Cold pressed' is the name used to describe the first pressing of other types of oils.

Do I need plant omega-3?

Yes. The plant omega-3, alpha linolenic acid (ALA), is essential and must be provided by the diet. Adequate amounts are 1.3g per day for men, and 0.8g per day for women; however, it is recommended to consume more than this (around 2g) to help reduce heart disease risk.

While marine omega-3 are known for the heart protective properties, it is now thought that ALA from plants also reduces the risk of coronary heart disease and fatal heart attack in both women and men.

To spread or not to spread?

Many people stop using margarine (oil spread) when they find out they have high cholesterol but this makes no nutritional sense. To lower cholesterol only saturated fats need to come down, whereas the good polyunsaturated and monounsaturated fats need to take a leading role.

Margarines are important sources of healthy unsaturated fats including essential omega-6 and -3 fats and fat-soluble vitamins. Just in case you're still not convinced, a New Zealand study found that a diet including a spread with plant sterols produced lower cholesterol results than a diet lower in fat without margarine.

> ### Margarine terms
> 'Spread' is a term used to describe reduced-fat soft margarines in Australia and New Zealand that are less than 80 per cent fat, and these are the most commonly available products used for spreading. The hard yellow blocks used for cooking—called 'stick' margarines in the US—tend to be higher in saturated and trans-fats and not recommended. Soft margarines (or spreads) are considered essential foods similar to oils in food guides around the world and virtually free of trans fats.

Butter or margarine?

This question has been well and truly answered by scientific research. Butter increases cholesterol, while unsaturated spreads help to lower cholesterol—especially if they are enriched with plant sterols. Heart associations and health authorities around the world recommend using unsaturated soft margarine spread instead of butter.

For spreading and for baking, choose (reduced-salt) soft unsaturated margarine rich in omega-6 and omega-3, made from canola, sunflower, safflower and olive oil rather than butter or hard (stick) margarine, preferably enriched with plant sterols that actively lower cholesterol.

Case study: the right fats make a difference

A population study conducted in Poland found a clear association between an increasing amount of unsaturated margarine spreads and oils in the diet and a reduction in coronary heart disease risk. During the 1990s consumption of polyunsaturated fat increased by 57 per cent as the supply of affordable canola and soy bean oil margarines increased, and butter became more expensive due to a reduction in government subsidies. The death rate from coronary heart disease fell by 40 per cent over the same period.

Do cholesterol-lowering margarines really work?

Cholesterol lowering margarines contains plant sterols (or stanols), which are naturally occurring vegetable fats that lower cholesterol. They do this by reducing the absorption of cholesterol from the digestive system which results in more cholesterol being passed out of the body. Plant sterols can be found in vegetable oils, nuts, seeds and wholegrains, but in quite small amounts. Much higher levels are found in plant sterol-enriched margarines. Clinical studies of plant sterols have shown that eating 2g a day can lower total and LDL (bad) cholesterol by around 10 per cent. This amount of plant sterols is present in 25g/1oz (5 teaspoons) of cholesterol lowering margarine. For best results you need them daily and keep eating them to ensure your cholesterol stays down.

Cholesterol lowering margarines are true 'functional foods' for heart health and an easy way to make a significant improvement in blood cholesterol levels. This effect is additional to the effects of cholesterol-lowering drugs (statins) so even if you take medication for cholesterol it's worth using cholesterol lowering margarines as well. Because there can be a small reduction in the absorption of carotenoid antioxidants while using plant sterol spreads, have an extra serve of orange/yellow vegetables or fruits to be on the safe side. While some research suggests the reduction in absorption is insignificant, vegetables and fruits are heart-friendly foods so go ahead and eat more anyway!

What about trans fats?

Trans fats are worse than saturated fats for cholesterol because they raise bad LDL cholesterol and reduce the good HDL cholesterol: a double whammy. Heart health organisations around the world agree they should be minimised in the diet. Trans fats occur naturally in animal and dairy fat (yet another reason to choose lean meat and low-fat dairy foods); however, they are also produced in the partial hydrogenation, or hardening, of oils during commercial food manufacturing. Cooking (stick) margarine and shortening used by commercial bakers may be high in trans fats, so pies, pastries, cakes and biscuits can contain significant levels. Look for the words 'partially hydrogenated' on food labels to spot trans fats. Most soft margarines are virtually free of trans fats—check the label. Cook at home with soft margarines instead of hard cooking margarine.

Saturated fats to avoid

Saturated fats increase cholesterol and also increase the risk of cardiovascular disease. They also worsen insulin resistance—a key feature of the metabolic syndrome. A rule of thumb is that saturated fats are usually of animal origin, such as butter and lard. However, there are always exceptions! For example, coconut and palm oil despite being of plant origin are highly saturated and best eaten occasionally.

When it comes to healthy eating and lowering your cholesterol, it's what we do most days that really counts. Enjoying the occasional treat won't be a cholesterol disaster, but make sure that foods high in saturated fat aren't on your daily menu.

For optimal cholesterol levels and to reduce the risk of heart disease, saturated fats must be replaced with unsaturated fats, especially polyunsaturated ones. Swapping butter for margarine is a simple example of how this can be achieved, or snacking on nuts instead of chocolate biscuits.

Typical amounts of saturated fat in foods (daily target 20g or less, the lower the better)	
Food + serving size	Saturated fat per serve (g)
Apple pie, individual commercial frozen	7
Bacon, 1 long rasher	6
Butter, 2 teaspoons (10g)	5
Chocolate bar, nougat and caramel filling, 60g	8
Chocolate cheesecake, 1 slice, 150g	19
Cream filled choc coated biscuits, 2	6
Croissant, 1 average	13
French fries, take-away, small	7
Hamburger with cheese, take-away	9.5
Meat pie, individual	10
Pasta carbonara creamy style (½ cup sauce)	23
Pizza, ¼ family size supreme	7
Rich vanilla ice cream, 1 cup	8.5
Salami, 40g	5
Sausages, 2 thin	14
*Average figures from FSANZ (AUSNUT)	

What about weight?

It is now clear that low-fat diets are not the answer to prevent overweight and obesity, and are not the best diet for weight loss either. It is the amount of kilojoules (calories) eaten, not the proportion of fat in the diet, that is important for weight control. A 6000 kilojoule (1400 calories) weight loss diet containing 30 per cent of kilojoules from fat is just as effective as a 6000 kilojoule diet with 20 per cent kilojoules from fat. The 30 per cent fat diet is better because very low-fat diets don't provide enough essential omega-3 and omega-6 fats and fat-soluble vitamins.

For cholesterol lowering, very low-fat diets aren't the best because they lower good HDL cholesterol (and aren't very much fun either). You can include 6 teaspoons of added healthy oils and spreads in a balanced low-kilojoule eating plan for weight loss, or even more if you use a fat-reduced spread. See part 4 starting on page 252 for an eating plan to beat cholesterol.

How do I enjoy healthy oils?

Breakfast

- Spread cholesterol-lowering margarine on hot wholegrain toast or English muffin and top with orange marmalade—enjoy with some fruit salad and a cup of tea.
- Partner a wholemeal fruit muffin with soft margarine and a skim latte.
- Brush a thick slice of sour dough or soy and linseed bread with oil and toast on a griddle pan. Top with sliced avocado and a little smoked salmon and a dollop of low-fat ricotta.
- Pan-fry mushrooms in a little oil, add a dash of sweet smoked paprika and a squeeze of lemon juice. Serve on a wholemeal crumpet.

Lunch

- Spread wholegrain bread with cholesterol-lowering margarine and top with salmon and plenty of salad.
- Dress a tomato, rocket and cucumber salad with extra virgin olive oil and balsamic vinegar and enjoy with crusty wholegrain bread and tuna in springwater.
- Make a sandwich with lean chicken, soybean oil mayonnaise and plenty of coloured lettuce on wholegrain bread.
- Dress a cos lettuce, red cabbage and orange salad with avocado oil and raspberry vinegar and serve with wholemeal pita bread with slices of cold lean roast pork.
- Toss a kidney bean, sprout and onion salad in a dressing of walnut oil and white wine vinegar and enjoy with drained sardines in springwater and multi-grain crispbreads spread with polyunsaturated margarine.

Did you know?

Healthy oils contain antioxidants

- Seed and nut oils and rice bran oil contain high amounts of Vitamin E—a powerful antioxidant thought to play a protective role against heart disease.
- Virgin olive oil is known for its polyphenolic antioxidants that can reduce oxidation of LDL cholesterol in the body.
- Rice bran oil contains small amounts of oryzanol and avocado oil contains small amounts of beta-sitosterol—both plant sterols that can help lower cholesterol absorption and reduce LDL cholesterol levels.
- Grapeseed oil contains proanthocyanidins thought to protect the heart.

Dinner

- Start an Indian curry by sautéeing spices in canola or peanut oil.
- Start an Italian tomato sauce by sautéeing garlic, onions and capsicum in olive oil.
- Finish an Asian stir-fry or chicken and corn or vegetable, tofu and noodle soup by adding some sesame oil just before serving.
- Melt some plant sterol-enriched spread into mashed or baked potato.
- Dress steamed/microwaved carrots with walnut oil and a little orange juice and zest.
- Sprinkle mustard seed oil and apple cider vinegar on sautéed cabbage and onion.
- Combine canola oil and dried rosemary to coat potato wedges before baking.
- As a starter serve wholemeal Turkish bread pieces for dipping into a small dish of avocado oil and Middle Eastern dukkah.
- Dress steamed/microwaved Asian greens with a mixture of peanut oil and salt-reduced soy sauce.
- Coat a mix of vegetables such as capsicum, zucchini (courgette) and eggplant (aubergine) in olive oil before roasting.
- Dress cooked vegetables in a mixture of virgin olive oil, lemon juice, chopped parsley and crushed garlic for a great Mediterranean flavour.
- Make a potato and bean salad with cooled boiled potato cubes, drained four bean mix and a mixture of soybean oil or canola mayonnaise, natural (plain) yoghurt and a dash of curry powder.
- Drizzle corn on the cob with melted cholesterol-lowering margarine mixed with chopped herbs.

TIPS WITH OILS

- If you're cooking a stir-fry or curry allow 2 teaspoons per person (or per serving). Measure the oil out rather than pour it straight in. Always add oil to an already hot pan as it will spread more easily to prevent sticking.
- Store spreads in the fridge, and oils in a cool dark place.
- It's best to buy oils in smaller quantities and replace them regularly to ensure your oil is fresh.
- When deep-frying, ensure oil is hot to prevent food soaking up too much oil and cook food in small batches. Use oils with a higher smoke point that remain stable at high temperatures such as rice bran, camellia tea oil, olive (refined) or peanut oil (deep-frying is a higher kilojoule cooking method).
- Virgin olive oil is not the best for deep-frying as it has a lower smoke point than more refined olive oil. It's also more expensive, so save the good stuff for your salads.
- Use a screw-top jar and shake well to make dressings—store any remainder in the fridge.

17: Dairy foods and the alternatives

There's no need to give milk a miss if your cholesterol is high. In fact, provided you make the smart choice of reduced or low-fat types, count dairy in as a heart-friendly food group. How does dairy do it?

Dairy foods include milk, yoghurt, custard and cheese. Dairy foods are core foods, which means they contribute important amounts of essential nutrients, protein, calcium, phosphorous, magnesium, riboflavin and vitamin B12. You need the nutrients from dairy foods every day, or choose suitable calcium-enriched alternatives.

Whole milk and regular-fat dairy products contain significant amounts of saturated fats, which tend to raise blood cholesterol but luckily there are plenty of reduced-fat and low-fat options available. Enjoying lighter options is a great way to get all the nutritional benefits with no downside. And they have a low GI, providing sustained energy throughout the day.

Butter is made from cream, and is almost entirely milk fat and therefore not considered part of the dairy food group. The same goes for cream and sour cream. Butter and cream increase blood cholesterol, so use them sparingly and occasionally. An unsaturated margarine is the best spread to use every day.

How many serves?

Dairy foods are our main source of calcium, and 2–3 serves a day are recommended. Women over 50 years of age and men over 70 need even more calcium in order to keep bones strong and account for reduced absorption with age. Calcium-enriched dairy products such as milk and yoghurt with added calcium are useful in meeting higher calcium needs.

What is a serve?

1 cup (250ml/9fl oz) milk
200g (7oz) yoghurt
40g (1½oz) cheese
Choose low or reduced-fat types.

What if I can't drink milk?

For those who are lactose intolerant, there are lactose-free milks and yoghurt. Cheese contains virtually no lactose. Yoghurt is also usually well digested due to the natural bacterial cultures it contains.

If you have a medically diagnosed cows milk allergy, try a milk alternative like soy milk (see below) and make sure it has added calcium. Chinese green vegetables, other leafy green vegetables such as kale, hard tofu, fish with edible bones (like salmon and sardines), nuts, seeds, oranges, cereals and vegetables contain calcium, but in much smaller amounts than dairy foods.

Soy milk has unique heart-health benefits and is a good alternative to dairy, provided it has added calcium. It is naturally low in saturated fat so there's no need to choose low-fat versions unless you're reducing kilojoules to lose weight—1 cup of soy milk contains 663kJ (158 cals) and a cup of low-fat soy milk contains 446kJ (107 cals). You can just swap soy milk for dairy milk in recipes, or enjoy it as a drink or on breakfast cereal.

Say cheese!

Cheese is higher in kilojoules (calories) and saturated fat than milk and yoghurt. Best everyday choices are reduced-fat hard cheese and low-fat cottage and ricotta, while the regular cheeses are best enjoyed in smaller portions, or less often—twice a week. There are low-cholesterol, low saturated fat cheeses and soy-cheese alternatives available. Hard cheese is high in sodium so choose reduced-salt types where possible.

What about dairy foods and blood pressure?

High blood pressure is a risk factor for cardiovascular disease. A major study called DASH (Dietary Approaches to Stop Hypertension) has convincingly shown that including low-fat dairy foods together with less salt and more vegetables and fruits can lower blood pressure.

Dairy foods and weight

Clinical studies have shown that including three serves of dairy foods (mostly lower fat varieties) daily in a kilojoule-controlled diet helped people lose more weight from around their waist—a real benefit for heart health. The calcium from dairy is thought to be the active fat-loss ingredient, but additional effects may be due to the protein (amino acid) content, low glycemic index (GI) or other bioactive substances. Dairy foods are also nutrient dense (they contain a lot of nutrients per gram), which is great for ensuring adequate amounts of nutrients within a weight-loss eating plan.

Dairy foods compared

The table on page 100 gives you an idea of the calcium and saturated fat content of various dairy foods. Choose lower saturated fat levels to help control blood cholesterol.

What's the difference between reduced-fat and low-fat?

Dairy foods labelled 'low-fat' contain less fat than those called 'reduced-fat'. Always check the nutrition information panel and choose dairy foods with lower levels of total and saturated fat.

Things to notice in the table on the next page

Fat-reduced and low-fat milks and cheeses have more calcium—a good choice.

Softer cheeses like cottage cheese contain less calcium—but they contain less saturated fat so they are also a good choice. Obtain your calcium from low-fat milk and yoghurt.

Creamed cheese is high in kilojoules and saturated fat and low in calcium—not a good choice.

Nutritional profile of dairy foods per 100g (3½oz)			
Dairy food (mg)	Kilojoules (calories)	Saturated fat (grams)	Calcium (mg)
Milk (less than 1% fat)	190	0.1	160
Reduced-fat milk (1–2% fat)	204	0.9	137
Skim milk (less than 0.16% fat)	145	0.1	123
Whole milk (3.8% fat)	272	2.5	114
Buttermilk (2% fat)	243	1.3	143
Evaporated milk (8% fat)	597	5.4	265
Evaporated skim milk (0.3% fat)	314	0.2	250
Yoghurt, Greek style (7% fat)	513	4.6	196
Yoghurt, whole milk, natural/plain (3.4% fat)	304	2.2	172
Yoghurt, skim/low-fat, natural/plain (0.2% fat)	223	0.1	210
Yoghurt, skim, low-fat, fruit flavour	320	0.1	179
Yoghurt, (2% fat), natural/plain	294	1.1	160
Fromage frais, flavoured (4% fat)	511	2.9	74
Fromage frais, low-fat (0.3% fat)	393	0.2	10
Hard cheese (cheddar, 34% fat)	1690	21.5	77
Hard cheese, reduced-fat (24% fat)	1370	15.1	805
Hard cheese, reduced-fat (15% fat)	1107	9.9	925
Cheese, brie	1410	18.6	470
Fetta cheese	1170	15.3	325
Fetta cheese, reduced-fat	974	9.3	370
Cream cheese	1410	21.2	104
Cream cheese, reduced-fat	803	10.9	100
Cottage cheese, creamed	509	3.6	70
Cottage cheese, low-fat	412	1.5	79
Ricotta cheese	616	7.2	225
Ricotta cheese, reduced-fat	530	5.6	245
Ice cream (vanilla) 10–12% fat	766	6.9	119
Ice cream, reduced-fat, less than 6.5% fat	607	3.6	130
Ice cream, low-fat, less than 4% fat	495	2	150
Custard, vanilla	392	2	100
Custard low-fat	328	0.6	127

* Average figures from SERVE Nutrition Management System Version 5.2.001 (AUSNUT data).

Which milk?

With so many choices in the dairy cabinet these days it may seem overwhelming. To lower cholesterol the most important factor when choosing milk is fat content—the lower the better. If you're used to the taste of whole milk, it's helpful to reduce fat content gradually to give your taste buds time to adjust. Instead of going straight to skim/fat-free milk, try 'light' milk (1–2 per cent fat) first. High calcium and added omega-3 fats are a bonus. Low-fat organic and A2 milk have no proven added health benefits, so they're a personal choice.

What is buttermilk?

Despite the name, buttermilk doesn't contain butter at all, and is actually reduced-fat milk (2 per cent). It's called buttermilk because it was originally a by-product of making butter. Nowadays, buttermilk is produced by adding friendly bacteria to reduced-fat milk. Buttermilk is slightly thicker in texture and sour in taste and great to use in cooking.

How to enjoy low-fat dairy foods

Breakfast

- Enjoy a wholegrain breakfast cereal like porridge or muesli (granola) with skim milk and some sliced fruit.
- Top an apple, pear and peach salad with some low-fat yoghurt, drizzle with maple syrup and sprinkle with muesli and chopped hazelnuts.
- Whiz up a smoothie for a quick breakfast using skim milk, fruit of your choice (try banana, berries or mango), low-fat yoghurt, wheatgerm and honey.
- Make cheesy beans on toast with reduced-salt baked beans and grated reduced-fat cheese.

- Spread wholegrain toast with soft margarine spread and wholegrain mustard and top with sliced tomato, freshly ground pepper and a thin slice of reduced-fat cheese—grill (broiler) until cheese has melted.

Lunch

- Mix low-fat cottage cheese with mango chutney and chopped fresh coriander and spread on wholegrain crispbread—top with sliced tomato and baby spinach leaves.
- Stir in some low-fat plain (natural) yoghurt to a soup made with puréed pumpkin, water and a little reduced-salt chicken stock, caramelised onion and curry powder—serve with toasted wholegrain bread.
- Enrich an instant salt-reduced soup by adding half boiling water, half warmed skim milk or buttermilk.
- Fill a wholemeal flatbread wrap with low-fat cottage cheese, chopped walnuts, dried apricots, grated carrot and bean sprouts.
- Layer a wholegrain bread roll with pickles, reduced-fat cheese, cucumber and coloured lettuce.

Dinner

- Top a vegetable and chickpea curry and brown rice with a dollop of low-fat natural (plain) yoghurt and fresh coriander (cilantro) leaves.
- Make a creamy-style chicken and vegetable curry using lean skinless chicken pieces and mixed chopped vegetables simmered in evaporated skim milk and prepared curry paste* (or powder).
- Make a potato gratin by combining sliced potatoes with a cheese sauce made with soft margarine spread, flour, skim milk and reduced-fat cheese—serve with grilled (broiled) steak or fish, and steamed mixed vegetables.
- Create a healthy and creamy pasta dish with low-fat ricotta, canned salmon, capers, lemon zest, halved cherry tomatoes, steamed zucchini (courgette) and broccoli stirred through cooked wholemeal pasta.
- For a delicious dessert, grill halved peaches or nectarines with a sprinkling of brown sugar until golden, and serve with low-fat ricotta sweetened with honey and a little cinnamon.
- For a sweet finish to a meal, enjoy a scoop or two of low-fat ice cream on top of fruit salad, or with a little fruit sauce and a sprinkling of mixed chopped nuts.

Snacks

- Have a low-fat fruit yoghurt—sweet and sustaining.
- Try a low-fat fruit-flavoured fromage frais for something different.
- Drink a glass of skim milk to keep hunger at bay.
- Whip up a skim milkshake with a spoon or two of yoghurt for added creaminess.
- Have a skim café latte or hot chocolate to warm the cockles and boost energy.

- Snack on cooked brown rice or barley with low-fat milk and a sprinkling of brown sugar.
- Make a dip with low-fat plain yoghurt and curry paste* and serve with carrot, celery, capsicum and cucumber strips and microwaved pappadums.
- Enjoy wholegrain rice or corn cakes with sliced green apple with thinly sliced reduced-fat hard cheese (cheddar or edam).
- Recharge when out and about with a low-fat ice cream on a stick, or small portion of low-fat softserve ice cream or frozen yoghurt in a cup.

* Compare the sodium content of curry pastes and choose the one with the lowest.

Did you know?

Lactose is the name of the naturally occurring sugar in milk. Lactose has a low glycemic index (GI) and dairy foods like milk, yoghurt and custard also have a low GI so they keep you going for longer. Enjoy reduced and low-fat varieties for deliciously sweet and nutritious treats that really satisfy.

DAIRY TIPS
- Evaporated skim milk is a great alternative for cream in cooked savoury dishes and sauces.
- Add coconut essence (extract) to evaporated skim milk for Asian-style creamy curries.
- Natural (plain) yoghurt is a great alternative for sour cream in dips and soups.
- Ricotta cheese is a great alternative to cream for desserts and cakes.
- Use buttermilk instead of regular milk in baking and pancakes.

18: Alcohol and chocolate

Wine and chocolate are foods that many people love and they can fit into a cholesterol-lowering eating plan, but enjoying them in moderation is the key. Being foods derived from plants, wine and chocolate contain natural antioxidants that may actually be beneficial for a healthy heart.

Alcohol

Taking alcohol 'for medicinal purposes' goes back a long way and now there is evidence that drinking alcohol in moderation may be beneficial—especially for heart health.

Population studies show that people who drink a little alcohol regularly seem to have a lower risk of cardiovascular disease compared to those who don't drink any alcohol at all. This protection particularly applies for those middle-aged or older and those already at risk of developing coronary heart disease. The reason for this protective effect is not clear. It might be because alcohol raises good HDL cholesterol levels, or it may be that alcohol enhances the absorption of other protective dietary factors.

What about red wine?

Wine has been of interest to nutrition researchers for years because of the so-called French paradox. This term was coined to describe the unexpectedly low death rates from coronary heart disease in France despite the fact the French are traditionally known to eat foods high in saturated fat such as cheese, cream and pastry.

Researchers began to search for what else they were consuming that might be protecting their hearts. The French drink a lot of wine, so wine was identified as being a good candidate because of its high antioxidant content. It must be said, however, that this link is far from proven and lifestyle is important.

Studies of drinkers in France have shown those who drink wine in moderation are also less likely to be overweight and more likely to be active and eat a healthy diet. Visitors to Paris will notice for example that Parisians walk a lot (driving in Paris is a health hazard in itself!), almost always take time to enjoy meals, they don't snack much between meals, and they eat smaller portions.

In fact, the rates of cardiovascular disease in France are not much different to those of Southern Europe, indicating the protective factors are not particularly French (perhaps we should re-name it the Mediterranean paradox?).

A review of population studies concluded that daily consumption of 150ml (5fl oz) of wine (that's a little more than ½ cup) reduces cardiovascular disease by 32 per cent.

But wait! Because there are health risks involved in drinking alcohol—especially to excess—it's important to see wine as an enjoyable option in moderation rather than an essential for heart disease protection. Heart Associations around the world do not suggest you start drinking alcohol to protect your heart, but rather if you already drink, to do so in moderation. Drinking too much alcohol is associated with an increased risk of other health problems including breast cancer, suicide and accidents.

What's the best tipple?

In short, the jury is still out about which type of alcoholic drink is best. Alcohol itself, no matter where it comes from, appears to be protective by increasing good HDL cholesterol and 'thinning' the blood. Although some studies show wine to have the protective edge, other more recent studies show beer and spirits have similar effects.

If wine does have an edge, and especially red wine, it's probably due to high levels of antioxidants. The polyphenolic antioxidants in red wine have been shown to reduce the oxidation of bad LDL cholesterol, increase good HDL, reduce inflammation, improve flexibility of blood vessels (endothelial function), reduce the sticky-ness of the blood and reduce the risk of clots. Or it might how wine is traditionally consumed with meals, whereas beer and spirits have a reputation of being downed quickly in order feel the effects of the alcohol.

How much is OK to drink?

For protecting your heart, it seems it is not what you drink but HOW you drink it that makes the difference. A little alcohol each day is protective, yet 'binge' drinking, or drinking large amounts less often (like on weekends), is actually harmful. The consensus of health authorities around the world is no more than 1–2 drinks a day for men and 1 for women. If weight is a problem, then less is best.

Studies indicate 1–2 standard drinks a day is protective against heart disease.

For people with diabetes, drinking small amounts of alcohol is also protective against coronary heart disease, but drinking more than 1 standard drink a day may actually increase the risk. Interestingly, drinking alcohol in moderation helps insulin to work better (improves insulin sensitivity).

The downside

Unfortunately, drinking alcohol can raise triglyceride levels and blood pressure. It is also high in kilojoules and can cause weight gain. Again, limiting how much you drink makes the difference.

What is a standard drink?

To confuse matters, there are differences in what constitutes a standard drink between countries. The amount of pure alcohol classified as 'standard' varies from 6g in Austria through to 19.75g in Japan! The average sits around 12g (used by France, Denmark). The UK uses 7.9g. The other confounder is that similar drinks vary in alcohol content. Consult your local health authority to obtain correct figures and also check the label of your alcohol drinks for their alcohol content.

A standard drink in Australia, New Zealand, Ireland Italy, Spain (10g pure alcohol). These are similar for the UK.

100ml (3½ fl oz) wine/sparkling wine
285ml (9½ fl oz) beer (middie)
450ml (15fl oz) light (2 per cent alcohol) beer (schooner)
30ml (1fl oz) spirits (1 nip)
60ml (2fl oz) fortified wine (port, sherry)

A standard drink in the USA and Canada (14g pure alcohol)

150ml (5fl oz) wine
350ml (12fl oz) beer
45ml (1.5fl oz) 80-proof spirits
30ml (1fl oz) 100-proof spirits
85–120ml (3–4 fl oz) fortified wine (port, sherry)

How do I enjoy alcohol in moderation?

The trick with alcohol is to enjoy 1–2 drinks a day and no more. This can be challenging, especially if there is social pressure to drink more, or you really like the taste! Try the following ideas to slow down your drinking:

- Have your drinks in smaller, attractive glasses—a glass half full rather than half empty!
- Drink slowly, taking small mouthfuls with good breaks between mouthfuls to really savour the flavour.
- Pace your eating and drinking at meal times by putting your fork and glass down between mouthfuls and making conversation.
- Alternate your alcoholic drinks with non-alcoholic drinks. If weight is an issue, choose low-kilojoule options such as water (with a slice of lemon or a dash of lime juice), soda water, diet soft drinks or weak cordial.
- Choose light beer.
- Have half-nips of spirits with plenty of ice, with water or mixers.
- In warm weather, mix your white wine with soda— a spritzer.
- Keep your wine glass close to you so as to monitor how often it is refilled.
- Be assertive in controlling how much you drink. A firm 'no thank you' with a smile while placing your hand over your glass is usually effective.
- If you are given too much, don't feel you need to finish it all (same goes for food).
- Pre-mixed drinks can vary in their alcohol content. Check the label for the number of standard drinks they contain.
- Sweet pre-mixed drinks can have loads of sugar—avoid or limit these.
- Beware of creamy cocktails as they are very high in alcohol, saturated fat and kilojoules—not very heart-friendly at all.

Did you know?

Cooking wine causes much of the alcohol to evaporate, but most of the antioxidants remain.

How do different standard drinks compare?		
Amount of 1 standard drink (10g alcohol)	Kilojoules	Calories
100ml sparkling wine/ Champagne	271	65
30ml spirits	275	66
100ml white wine	276	66
30ml spirit + 200ml diet cola	278	66
100ml red wine	285	68
60ml port	360	86
285ml beer	440	105
30ml sweet liqueur	490	117
30ml spirit + 200ml cola	625	149
30ml sweet liqueur + 200ml skim milk	780	186
30ml sweet liqueur + 200ml full cream milk	1034	247

Cooking with wine

Cooking with wine is a great way to add flavour without salt to savoury dishes, and richness without saturated fat to sweet dishes.

- Add some red wine to tomato-based pasta sauce or casseroles.
- Add red wine to marinades for red meats, and white wine for chicken and fish.
- Port is delicious in a gravy or sauce for beef.
- Mirin is Japanese rice wine and is delicious added to Asian-style sauces and dressings.
- White wine is great for seafood soups and risottos.
- Sweet liqueurs add delicious flavour to low-fat puddings and desserts.

TIPS WITH WINE
- An opened bottle of wine will last three days if sealed and stored in the fridge—there's no need to finish the bottle! Just pour red wine half an hour before serving to take the chill off.
- A typical bottle of wine (12 per cent alcohol) contains seven standard drinks.
- Glasses of wine served in restaurants, bars and clubs (especially in those stylish large glasses) are always more than one standard drink and can be up to three in just one glass.
- Alcoholic drinks should list the number of standard drinks they contain on the label.

WINE FACT

Red and white wine can be made from red-skinned grapes, however the skins are left to ferment with the juice in red wine whereas the skins are removed when making white wine. The skins are a rich source of antioxidants and are responsible for the higher antioxidant levels in red wine.

Chocolate

What's good about chocolate (besides the obvious!)? Chocolate is made from cocoa beans that are naturally rich in flavonoid antioxidants called procyanidins (catechin and epicatechin). These antioxidants have been shown in scientific studies to reduce oxidation of LDL cholesterol, increase good HDL cholesterol, help blood vessels be more flexible and less stiff (improve endothelial function), prevent the blood becoming 'sticky' and forming clots, reduce inflammation, improve insulin sensitivity and lower blood pressure.

Good quality chocolate is an indulgence food you can feel good about

Chocolate comes in several forms. Cocoa powder contains the most antioxidants, containing 10 per cent by weight of flavonoids. Next comes dark chocolate, and the higher the cocoa content, the more antioxidants it contains. Milk chocolate contains half as much as dark chocolate, and white chocolate contains no antioxidants. Remember chocolate is high in saturated fat and kilojoules so go easy. Cocoa powder is a delicious way to enjoy chocolate (as a drink or in cooking) and contains much less fat than solid chocolate. Enjoying chocolate with nuts is a good way to combine heart-friendly nutrients in an indulgent and enjoyable way.

Different types of chocolate

A good rule of thumb is 'dark and rich' is best. In terms of antioxidant content, dark chocolate is top of the heart-benefit hierarchy tree—high cocoa content chocolate contains up to 70 per cent cocoa and the percentage is usually on the label.

BEST: Cocoa powder

GOOD: Dark chocolate (semi-sweet/bitter sweet/high cocoa) are basically the same thing—dark chocolate with no milk solids and more than 35–40 per cent cocoa content

GOOD: Drinking chocolate (cocoa + sugar)

OK: Milk chocolate

NOT GOOD: Compound chocolate

NOT GOOD: White chocolate contains only the cocoa butter and no cocoa solids at all so technically it's not really chocolate.

What about chocolate bars?

Chocolate bars with added ingredients like caramel, nougat, marshmallow and biscuit/wafer are lower in chocolate flavonoids and high in kilojoules. They are also getting bigger in size and more and more widely available. Avoid grabbing these as a quick snack and instead take some time to enjoy a modest portion of rich, dark chocolate in a relaxed way. Many people say dark chocolate is easier to stop eating because its richness and intensity is more satisfying.

What is a serve?

How much chocolate you can eat depends on your daily energy needs. Healthy eating guides around the world agree we should limit the amount of 'extra' (non-core) foods we eat: chocolate is an example of a high-fat, high-sugar 'extra' food. In general, enjoy chocolate in small portions as a treat.

A dietary 'extra' or treat food is suggested as equivalent to 600 kilojoules (150 calories).

A serve of chocolate (600 kilojoules/150 calories) is around 25g (1oz) chocolate = 6 small squares, $^1/_2$ small bar.

Case Study: Antioxidants in beverages

Researchers from Cornell University in the US discovered that hot cocoa had a higher total antioxidant capacity than red wine or tea. Hot cocoa had the highest amount of phenolics and flavonoids, followed by red wine, then green tea and black tea.

Can chocolate lower cholesterol?

Chocolate is high in saturated fat, so it's not a cholesterol-lowering food (sorry!). But interestingly chocolate feeding studies have shown that eating chocolate regularly does not increase cholesterol either. Forget about eating chocolate to lower cholesterol, but savour it in small portions as an indulgent treat that contains beneficial antioxidants and just for the taste of it!

Did you know?

Chocolate originated in South America, where the ancient Aztec and Mayan people used ground cacao seeds mixed with spices (including chilli) and water to make a bitter-tasting drink. The Aztecs used cacao seeds as a type of currency, such was their value and appreciation. Chocolate has a long history of traditional use as a medicine for many ailments including poor digestion, mental fatigue and lethargy.

How do I enjoy quality chocolate in moderation?

- Take time to savour your chocolate slowly so as to fully appreciate the mouth-filling flavour and creamy texture.
- Enjoy a small portion of plain (semisweet) dark chocolate or dark chocolate with nuts with a short black (espresso coffee) or small glass of port to finish a meal.
- Enjoy a dark chocolate fondue (melted chocolate and evaporated skim milk) with fruit like strawberries, banana slices and raspberries for an indulgent dessert.
- Make a hot chocolate or iced chocolate using skim milk or soy milk, cocoa powder and a little sugar.
- Add a scoop of cocoa powder to a banana smoothie made on low-fat milk or soy milk.
- Sprinkle cocoa powder and a little sugar on hot wholegrain toast with cholesterol-lowering margarine (a variation on cinnamon toast).
- Sprinkle a combination of grated dark chocolate and roasted slivered (flaked) almonds over a scoop or two of low-fat ice cream.
- For an indulgent sweet snack on the go, combine dark chocolate pieces with chopped apricots, raisins and hazelnuts.

19: Tea and coffee

Both tea and coffee are derived from plants and therefore contain antioxidants as well as caffeine (a stimulant). They also contribute towards your daily fluid needs. However, you can have too much of a good thing, so balance your tea and coffee with a variety of other beverages, including plenty of water.

Tea

Tea is made from the leaves of a plant called *Camellia sinensis*. The leaves are picked and dried to make green or black (regular) tea. Green tea is lightly steamed soon after picking to suspend oxidative changes, while black tea is allowed to oxidise. Oolong tea is made by partial oxidation of the tea leaves. Herb tea is not technically tea at all as it is not made from *Camellia sinensis* but rather herbs, flowers and spices. Herb 'tea' contain phytochemicals as well but these are far less studied.

Black, green and Oolong teas contain flavonoid antioxidants, they are just different types. Green tea contains more simple flavonoids called catechins, while black tea contains more complex flavonoids called theaflavins and thearubigins.

Tea and heart disease

A number of population studies have shown that drinking tea is associated with a decreased risk of cardiovascular disease. There are a number of different ways tea is thought to offer this protection, mostly related to the flavonoid antioxidant content.

Flavonoid antioxidants in tea have been shown to reduce the oxidation of bad LDL cholesterol, one of the mechanisms contributing to atherosclerosis or 'hardening' of the arteries. Drinking tea has also been shown to improve the elasticity and flexibility of blood vessels (endothelial function).

There are other things in tea that could also be protective against heart disease. Tea contains the B vitamin folate that reduces homocysteine in the blood—high homocysteine levels are believed to be bad news for heart disease risk. Tea flavonoids can also reduce homocysteine levels. Population studies also link drinking tea with lower blood pressure—another risk factor for heart disease.

Tea and cholesterol

Although it's not 100 per cent proven at this stage, drinking black and green tea has been shown to lower total and bad LDL cholesterol in human studies. Even so, it has enough other benefits to support a role in a heart-friendly eating plan.

How much tea?

The benefits for heart health appear at around 3–4 cups a day in scientific studies. Keep in mind you can drink up to 6 cups of tea without going into the 'high' level for caffeine consumption (see page 113). However, if you drink coffee as well then you'll need to factor in the caffeine from all your beverages.

Does green tea aid weight loss?

Green tea and the flavonoid antioxidants it contains is by no means a magic bullet for weight loss, but it might have positive effects—especially if you drink it instead of other sweetened drinks and you drink it as part of a heart-friendly eating plan.

Experiments with green tea have shown increases in the amount of energy burned and the use of fat as fuel in the body, and better weight and body fat loss. While this sounds promising, more research is needed.

TEA FACTS
- Tea is the second most widely consumed beverage after water in the world.
- The longer tea is left to brew, the higher the flavonoid antioxidant content.
- Adding milk does not affect the antioxidant activity.

What about herbal infusions?

Herbal infusions such as chamomile and peppermint are caffeine-free and virtually kilojoule-free when taken without additions. They don't contain the flavonoid antioxidants in tea but they can contribute to daily fluids for hydration.

How do I enjoy tea in moderation?
- Take time to enjoy 'taking tea'.
- Embrace the ceremony of tea-drinking by serving it in attractive cups.
- If you add milk, ensure it is low-fat.
- If you use sugar, gradually use less.

How to make the perfect cuppa

1. Always refill your jug with fresh water rather than reboil old water as this adds oxygen to the water, which improves flavour.
2. When brewing loose-leaf tea in a pot, use 1 rounded teaspoon per person.
3. Allow regular black tea to brew for 3 minutes, green tea for 4 minutes and Oolong tea for 6 minutes.
4. Don't add milk to green tea, Oolong or Lapsang Souchong.
5. Try making loose-leaf tea in a plunger pot (also used to make coffee) and you won't need to use a tea strainer.
6. Don't try to re-use tea leaves—always make a fresh pot with new tea.
7. Visit a tea shop and try new and unusual blends and varieties.
8. For interest and variety, try flavoured black tea.
9. Green tea is an acquired taste but flavoured green tea can be a nice introduction.

TEA TIPS

Store tea in a cool dry place. Keep loose-leaf tea and tea bags in an airtight container away from other strong smelling foods (such as herbal infusion bags).

What is white tea?

White tea is a premium type of tea also known as silver tip; the unopened buds of new tea leaves.

What is chai?

Chai is tea flavoured with spices and originates from India. It is traditionally served very sweet with lots of milk; however, chai loose-leaf tea and tea bags are now available for you to prepare chai tea with low-fat milk and less sugar.

Caffeine

Caffeine is found naturally in the leaves, seeds and fruits of over 60 plants, including tea leaves, coffee beans, cocoa beans and guarana. Caffeine has a mild stimulating affect that helps boost alertness, concentration and energy levels, but having too much can cause anxiety, increased blood pressure and sleeping difficulties. Drinking some types of coffee to excess may increase cholesterol levels.

The caffeine content of tea and coffee varies a lot according to how it's made. If it tastes strong, then it's likely to contain more caffeine (and also more antioxidants). For example, an espresso tastes quite strong and contains much more caffeine than a cup of instant coffee or tea. The table below gives you a rough idea of caffeine content of foods and drinks.

Caffeine content of foods and beverages	
Food/drink	**Caffeine (mg)**
Tea (250ml)	10–50
Instant coffee, 1 teaspoon in 250ml (9fl oz)	60–80
Decaf instant coffee, 1 teaspoon in 250ml (9fl oz)	3
Percolated/plunger coffee 250ml (9fl oz)	60–120
Espresso coffee (1 shot, 30ml/1fl oz) used to make long black, cappuccino and latte	100 (av.)
Cola-type soft drinks (1 cup/250ml/9fl oz)	36
"Energy" drinks (1½ cups/375ml/13½fl oz)	80
Hot chocolate (1 cup/250ml/9fl oz)	6
Milk chocolate (100g/3½oz)	20
Dark chocolate (30g/1oz)	20
Source: Adapted from Food Standards Australia & New Zealand. http://www.foodstandards.gov.au/whatsinfood/caffeine/index.cfm	

How much caffeine?

More than 300mg of caffeine a day is considered high, although some international recommendations say up to 400mg is fine. More than 500mg is associated with anxiety, irritability, headache and sleep disturbance. What confuses the issue is that everyone is different in how they tolerate caffeine, with regular users developing greater tolerance. People with high blood pressure, children, adolescents, and the elderly may be more vulnerable to the adverse effects of caffeine. Pregnant women are advised to avoid or limit caffeine intake, and those with reflux may find coffee aggravates their symptoms.

300mg of caffeine a day is roughly equal to:
- Four average cups, or three average size mugs, of instant coffee.
- Three average cups of brewed coffee.
- Six average cups of tea.

Caffeine and hydration

Enjoying caffeine-containing drinks such as tea and coffee in moderation does not cause dehydration and they can contribute to your daily fluid quota. This is because the diuretic effect is very mild and regular drinkers develop a tolerance.

Is caffeine addictive?

You don't get addicted to caffeine like other drugs such as alcohol or illegal drugs, but if you enjoy tea or coffee regularly, you may notice mild symptoms if you stop, such as headaches, fatigue and irritability. If you're currently having too much, then cut down gradually.

Coffee

Coffee can be enjoyed in moderation as part of a heart-friendly eating plan. To enjoy the likely benefits without the downsides avoid the 'add-ons' such as full cream milk, cakes and biscuits.

From the bush to barista

Coffee beans grow inside a red-coloured berry on the coffee bush. There are two main species, *Robusta* and *Arabica*, with *Arabica* being of higher quality. After harvest, the beans are removed from inside the fleshy fruit and then hulled to leave 'green' coffee beans. The beans are then roasted to fully develop the flavour and aroma, ready for packaging as whole or ground coffee.

What's good about coffee?

Coffee beans contain antioxidants from the polyphenol family, namely chlorogenic and caffeic acids, and clinical studies have shown that coffee drinking increases antioxidant activity inside the body. Drinking coffee appears to have health benefits. Regular coffee drinkers have a lower risk of developing gallstones, Parkinson's disease, liver disease and type 2 diabetes. The research is not entirely clear as to why, but the antioxidants are likely to play a role.

Coffee and cholesterol

Unfiltered boiled coffee contains cafestol and kahweol (diterpenes) that can increase cholesterol levels. Boiled and plunger coffee contains the highest amounts, espresso contains moderate amounts, while instant coffee contains very low amounts. Using filter paper tends to remove these substances, but again the general message is, don't have too much and enjoy coffee in moderation as part of your heart-friendly lifestyle.

Coffee and coronary heart disease

While population studies suggest drinking coffee may actually be protective against several diseases, it has been considered risky for the heart. This is because coffee consumption affects some risk factors for heart disease: blood pressure, homocysteine levels and blood vessel stiffness.

However studies to date do not link coffee with an increased risk of cardiovascular disease. In fact, some coffee appears to be better than drinking none at all for heart disease risk (an effect similar to alcohol). The beneficial effects for the heart appear to kick in at 2–3 cups of brewed coffee a day (providing 200–300mg caffeine), which fits neatly into the generally recommended moderate limit of caffeine intake.

If you have high blood pressure, you're probably best to err on the side of caution. Enjoy less coffee (1–2 cups brewed coffee a day, providing 100–200mg caffeine) and focus on healthy living to get it down—less salt and plenty of vegetables, fruit, low-fat dairy products and physical activity.

How do I enjoy coffee in moderation?

- Resist the temptation to up-size your coffee—use a regular sized cup and order regular sized servings at cafes.
- Enjoy your coffee less strong (by using less).
- Always ask for low-fat milk.
- Use the single shot function of your home espresso machine.
- If you're trying to cut down on caffeine, try decaf.

Watch the extras!

Adding full cream milk, especially in a cafe latte, is not recommended for cholesterol lowering—use skim or low-fat milk instead. Adding sugar won't affect your cholesterol, but does add kilojoules, so add as little as you can. The big risk to watch is for high saturated fat treats that tend to go with coffee like biscuits and cakes—limit these to special occasions.

What about decaf?

Drinking decaffeinated coffee is a good way to keep enjoying coffee while trying to cut back on caffeine. Decaf coffee is available as instant, ground and whole beans and has almost all the caffeine removed, leaving around 3mg per cup.

Different ways of making coffee

The coffee-making method you choose is a matter of personal taste, but remember the more coffee you use, the stronger the taste and the higher the caffeine content. Instant coffee generally has the least caffeine. Home espresso machines are increasingly popular and provide café quality coffee at home.

Instant – Boiling water is added to powder or granules of dehydrated coffee.

Percolated – Boiling water is bubbled under pressure through ground coffee on the stove-top (in a cafeteria).

Drip filter – Hot water is dripped over coffee grounds and sometimes filtered through paper.

French press /plunger/cafetiere – Hot water is poured over coarsely ground coffee and then the grounds are pushed to the bottom by a plunger.

Espresso – Hot water is forced through finely ground coffee under pressure.

Different ways of serving espresso coffee

These are typically all made with one shot of espresso (30ml, 100mg caffeine on average)

Short black – A tiny cup or glass with a single shot of espresso.

Long black – A tall cup or mug with espresso plus hot water.

Flat white – A cup with espresso, hot water and hot milk.

Cappuccino – A cup with espresso, hot milk and lots of milk froth (sprinkled with powdered chocolate).

Cafe latte – A tall cup or glass with espresso, lots of hot milk and a little milk froth.

Machiato – A short glass with just a dash of steamed milk to 'stain' the coffee (macchiato means 'stained' in Italian).

TIPS

- For superior flavour, buy your ground coffee fresh or vacuum packed in small amounts.
- Store ground coffee or beans at room temperature in an airtight container for up to 2 weeks.
- When making plunger coffee, allow 2 tablespoons of coffee per person. The longer you leave it, the stronger the brew.
- You can heat milk in the microwave to make cafe latte, pronto!

Did you know?

The coffee plant originated in Eastern Africa and then travelled to the Middle East, Turkey and then to Europe where coffee houses became the place for intellectuals to hang out and talk about art, philosophy and politics. It reached America in the 17th century and went on to be heavily promoted in the US as a form of protest to the high taxes on tea imposed by the British.

Part 3

Eat to beat cholesterol in your kitchen

20: Getting your kitchen into gear

Your kitchen is the powerhouse of heart-healthy nutrition. To ensure the meals and snacks you produce are the best for lowering your cholesterol and protecting your heart, all the equipment and materials need to be in place to make preparing food easier.

You've heard the adage that a shoddy tradesman always blames his tools, so make sure this doesn't apply to you in your kitchen. Having a good selection of tools and utensils is important for you to produce your best results—healthy food that looks appealing, tastes great and makes you look good in the kitchen!

Knives
Using quality knives and sharpening them regularly will make cooking a breeze. You'll need around 4 5 of different sizes, including a long serrated edge knife for slicing crusty wholegrain bread. Storing your knives in a block, or on a magnetised rack will keep them in top condition and reduces the chances of cutting yourself while rummaging through your kitchen drawers.

Chopping boards
Plastic boards are best because bugs can't hide away in the grain like in wooden ones. Ideally, buy several different coloured boards and allocate separate boards for raw meat/fish/chicken and another for uncooked/raw foods to prevent cross contamination.

Mixing bowls
A set of stainless steel kitchen bowls of different sizes will keep you organised as you cook because you can keep chopped ingredients separate. They're also great for mixing and coating. You'll need a glass, ceramic or pyrex dish for marinating foods.

Pots and pans

Solid-based saucepans with well-fitting lids will help you cook pasta, rice, noodles and couscous like a pro, as well as make sauces. Around 3–4 of varying sizes should do. A steamer attachment will produce moist and tender vegetables and meat, chicken or fish.

A wok is essential for Asian-style cooking. Stir-frying produces fabulously crisp and colourful vegetables and is marvelously quick and simple. Non-stick frying pans are ideal for healthy pan-frying meat, vegetable and egg recipes.

Microwave

A microwave cooks fast and uses less energy so it's a great time saver. It also preserves nutrients, especially in vegetables. No water is needed, just place vegetables in a microwave cooking container and press go! Have a couple of microwave cooking containers of different sizes. You can also use microwave-safe glass and ceramics in the microwave and these are best for foods that are oilier or sweeter as these can stain plastic cookware.

Measuring

Invest in a set of measuring cups and spoons so you can follow recipes accurately. These also help you stay in control of portion sizes where these are important, such as in oil, pasta and rice. A liquid measuring jug is an essential for measuring liquid ingredients. A set of kitchen scales are also useful. For example, for measuring accurate portions of meat, chicken and fish. After a while you'll have a better understanding of what the right amounts look like and be able to estimate more accurately without weighing.

Gadgets and gizmos

There are some pieces of kitchen equipment that just make things easier and more fun. A quality can-opener, vegetable peeler, grater and garlic crush are essential. A coffee machine will provide café quality at home, or a coffee plunger can make for a nicer experience than instant coffee. A teapot and china cups also take a 'tea break' to a whole new level. A juicer can make phytochemical-rich vegetable and fruit juices (look for machines which preserve more of the pulp and fibre). Bread lovers, you can bake your own with a bread machine—wholegrain and low sodium mixes are available.

Containers

Good sealable plastic containers that can go from the fridge or freezer to the microwave make food storage safer, prevent mess and smells in your fridge, and allow you to use leftovers wisely—great for the food budget, and saves time. A good lunchbox will keep your food fresh and in good shape to help you enjoy healthier options at work or play. Re-sealable plastic bags also come in handy for nuts and dried fruit. A small screwtop glass jar is excellent for making dressings.

Tableware

Food is meant to be a social and enjoyable experience. If you're serious about eating well, pay attention to your table. What does it say about you? If you've made your mind up to be a healthy person, be kind to yourself and believe that you deserve good health and wellbeing, then you will make time to enjoy your meal in a pleasant setting. Attractive plates, cutlery, glasses and serviettes add to the sense of occasion and add to the enjoyment of your cooking. A little relaxing music is a nice finishing touch, and stopping between mouthfuls to talk is a great way to slow your pace of eating and improve digestion and satisfaction.

Smart cooking

Let's review the Eat to Beat Cholesterol heart-friendly diet:

1. 5+ vegetables a day
2. 2+ fruit a day
3. Herbs and spices not salt
4. 2+ wholegrains a day
5. Low GI foods at most meals
6. 2+ meals a week with legumes
7. 30g/1oz nuts most days
8. 2+ fish meals a week
9. At least 30–45g (6–8 teaspoons) healthy oils and spreads daily
10. 25g of cholesterol-lowering margarine a day (to provide 2g plant sterols daily)
11. Perhaps 1–2 standard alcoholic drinks daily
12. Tea and coffee in moderation (Up to 3–4 teas plus 1 strong coffee or 2–3 weak coffees daily)

Healthy-heart tips for preparing food

To make the most of heart-friendly goodness in vegetables and fruit:

- Leave the skin on where you can.
- Don't leave chopped vegetables in the air too long before cooking (this will prevent oxidation and nutrient losses).
- Cook with little or no water to preserve vitamins.
- Use quicker cooking methods such as microwaving, stir-frying and steaming.

To remove saturated fat from meat:

- Trim visible fat from meat and chicken before cooking.
- Buy leaner cuts such as lean/trim mince.
- Remove the skin from chicken (fish skin is OK).

To make pulses and legumes less 'windy':

- Discard the water used for soaking dried peas and beans.
- Discard the water in canned legumes, and rinse well.

To keep food safe:

- Store food in the fridge or freezer.
- Keep food well wrapped or covered.
- Defrost food in the fridge or microwave, not on the bench/sink.
- Wash hands and equipment with hot soapy water.
- Keep raw and cooked food in different bowls when cooking in batches.
- Use different utensils and chopping boards for raw and cooked ingredients.
- Ensure you discard the marinade from raw meat, unless it is to be cooked.
- Always re-heat food until piping hot.

The perfectly balanced plate

Use the following dinner plate-guide to make sure you are eating a variety of foods in the right proportions. About half your plate should be filled with vegetables or salad, a quarter with lean meat and a quarter with grain foods (preferably wholegrain) such as pasta, rice or bread. For weight loss, consider using a smaller plate. For bigger appetites, use a bigger plate but the proportion stays the same. It's nutritionally a good idea for a smaller woman to use a smaller plate and a larger man to use a larger one–a situation where equality is not the aim!

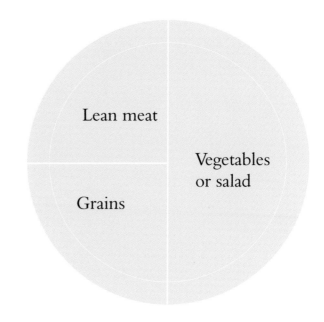

How to eat to beat cholesterol with your favourite recipes

There's no need to do away with your favourite recipes, just make them heart-friendly!

Lasagna:
- For white sauce: use sterol-enriched margarine spread instead of butter, low-fat milk and reduced-fat cheese; or use ricotta instead of white sauce.
- For meat filling: Use extra lean mince and substitute red lentils (or grated vegetables) for one-third of the meat.

Pasta:
- Use wholemeal lasagna sheets.
- For topping: use reduced-fat cheese.
- Serve with a salad.

Spaghetti bolognaise:
- Use extra lean mince.
- Salt-reduced canned tomatoes.
- Add red lentils or kidney beans, or grated vegetables.
- Use wholemeal spaghetti.
- Serve with a salad.

Roast dinner:
- Use kangaroo or venison roast, lean lamb roast, lean turkey roast.
- Use spray oil on vegetables.
- Include a variety of vegetables such as garlic, onion, sweet potato, parsnip, zucchini (courgette), pumpkin, squash, capsicum (pepper), baby eggplant (aubergine).
- Use reduced-salt gravy powder.

Quiche:
- Use filo pastry or brown rice base, or omit pastry (making it a frittata).
- Use high omega-3 eggs.
- Use salmon in springwater rather than bacon.
- Serve a small piece with lots of fresh salad and a slice of wholegrain bread.

Smart shopping in the supermarket

Shop regularly

When you have healthy food on hand, there's less reason to order takeaway. Ensure you shop regularly for fresh ingredients such as vegetables, fruit and dairy, and keep your pantry stocked with dry and canned goods. Meat, chicken and fish can be stored in the freezer—bag into meal sized amounts and take the right amount out when needed. Keep your bread in the freezer and take it out as you need it so it stays fresh. If shopping is a struggle, shop online and have your groceries delivered, or order a weekly box of fruit and vegetables from your greengrocer. Produce markets are very popular so why not make a day of it and select the freshest locally grown food?

SHOPPING TIPS
- Take a list so you don't forget anything. Using a list also helps to resist impulse buying of items you don't really need.
- Get to know your local shops. This will save time wandering around looking for things
- Keep your re-usable shopping bags in the car so you don't forget them
- Use an insulated bag to keep your chilled foods cold on the way home.

Balance your trolley

Much like the proportion of foods on your dinner plate needs to reflect a healthy balance, your shopping trolley needs to have the right foods to look after your heart.

Remember what you need to eat so you know what to buy:

- Vegetables in a variety of colours and types
- Fruits 2-a-day in a variety of colours and types
- Fresh and dried herbs and spices
- Lean meat (red and white)
- Fish (fresh and canned)
- Eggs
- Wholegrains: breads, crispbreads, pasta, rice, noodles and breakfast cereals (preferably low GI)
- Low-fat milk and yoghurt
- Margarine and oil
- Dried or canned legumes (beans, lentils, chickpeas)
- Nuts and seeds
- Tea and coffee

Treats and extras such as cakes, biscuits and confectionery should take up very little space in your trolley.

Reading the food labels

The nutrition information panel lists the energy (kilojoules/calories), protein, total fat, saturated fat, carbohydrate, sugars and sodium content per 100g/3½oz and per serve, and sometimes other nutrients as well such as fibre, polyunsaturated fat, monounsaturated fat, omega-3 and minerals such as calcium and iron.

Guideline daily amounts (expressed as a percentage) are a way of telling you how much of an average person's daily nutrient and energy needs are provided in a single serve of a food. If you need to lose weight, your energy needs will be less.

Example of Guideline Daily Amount (GDA) labelling

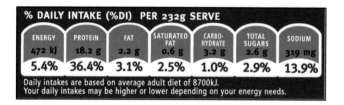

The most important nutrients to look out for to lower your cholesterol and look after your heart are saturated fat and sodium: look for the lowest in these, and also the highest in fibre. How much saturated fat and sodium is okay depends on the type of food and serving size. As you might imagine, you can't use the same criteria for a cooking oil and pasta because they have a different place in the diet. Compare the 'per 100g' column to compare products within a category, but always consider how much of the food you will actually eat as it could be more or less than 100g.

Tips for finding healthier products from food labels

Food category	Examples	Look for
Breads and cereals	Bread, crispbread, muffins, crumpets, breakfast cereals	Highest in fibre Lowest in sodium
Dairy products	Milk, yoghurt, cheese, ice cream	Lowest fat
	Dairy alternatives such as soy	Added calcium
Savoury	Sauces, ready-meals, snacks, meat products, soups	Lowest saturated fat Lowest sodium
Sweet	Biscuits, cakes, slices, muesli bars	Lowest saturated fat Lowest kilojoules Highest fibre
Spreads	Margarine spreads, peanut butter	Polyunsaturated Monounsaturated Lowest trans fat Lowest sodium

A note about 'low-fat' and 'fat-free'

By now you know that to lower cholesterol you need to eat healthy oils, so low-fat doesn't always mean a healthier choice. Low-fat milk and yoghurt are good options because most fat in whole milk is saturated, however 'low-fat' starchy foods such as crackers, potato chips or muffins are still high in kilojoules (calories), low in nutrients and likely to be high GI (and possibly trick you into eating more). Reduced-fat margarine and low-fat salad dressings are counter-productive because they have removed the very healthy unsaturated oils that we need to eat.

Additives

Food additives are listed by number on food labels and you can find out what the numbers mean easily online from your country's health authority. If you or anyone in your family is sensitive to particular additives, understanding the numbers allows you to avoid buying products that contain the problem ingredient.

Natural vs artificial

Just because a food is labelled 'natural' or contains 'no artificial colourings, flavourings or preservatives' doesn't mean it's good for you and your heart. Lard and butter are 100 per cent natural but loaded with artery clogging saturated fats! Don't be coaxed by 'natural' claims as they are often nutritionally meaningless. Look to the nutrition information panel instead.

21: Cooking to beat cholesterol

Sharing delicious food with those you love is a great way to boost your wellbeing. To help you lower your cholesterol, we've put together recipes that you and your family and friends will love eating because we really believe that enjoying food (we do) is essential for a happy life.

About the recipes

Adventure

Food should be fun! Enjoying foods and ingredients from different cultures is like taking a holiday at your dining table. Try new and interesting ingredients and flavours with the added bonus that they're good for you and your cholesterol. If you can't get hold of ingredients that are a bit different or exotic, we give you an alternative.

Convenience

We know many people don't have a lot of spare time, so we have kept the cooking and preparation times as short as possible for most recipes and we make the most of convenience foods such as canned foods and curry pastes to help you get dinner on the table. You'll also find there's a speedy microwave option for some recipes as well as the conventional cooking alternative.

The healthy stuff

Many of our recipes are complete and balanced meals packed with the heart-friendly, 'eat-to-beat-cholesterol' ingredients we talked about in earlier chapters. You don't have to worry about fat or sugar or kilojoules (calories) because we have done all the calculations for you. All you have to do is serve up your portion.

The technical stuff

If you're not into the technical stuff, then flick over this next bit and head straight to the recipes.

Nutrition information

You'll find 'Nutrition information per serve' for each of the recipes if you'd like to keep track (except the quickies at the end of each section). There are example daily eating menus in part 4 on page 252 if you'd like something specific to follow. We've used nutrient tags to help you identify recipes with particular characteristics. For example, if you want to lose weight you can watch out for 'Low kilojoule' tags, and if you're cutting back on sodium to reduce blood pressure you can look for 'Low sodium' tags.

Nutrient tag	When it is used
Low kilojoule	Main meal 2000kJ (480 cals) or less Light meal 1500kJ (360 cals) or less Snack 600kJ (150 cals) or less
Fibre	Main meal 8g or more Light meal 6g or more Snack 4g or more
Low sodium	Less than 120mg/100g AND Main meal 500mg or less Light meal 300mg or less Snack 50mg or less
Omega-3 (long chain from fish) DHA & EPA	Excellent source contains more than 900mg Great source contains 250-900mg Good source contains less than 250mg
GI rating*	In low GI recipes, the predominant carbohydrate ingredient(s) is/are low GI

Recipe nutrition guidelines

Our recipes were developed with lowering cholesterol and heart health in mind. We calculated how much of the key nutrients were ideal, the heart-healthy ingredients to include, added culinary creativity, and came up with the final healthy and delicious recipes for you to enjoy.

Daily nutrient targets

The daily targets for key nutrients such as saturated fat, cholesterol and fibre were derived from key recommendations from major health bodies. They are suitable for people with elevated cholesterol levels and designed to reduce the risk of cardiovascular disease. They're also good for healthy people who want to stay that way.

Daily Nutrient Targets for Lowering Cholesterol and Reducing Heart Disease Risk (Adults)

Nutrient	Daily targets
Total fat	25–35% total kJ/cals
Saturated fat	Saturated + trans 8% total kJ/cals or less
Polyunsaturated fat (total)	Up to 10% kJ/cals
Plant omega 3 polyunsaturates (ALA)	2g or more 1% total kJ/cals
Marine omega-3 polyunsaturates (EPA & DHA)	500mg (av.) At least 2 fish meals/week (preferably oily fish)
Monounsaturated fat	10–20% kJ/cals
Cholesterol	Less than 200mg
Total dietary fibre	38g men 28g women
Plant sterols	2g/day
Sodium	1600mg or less

Daily meal targets

Key nutrient targets for different meals were developed from the figures above using an average adult energy (kilojoule) intake of 9000kJ/2000 calories. A daily pattern of 3 meals and 2 snacks was assumed. A 6000kJ level suitable for weight loss was also used to derive the 'low kilojoule' tag.

Energy (kilojoule/calorie) targets for Recipes

Meal/snack	Kilojoules (calories)	Low kilojoule (calorie) for weight loss
Light meal (x 2 daily)	2000 (478) or less	1500 (358) or less
Main meal	3000 (717) or less	2000 (478) or less
Snack (x 2 daily)	1000 (239) or less	600 (143) or less
TOTAL	**9000kJ (2151 cals)**	**6200kJ (1480 cals)**

Meal targets for key heart-health nutrients

	Saturated fat (g)		Cholesterol (mg)	Sodium (mg)	Fibre (g)
	9000kJ	6000kJ			
Main meal	8 or less	6 or less	80 or less	600 or less	8 or more
Light meal x 2	4 or less	2 or less	40 or less	400 or less	6 or more
Snack x 2	2 or less	1 or less	20 or less	100 or less	4 or more
TOTAL	18 or less	12 or less	180 or less	1600 or less	28 or more

There are always exceptions to every rule

These targets have been applied as much as possible, however the occasional recipe may be a little over on one nutrient. This is because, thankfully, not all meals are nutritionally identical. This is okay because a little extra at one meal is likely to be balanced out by a little less at other meals. The recipe is still a healthy choice and contains heart-friendly foods. For example when a recipe includes an egg, this exceeds the cholesterol target for that meal, but the whole day's intake can still be on track for heart health. See page 82 for more information on eggs.

What about children?

High cholesterol is an increasing problem for children and teens, but the best cure is prevention. Nutritious heart-friendly meals like ours are great for the whole family. Please note energy needs of children and teens may be slightly different to the needs for adults. A good rule of thumb is: you provide healthy meals and snacks and they decide how much they eat.

You may notice an advisory statement on some cholesterol lowering margarines (containing plant sterols, see page 93) saying they are not suitable for children. Be assured this is not because they are unsafe, but because care is required to undertake a cholesterol-lowering diet in children. While there is no problem with baking a cake for the whole family with a cholesterol-slowering margarine, seek expert dietary advice from a Registered or Accredited Practising Dietitian if your child or teen has high cholesterol. If your child's cholesterol is normal, it's more economical to give them a standard soft margarine and leave the expensive cholesterol-lowering stuff to the grown-ups.

22: Breakfast and brunch

Cereal Mix

Low kilojoule, low sodium, low–medium GI

This cereal recipe includes only heart-friendly ingredients and delivers a great-tasting combination of crunch, puff and soft textures. The proportions of each ingredient can be changed to taste and the mix is great as a quick snack any time. If you can't find soy flakes, try using high-fibre, low-GI wheat flakes.

Preparation time: 5 minutes
Cooking time: 10 minutes
Storage time: 1 week in an airtight container
Makes: 3½ cups (7 serves)

½ cup (60g/2¼oz) walnut pieces
1 cup (30g/1oz) puffed wheat
1 cup (55g/2oz) soy flakes
½ cup (50g/1¾oz) traditional rolled oats
½ cup (60g/2¼oz) LSA (linseed, sunflower and almond blend)
2 teaspoons ground cinnamon

Preheat oven to cool 150°C/300°F/Gas Mark 2. Spread the walnuts on a baking tray and bake for 6–8 minutes or until lightly golden. Cool. Meanwhile, place the puffed wheat, soy flakes, oats, LSA and cinnamon in an airtight cereal storage container. Add the cooled walnut pieces and shake to combine. Shake container well before serving to make sure you get a taste of all the flavours and textures.

Cook's tips

Try different nuts such as pecans or almonds.
Add some dried fruits, such as pear, apple, apricots or raisins.
Try adding a soy flake cereal that has dried fruits or nuts added.

Nutrition note

Look for wholegrain rolled oats, commonly labelled traditional rolled oats, rather than instant oats, as they have a lower GI. Also use rolled barley, which is low GI.

Nutrition per serve

Energy kJ (cals) 727 (173)
Protein 8g
Total fat 10.8g
Saturated fat 0.9g
Fibre 4.1g
Carbohydrate 11.6g
Cholesterol 0mg
Sodium 4mg

Brunch Muffins

High fibre, low GI

A mixed-grain English muffin is used for this recipe. The grains are kibbled rye, kibbled wheat, linseed, linola seed, kibbled corn, sunflower kernels, triticale, kibbled barley and rolled oats—an excellent way of enjoying a variety of healthy grains in the diet.

Preparation time: 5 minutes
Cooking time: 10 minutes
Serves: 2

3 teaspoons sunflower oil
2 x 60g/2¼oz flat mushrooms, trimmed
½ cup (150g/5½oz) salt-reduced baked beans in tomato sauce
2 x 50g/1¾oz eggs
2 x 60g/2¼oz mixed wholegrain muffins
1 tablespoon light cholesterol-lowering margarine
2 teaspoons chopped flat-leaf parsley

Heat the oil in a non-stick pan over a medium heat. Cook the mushrooms, stem side down, until golden, 2–3 minutes, turn and cook the other side. Spoon the baked beans into the tops of the mushrooms to heat while the mushrooms are cooking. Add the eggs to the pan and cook to liking or poach in a separate pan. Toast the muffins and spread with cholesterol-lowering margarine. Serve the mushroom and beans on one half of the muffin and the egg on the other. Sprinkle with parsley.

Nutrition note

This is a good example of a recipe that is higher in fat, but as a breakfast meal is still low in saturated fat. If you're watching your weight, kilojoules are the most important thing to limit and the kilojoules in this recipe are on target (between 1500–2000kJ/350-475cals).

Nutrition per serve

Energy kJ (cals) 1484 (354)
Protein 18g
Total fat 17g
Saturated fat 3g
Fibre 8g
Carbohydrate 32g
Cholesterol 188mg
Sodium 442mg

Breakfast in a Flash

Low kilojoule, low sodium, low–medium GI

Keep a measuring cup in the cereal container for portion control and quick measuring when you are trying to tackle the early morning breakfast rush—the perfect guarantee of the recommended serve and a heart-healthy start to the day.

Preparation time: 5 minutes
Serves: 2

1 cup (30g/1oz) Cereal Mix (see page 132)
½ cup (125g/4½oz) low-fat yoghurt
2 x 150g/5½oz apples, chopped
½ cup (125ml/4fl oz) low-fat milk (semi-skimmed) or soy milk

Divide cereal between two bowls. Top with yoghurt and apple. Pour on the milk.

Nutrition per serve
Energy kJ (cals) 1002 (240)
Protein 11g
Total fat 5.8g
Saturated fat 0.6g
Fibre 5g
Carbohydrate 36g
Cholesterol 6.5g
Sodium 92mg

Strawberry Smoothie

Low kilojoule, low GI

Keep a measuring cup in the cereal container for portion control and quick measuring when you are trying to tackle the early morning breakfast rush—the perfect guarantee of the recommended serve and a heart-healthy start to the day.

Preparation time: 3 minutes
Blending time: 2 minutes
Serves: 2

Smoothie
1 cup (250ml/9fl oz) low-fat or soy milk
¾ cup (185g/6½oz) low-fat vanilla yoghurt
½ cup (80g/2¾oz) diced strawberries
¼ cup (30g/1oz) LSA (soy, linseed, sunflower and almond blend)

Topping
¾ teaspoon ground cinnamon
½ teaspoon sugar
¼ teaspoon cocoa powder

Place milk, yoghurt, strawberries and LSA into a blender. Blend for 1–2 minutes. Pour into glasses. Mix together the cinnamon, sugar and cocoa in a small bowl and sprinkle on the shake.

Nutrition per serve
Energy kJ (cals) 915 (218)
Protein 15.4g
Total fat 7g
Saturated fat 0.9g
Fibre 3.7g
Carbohydrate 24g
Cholesterol 11mg
Sodium 154mg

Corncakes, Salsa and Avocado

Low kilojoule, low GI

It's always fun making up a batch of hotcakes. These corncakes are a variation of the traditional hotcake and are made with a combination of buckwheat and wholemeal flours. They are perfect for breakfast and brunch, and even for lunch or dinner. This recipe is a double quantity—enjoy a serve for two when freshly cooked and freeze the remaining corncakes for later.

Preparation time: 10 minutes
Cooking time: 15 minutes
Storage time: Freeze for up to 2 weeks
Makes: 8 corncakes (4 serves)

¼ cup (45g/1½oz) buckwheat flour
½ teaspoon baking powder
½ teaspoon bicarbonate of soda (baking soda)
½ cup (75g/2½oz) wholemeal plain flour
½ teaspoon brown sugar
1 (50g/1¾oz) egg
1 cup (250ml/9fl oz) buttermilk
1 cup (185g/6½oz) drained canned sweet corn kernels
¼ cup (50g/1¼oz) drained canned lentils
3 teaspoons chopped chives
Olive oil spray

Sift the buckwheat flour, baking powder and bicarbonate of soda into a mixing bowl. Stir in the wholemeal flour and sugar. Beat the egg, mix with the buttermilk and blend into the flour mixture until smooth. Stir in the corn, lentils and chives. Set aside while preparing the salsa. Heat a large non-stick frying pan over a medium heat and coat lightly with oil spray. Place about two tablespoons of mixture in the pan for each corncake and cook until bubbles appear on the top, about 2–3 minutes (cook 2–3 at a time). Turn the corncakes with a spatula and cook until lightly browned, about 1–2 minutes. Keep warm and continue cooking with the remaining mixture. Serve two corncakes per person, spread with avocado, topped with salsa (see page 143).

Nutrition per serve
(2 corncakes with salsa)
Energy kJ (cals) 1295 (309)
Protein 12g
Total fat 12.7g
Saturated fat 3.2g
Fibre 5.2g
Carbohydrate 37g
Cholesterol 47mg
Sodium 433mg

Salsa

Low kilojoule

We created this recipe to serve with the Corncakes (page 140). It would also be perfect served over poached chicken breast, grilled (broiled) fish or lean lamb cutlets, or stirred through cooked pasta, with tuna and the avocado sliced on top.

Preparation time: 5 minutes
Storage time: Refrigerate up to 1 day
Serves: 2

½ cup (80g/2¾oz) finely diced red capsicum (pepper)
1 tablespoon drained canned lentils
2 teaspoons chopped chives
1 teaspoon white wine vinegar
½ teaspoon brown sugar
⅓ cup (75g/2½oz) mashed avocado
Freshly ground black pepper

Place capsicum, lentils, chives, vinegar and sugar in a bowl and mix to combine. Set aside to allow the flavours to develop. If you make it in advance it will keep for a day in the refrigerator in a covered container.

Nutrition per serve
Energy kJ (cals) 398 (95)
Protein 1.7g
Total fat 8.6g
Saturated fat 1.8g
Fibre 1.2g
Carbohydrate 3g
Cholesterol 0mg
Sodium 16mg

Banana Bread

Low kilojoule, low sodium, medium GI

Preparation time: 15 minutes
Cooking time: 1½ hours
Storage time: Up to 1 week in the refrigerator
Makes: 14 slices

½ cup (60g/2¼oz) walnut pieces
1 cup (270g/10oz) mashed very ripe bananas (3)
2 x 50g/1¾oz eggs, lightly beaten
¼ cup (60ml/2fl oz) buttermilk
½ cup (125g/4½oz) melted and cooled cholesterol-lowering margarine
¼ teaspoon vanilla extract
¾ cup (90g/3oz) extra walnut pieces
½ cup (90g/3oz) brown sugar
¾ cup (90g /3oz) plain (all-purpose) flour
¾ cup (110g/3¾oz) wholemeal plain (all purpose) flour
2 teaspoons baking powder
½ teaspoon bicarbonate of soda (baking soda)

Preheat oven to cool 150°C (300°F/Gas Mark 2) and grease a 21 x 9 x 6.5cm (8¼ x 3½ x 2½ inch) loaf tin. Spread walnuts on a baking tray and bake for 6–8 minutes, until lightly golden. Cool. Combine the bananas, eggs, buttermilk, margarine and vanilla together and stir until well mixed. Place the extra walnuts in the bowl of a food processor and process until they are fine, 20–30 seconds. Add the sugar, plain and wholemeal flours, baking powder and bicarbonate of soda. Process for 30–40 seconds, until the ingredients are combined. With the motor running, pour the banana mixture through the funnel of the food processor and process for 30 seconds or until the mixture is well combined. Stir in the toasted walnuts. Place the mixture into the prepared tin and bake for 1½ hours or until a skewer inserted in the centre comes out clean. Cool in the tin before transferring to a wire rack.

Nutrition per serve
(1 slice)
Energy kJ (cals) 985 (236)
Protein 4.8g
Total fat 15.4g
Saturated fat 2g
Fibre 2.3g
Carbohydrate 20g
Cholesterol 27g
Sodium 134mg

Whip It Up Breakfasts and Brunches—Quickies

Bircher Muesli

A great start to the day—just like a breakfast take-away from your own fridge since you prepared it the night before and it is now ready to be enjoyed.

Combine ½ cup natural muesli with 2 teaspoons each of LSA mix and wheatgerm. Stir in a grated apple, a pinch of ground cinnamon and about ¼ cup of low-fat natural (plain) or vanilla yoghurt.

Refrigerate overnight and serve with an extra dollop of yoghurt the next morning and perhaps a little low-fat milk. Serves 2

Mixed Grain and Fruit Porridge

This recipe makes about 1½ cups of porridge.

Bring 1½ cups water to the boil. Stir in 2 tablespoons each of linseed (flax seed), brown rice and traditional rolled oats, cover, reduce heat and simmer for about 25 minutes, until the rice is tender. Stir occasionally to prevent sticking. Stir in 1 tablespoon each of chopped raisins and dried apricots and stir for a couple of minutes until the porridge is thick. Serve with soy or low-fat milk. Serves 2

Soy-Good Breakfast

This gives you around 10g (½oz) of soy protein per serve. Divide 2 cups of a commercial soy-based breakfast cereal between two bowls. Pour around ¾ cup (200ml/7fl oz) of soy milk over each and top with 100g/3½oz (½ tub) of soy yoghurt and ½ cup chopped fresh fruit. Serves 2

Spiced Apple Compote

Try this compote on its own, or with a dollop of low-fat yoghurt, custard or ricotta cheese, or serve it on cereal.

Make up a cup of tea with a tea bag (your favourite flavour). Cut an apple into eight wedges (no need to peel), core and gently simmer in the tea with a cinnamon quill (broken into three pieces) and three cloves until the apple is tender. Sweeten to taste with honey. Remove cinnamon and cloves before serving. Serves 1–2

Wholegrain Ricotta and Banana Toast

Choose a dense grainy bread full of wholegrains such as wheat, barley, rye, oats, corn (maize) and seeds (sunflower, sesame, poppy, linseeds)—choose the brand lowest in sodium (less than 450mg/½g).

Mix together 1 teaspoon brown sugar and 1 teaspoon ground cinnamon (or to taste) in a small dish. Peel and slice a banana, drizzle with a little lime or lemon juice, and sprinkle over the sugar-cinnamon mix. Toast two thick slices of bread and top each slice with about ¼ cup fresh low-fat ricotta cheese and banana slices. Apple slices would be a delicious substitute for banana. Serves 2

Vegetable Frittata

Great for a weekend breakfast to share.

Heat 2 teaspoons canola oil in a small non-stick pan. Add 1½ cups diced vegetables, such as carrot, cucumber (seeds removed), zucchini (courgettes) or celery, and cook, stirring occasionally, for 2–3 minutes. Stir in 1 teaspoon salt-reduced soy and ½ teaspoon sesame oil. Beat 2 small eggs, add to the pan, swirling the pan to coat the vegetables. Cook until the egg is almost set, then heat under the grill (broiler) to just complete the cooking. Invert frittata onto a warmed plate. Serve topped with baby herbs or salad leaves, such as lettuce or baby spinach. Serves 1–2

23: Snacks

PM Snack

High fibre, low sodium, low–medium GI

Rich in heart-healthy oils and fibre, this is a great cure for the mid-afternoon munchies. Purchased popped or puffed corn is ideal to use in this recipe and can be warmed for a few minutes in a microwave. Alternatively, freshly pop your own corn. Try this mix with a low-fat vanilla yoghurt.

Preparation time: 10 minutes
Cooking time: 8 minutes
Makes: 1 cup
Serves: 2

1½ tablespoons (20g/¾oz) almond kernels with skin
2 tablespoons (30g/1oz) pumpkin seed kernels (pepitas)
½ cup (10g/1⅓oz) popped/puffed corn
1 tablespoon (15g/½oz) chopped dried paw paw (papaya)
1 tablespoon (15g/½oz) chopped dried pineapple

Preheat oven to moderate 180°C (350°F/Gas Mark 4). Spread almonds on a baking tray in a single layer and bake for 6–8 minutes, until golden. Cool. Combine the pumpkin kernels, popped corn, paw paw, pineapple and cooled almonds and mix well.

Nutrition note

Whole nuts with skin have more heart-friendly fibre.

Nutrition per serve

Energy kJ (cals) 821 (196)
Protein 7g
Total fat 12.7g
Saturated fat 1.4g
Fibre 5g
Carbohydrate 14g
Cholesterol 0mg
Sodium 6mg

Dukkah Dip, Vegetable Sticks and Crispbread

High fibre, low–medium GI

Dukkah, an Egyptian specialty spice blend of hazelnut, sesame, coriander seed, pistachio, cumin, salt and pepper, is available from specialty spice shops and delicatessens. This dip can be whipped up in a few minutes and turns snacking on vegetables into a real treat. Use red capsicum (peppers), carrot, zucchini (courgetttes). The dip can also be used to dress steamed vegetables such as asparagus, beans or broccoli.

Preparation time: 10 minutes
Makes: ¼ cup
Serves: 2

1½ tablespoons low-fat natural (plain) yoghurt
1 tablespoon soy mayonnaise (look for lowest sodium brand)
1 tablespoon dukkah
1 clove garlic, crushed
1 cup (150g/5½oz) raw vegetable sticks
2 x 9g (½oz) wholegrain rye crispbread

Mix the yoghurt with the mayonnaise until smooth and creamy. Stir in the dukkah and garlic and mix well. Serve in a small pot with the vegetables and crispbread.

Nutrition note

We used a soy mayonnaise with 73mg sodium per 100g.

Nutrition per serve

Energy kJ (cals) 748 (178)
Protein 5g
Total fat 13.3g
Saturated fat 1.6g
Fibre 4g
Carbohydrate 10g
Cholesterol 1mg or less
Sodium 119mg

Eggplant Dip with Za'atar Crisps

High fibre, low GI

Za'atar is a traditional Middle Eastern blend of thyme, oregano, sesame, sumac and a little salt. This dip can be made in larger quantities to kick-start a barbecue. If enjoying it as a snack, follow it with chilled orange quarters.

Preparation time: 10 minutes
Cooking time: 45 minutes
Chilling time: 30 minutes minimum
Serves: 2

Dip

2 large unpeeled garlic cloves
Olive oil spray
1 small (250g/9oz) eggplant (aubergine), trimmed
2 teaspoons low-fat natural (plain) yoghurt
¼ teaspoon finely grated lemon zest
1 teaspoon za'atar
150g/5½oz raw vegetables such as baby radishes,
   carrot and celery sticks

Za'atar Crisps

1 wholemeal pita pocket (lowest sodium brand)
Olive oil spray
1 teaspoon za'atar, extra

To make the eggplant dip, preheat oven to moderately hot 200°C (400°F/Gas Mark 6) and line a baking tray with foil. Place the garlic cloves on a piece of foil, spray with oil and wrap like a parcel. Place the eggplant and garlic on the baking tray and bake for 30 minutes.

Remove the garlic and continue to cook the eggplant for a further 15 minutes or until soft. Remove eggplant from oven and allow to cool. Peel the eggplant and place the flesh with the squeezed-out garlic cloves in a food processor. Add the yoghurt, lemon zest and za'atar. Process until smooth. Cover and chill for at least 30 minutes. Serve with the pita crisps, radishes, carrot and celery.

To make the za'atar crisps, preheat oven to moderately hot 200°C (400°F/Gas Mark 6) and spray a baking tray with oil. Place the pita bread on a cutting board, spray with oil and sprinkle with za'atar. Cut into long thin crisps and place on the baking tray and bake for 5 minutes. Cool.

Nutrition per serve
(½ pita bread + ¼ cup dip + vegetables)
Energy kJ (cals) 523 (125)
Protein 5g
Total fat 2.5g
Saturated fat 0.3g
Fibre 7g
Carbohydrate 19g
Cholesterol 1mg or less
Sodium 133mg

Creamy Rice and Fruit

High fibre, low–medium GI

This is an excellent snack to make with leftover cooked brown rice. The creamy yoghurt rice could be made a day ahead and refrigerated and would make a quick dessert. Serve with any fruits in season, canned or stewed fruits. It's high in fibre and very filling—ideal for larger appetites.

Preparation time: 10 minutes
Serves: 2

⅔ cup (150g/5½oz) cooked and cooled brown rice
2 tablespoons currants
2 tablespoons low-fat natural (plain) yoghurt
1 teaspoon honey
1 x 125g/4½oz mandarin, segmented
1 x 150g/5½oz apple, sliced
1 cup (125g/4½oz) sliced strawberries
Extra honey

Place the rice, currants, yoghurt and honey in a bowl and mix to combine.
Divide the mixture between two 125ml (4fl oz) plastic containers and press down firmly. Turn out onto serving plates. Serve with the fruit and drizzle with honey if desired.

Nutrition note

Using basmati, doongara or koshikari rice will lower the GI of this recipe, as will using yellowbox honey or pure maple syrup instead of regular honey.

Nutrition per serve

Energy kJ (cals) 1017 (243)
Protein 6g
Total fat 1.1g
Saturated fat 0.2g
Fibre 6g
Carbohydrate 52g
Cholesterol 1mg
Sodium 110mg

Honey Seed and Nut Slice

Low sodium, low GI

Jam-packed full of healthy oats, nuts and seeds, cut this slice into bars or squares. It makes a great snack to enjoy with an apple or a bunch of grapes. High in fibre and heart-healthy oils, this is a sweet treat that's good for you.

Preparation time: 10 minutes
Cooking time: 10–15 minutes
Makes: 10 pieces
Serving size: 1 piece

2 tablespoons cholesterol-lowering margarine
1 tablespoon brown sugar
¼ cup (80g/2¾oz) honey
1½ cups (150g/5½oz) traditional wholegrain rolled oats
½ cup (60g/2¼oz) walnut pieces, chopped
½ cup (70g/2½oz) sunflower kernels
¼ cup (30g/1oz) ground almonds (almond meal)
¼ cup (45g/1½oz) sesame seeds
1 tablespoon (20g/¾oz) linseeds

Preheat oven to moderately cool 170°C (325°F/Gas Mark 3) and grease and line a 21 x 9 x 6.5cm (8¼ x 3½ x 2½ inch) deep loaf tin. Melt the margarine, sugar and honey over a low heat, stir until the sugar dissolves. Continue to simmer very gently for 5 minutes. Mix together the oats, walnuts, sunflower kernels, ground almonds, sesame seeds and linseeds in a large bowl. Pour the melted mixture into the dry ingredients and mix until well combined. Press mixture very firmly into the prepared tin and bake for 10–15 minutes until light golden. If browning too quickly around the edges, cover the edges with foil. Cool completely in the tin. When cold, cut with a serrated knife into bars or squares and store in an airtight container.

Nutrition per serve
Energy kJ (cals) 822 (196)
Protein 4g
Total fat 12g
Saturated fat 1.4g
Fibre 2g
Carbohydrate 17g
Cholesterol 0mg
Sodium 17mg

Pistachio and Almond Biscuits

Low sodium, low GI

This recipe has been adapted from an almond macaroon. Oats have been added to increase the fibre. The mixture is rolled in pistachios and almonds before baking, making them look as delicious as they taste. Enjoy with morning or afternoon coffee or tea. Low in salt, and with the heart-friendly goodness of nuts.

Preparation time: 10 minutes
Refrigeration time: 1 hour
Cooking time: 20 minutes
Storage time: Store in an airtight container 5 days
Makes: 20

3 teaspoons cholesterol-lowering margarine
1 teaspoon honey
1 cup (100g/3½oz) flaked (slivered) almonds
¼ cup (30g/1oz) traditional wholegrain rolled oats
½ cup (110g/3¾oz) caster (superfine) sugar
1 egg white
¼ cup (30g/1oz) extra flaked (slivered) almonds
⅓ cup (45g/1½oz) pistachio kernels
Sifted icing (confectioner's) sugar for serving, optional

Place the margarine and honey in a microwave safe bowl and melt on 20 per cent power for 30–40 seconds. Place the almonds, rolled oats and caster sugar in the bowl of a food processor and process for 30 seconds or until fine. With the motor running, pour the egg white and honey mixture through the funnel of the food processor and process for 40 seconds or until the mixture forms a smooth paste.

Transfer mixture to a small bowl, cover and refrigerate for 1 hour. Preheat oven to cool 150°C (300°F/Gas Mark 2) and line a baking tray with baking paper. Roughly chop the extra almond flakes and pistachios and mix well to combine. Shape the biscuit mixture into small balls and roll in the combined almonds and pistachios, pressing the nuts firmly into the mixture. Place on the baking tray and press each biscuit gently with a fork. Bake for 20 minutes or until the biscuits are lightly browned. Cool on the baking tray before serving sprinkled lightly with icing sugar.

Nutrition per serve
(2 biscuits)
Energy kJ (cals) 707 (161)
Protein 4g
Total fat 10.6g
Saturated fat 1.0g
Fibre 2g
Carbohydrate 15g
Cholesterol 0mg
Sodium 11mg

Blueberry Crumble Muffins

Medium GI, low kilojoule

These mini muffins are delicious served warm when freshly baked or reheat well after refrigerating or freezing. A light sprinkling of icing (confectioner's) sugar is optional. These yummy baked treats have the benefits of a cholesterol-lowering margarine and oat bran as well as the goodness of wholegrains, nuts and seeds. Enjoy them with a glass of low-fat milk or skim milk café latte.

Preparation time: 10 minutes
Cooking time: 15–20 minutes
Makes: 24 mini-muffins
Serving size: 2 mini-muffins

2 tablespoons cholesterol-lowering margarine, melted
¾ teaspoon vanilla extract
1 (50g/1¾oz) egg, beaten
¾ cup (200ml /7fl oz) reduced-fat milk
¾ cup (110g/3¾oz) stoneground wholemeal
   self-raising (self-rising) flour
¼ teaspoon baking powder
¼ cup (30g/1oz) Soy and LSA mix (Soy, Linseed,
   Sunflower and Almond Blend)
1 tablespoon brown sugar
1 tablespoon oat bran
½ cup (75g/2½oz) blueberries

Topping

2 tablespoons stoneground wholemeal plain (all-purpose) flour
1½ tablespoons cholesterol-lowering margarine
1 tablespoon brown sugar
¼ cup (30g/1oz) soy, LSA mix

Preheat oven to moderately hot 200°C (400°F/Gas Mark 6) and grease 2 x 12 cup (30ml/1fl oz capacity) muffin trays. Mix together the margarine, vanilla, egg and milk. In a separate bowl, mix together the flour, baking powder, Soy LSA, sugar and bran. Add the wet ingredients to the dry ingredients and stir only until just combined. Fold the blueberries into the mixture. To make the topping, mix all the ingredients together in a bowl. Spoon the muffin mixture into the prepared tins and spread a little topping on each muffin. Bake for 15–20 minutes or until cooked. Cool and refrigerate or freeze.

Nutrition per serve
(2 mini muffins)
Energy kJ (cals) 494 (118)
Protein 4g
Total fat 6.4g
Saturated fat 1.2g
Fibre 2.4g
Carbohydrate 12g
Cholesterol 17mg
Sodium 105mg

Melon Energiser

Low sodium, high fibre

A great energy booster for that mid-morning or afternoon hunger attack. It looks and tastes great, with psyllium added to help beat cholesterol. Better than a juice because the fibre is retained, providing a thicker texture and more filling power. On a hot day enjoy it as a chilly smoothie over ice or try it as a 'mocktail', without the psyllium, over crushed ice when enjoying a drink with friends.

Preparation time: 10 minutes
Serves: 2

1 medium/1 cup (125g/4½oz) sliced carrot
1 teaspoon finely chopped ginger
1 x 250g/9oz orange, peeled, seeds removed and chopped
1 cup (170g/6oz) chopped watermelon
1 cup (170g/6oz) chopped rockmelon (cantaloupe)
1 tablespoon psyllium husks

Place the carrot, ginger, orange, watermelon and rock melon in a blender and blend for 1–2 minutes until well mixed. Add the psyllium and blend for 20 seconds until combined. Serve in glasses.

Nutrition per serve

Energy kJ (cals) 436 (104)
Protein 3g
Total fat 0.7g
Saturated fat 0.1g
Fibre 6g
Carbohydrate 21g
Cholesterol 0mg
Sodium 41mg

Whip It Up Snacks—Quickies

Citrus, Sultana and Oat Cakes

This is a variation on the traditional rock cake recipe; quick to make and quick to bake. Enjoy one or two freshly baked and freeze the rest for later—thaw and warm for that sweet snack attack. Preheat oven to 200°C (400°F/Gas Mark 6). Mix together 1 cup self-raising wholemeal flour, ¼ cup sugar, 2 tablespoons traditional rolled oats, 1½ tablespoons chopped mixed peel and 1 tablespoon chopped sultanas. Melt 1½ tablespoons salt-reduced cholesterol-lowering margarine and add it to a beaten egg, 1 tablespoon light milk and ¼ teaspoon vanilla essence. Mix the liquid and dry ingredients together—the mixture should be moist and firm (add a touch more milk if needed). Spoon ten mounds onto a tray lined with baking paper. Bake for about 10 minutes until golden. Makes 10 (we suggest 2 cakes per serving)

Mixed Grain Lemon and Dill Salmon Salad Sandwiches

Make a dressing with the juice and zest of 1 lemon and 1 tablespoon each of chopped dill and parsley. Mix together 1 cup each of baby spinach and baby rocket, ½ cup each of finely sliced red onion and cucumber; stir in the dressing. Spread 4 slices mixed grain bread with barley with 1 tablespoon cholesterol-lowering margarine. Evenly divide 90g (3oz) drained salmon in springwater and the spinach and rocket salad between two slices of bread and top each with a slice of cold baked kumara (orange sweet potato) and the other slice of bread. Cut each sandwich in half for easy eating. Serves 2

Hummus

This recipe makes about 2 cups, or 8 serves, so store leftovers, covered, in the refrigerator. Blend together 1 can (425g/15oz) drained and rinsed chickpeas, ⅓ cup tahini (sesame) paste, the juice of 2 large lemons, 2 tablespoons extra virgin olive oil, and 2 cloves fresh garlic, until smooth.

Hummus, Carrot and Baby Spinach Wrap

Spread 2 pieces wholemeal flat bread (lavash) each with 1 tablespoon cholesterol-lowering margarine and ¼ cup hummus. Top each with ½ cup grated carrot and ½ cup of baby spinach leaves between the wraps and roll each up tightly. Serves 2

Indian Yoghurt Dip (Raita)

This 'raita' is delicious as a snack with vegetable sticks (carrot, celery or cucumber, etc), pappadums or served as a cooling side dish for curries—each serve contains 280mg of calcium. Combine a 200g (7oz) tub low-fat yoghurt, 2 finely diced Lebanese cucumbers, 1 clove of crushed garlic and a teaspoon of finely chopped mint or to taste. Makes about 1 cup (4 serves)

Roasted Spiced Nuts

These nuts are very 'more-ish', so remember the '1–2 small handfuls' rule to avoid overdoing the kilojoules. You can also use these nuts in your cooking. You can use this recipe for one type of nut or a mixture of different nuts. Spread 1½ cups whole nuts in a single layer on a foil lined oven tray. Spray lightly with oil and sprinkle with about 1 teaspoon powdered spices (try chilli, cumin, coriander) and bake in a moderate oven 180°C (350°F /Gas Mark 4) until golden (only about 10–15 minutes). Keep a watchful eye on them as they can burn quickly. Allow to cool then store in an airtight container away from heat and light. Makes 8 small serves

24: Light meals

Asian Beef and Noodle Soup

Low kilojoule, high fibre, low GI

A complete meal in a bowl. The aromatic ginger, garlic and hoi sin sauce complement the beef, noodles and leafy green vegetables and, along with the mushrooms, combine to make a very heart healthy soup. Beef stocks vary in sodium content, so check the label to ensure you buy the lowest—less than 300mg/100ml is ideal.

Preparation time: 10 minutes
Cooking time: 25 minutes
Serves: 2

90g (3oz) soba noodles
¾ cup (185ml/6fl oz) salt-reduced beef stock
2 cups (500ml/17fl oz) water
2 cloves garlic, chopped
3 teaspoons finely grated ginger
1 cup (125g/4½oz) sliced carrot
2 cups (125g/4½oz) sliced mushrooms
1 cup (80g/2¾oz) thinly sliced Chinese chard (baby bok choy) stems
1 cup (60g/2¼oz) thinly sliced Chinese chard (baby bok choy) leaves
100g/3½oz thinly sliced lean beef (eye fillet)
3 teaspoons hoi sin sauce
½ teaspoon sesame oil

Bring 1 litre (1¾ pints) of water to the boil in a large pot. Add the noodles and rapidly boil for 4 minutes. Drain, rinse thoroughly in cold water and drain again. Place stock, water, garlic and ginger in a large pot over a medium heat, cover and bring to the boil. Reduce the heat and cook for 10 minutes. Add the carrot, mushrooms and Chinese chard stems and cook, covered, for a further 10 minutes. Stir in the Chinese chard leaves, beef and hoi sin sauce and cook until the leaves are just wilted and the beef is cooked, 2–3 minutes. Stir in sesame oil. Divide the noodles between two serving bowls, pour over the hot soup.

Nutrition per serve

Energy kJ (cals) 1213 (289)
Protein 20g
Total fat 5g
Saturated fat 1.2g
Fibre 8.4g
Carbohydrate 40g
Cholesterol 32mg
Sodium 420mg

Tuna and Cracked Wheat Salad

Good source omega-3, high fibre, low GI

This recipe is a variation of tabouli, and the flavours of the garlic, pepper sauce and herbs can be varied to suit your taste buds. It is a very portable salad and great to take to work for lunch, ideal for picnics or outdoor activities.

Preparation time: 20 minutes
Serves: 2

½ cup (90g/3oz) cracked wheat (bulgar/burghul)
185g (6½oz) can tuna in oil (eg, sunflower/canola/olive oil)
1–2 cloves garlic, crushed
Tabasco (pepper sauce) to taste
80g/2¾oz tomatoes, chopped
1 cup (125g/4½oz) diced red onion
1 cup (150g/5½oz) chopped yellow capsicum (pepper)
¼ cup chopped flat-leaf parsley
¼ cup torn basil leaves
Lemon wedges for serving

Place cracked wheat in a bowl and cover with boiling water. Allow to stand 15 minutes or until soft. Drain well. Drain the tuna, reserving 1 tablespoon of oil. Add the garlic and Tabasco to the reserved oil and mix well. Combine the tomatoes, onion, capsicum, parsley and drained cracked wheat in a large bowl. Stir in the oil. Divide salad between two serving bowls, top with the tuna and basil and a lemon wedge.

Nutrition per serve
Energy kJ (cals) 1718 (411)
Protein 31g
Total fat 13.8g
Saturated fat 2.2g
Fibre 10.9g
Carbohydrate 35g
Cholesterol 37mg
Sodium 443mg

Fish, Tomato and Saffron Soup

Low kilojoule, good source omega-3, high fibre, low GI

Saffron adds an authentic flavour and rich colour to this Mediterranean-influenced soup that could also be made with green peeled prawns or a marinara mix. If you have time you could use fresh tomatoes with the skins and seeds removed.

Preparation time: 10 minutes
Cooking time: 15 minutes
Serves: 2

1 tablespoon olive oil
1 clove garlic, finely chopped
½ cup (60g/2¼oz) diced white onion
½ cup (60g/2¼oz) diced carrot
Pinch saffron threads, dissolved in 2 tablespoons boiling water
1 cup (200g/7oz) canned whole peeled tomatoes in juice (no added salt)
½ cup (125ml/4fl oz) water
½ cup (75g/2½oz) drained and rinsed canned white beans (butter beans/fagioli)
150g/5½oz cubed boneless white fish
1 tablespoon chopped parsley
2 small warm mixed grain rolls or lite wholemeal pita breads

Heat the oil in a saucepan over a medium heat. Add the garlic, onion and carrot and stir until the onion is soft, 2–3 minutes. Stir in the dissolved saffron threads, tomatoes and water. Stir to break up the tomatoes while bringing to the boil, 1–2 minutes. Stir in the beans, reduce heat, cover and cook for 5 minutes, stirring occasionally. Add the fish and stir occasionally for 2–3 minutes or until the fish is cooked. Stir in the parsley and serve with the rolls.

Nutrition note

Try low sodium wholemeal pita rolls with only 200mg sodium per 100g.

Nutrition per serve	
Energy kJ (cals)	1501 (357)
Protein	25g
Total fat	12g
Saturated fat	2g
Fibre	8.5g
Carbohydrate	36g
Cholesterol	44mg
Sodium	345mg

Sardines and Capers on Rye

Excellent source omega-3, high fibre, low–medium GI

Mint was the inspiration for this recipe as it is one of the most popular of all herbs, tastes wonderful and is often growing in the garden. Combining mint with the sharpness of lemon, the subtle saltiness of the sardines and capers delivers a refreshing taste sensation. Look for wholegrain breads less than 400mg sodium per 100g.

Preparation time: 10 minutes
Serves: 2

4 slices wholegrain rye bread
2 tablespoons light cholesterol-lowering margarine
2 x 110g/3¾oz cans sardines in springwater, drained
¼–½ lemon, rind, pith and seeds removed and finely diced
3 teaspoons (15g/½oz) drained baby capers in wine vinegar
¼ cup torn mint leaves
¼ cup trimmed rocket (arugula)
⅔ cup (100g/3½oz) halved cherry tomatoes

Spread the bread with the spread. Place the sardines in a bowl and lightly mash with a fork, add the lemon, capers and mint and mix to combine. Place the bread on two serving plates, pile the sardine mixture onto each piece of bread and top with rocket. Scatter the tomatoes over or on the side of the sandwiches and serve.

Cook's tip
Two 110g/3¾oz cans of sardines in springwater yield a drained mass of 150g/5½oz that is the recommended serving size for two serves.

Nutrition note
We used rye bread with other mixed grains and seeds with 360mg sodium to 100g bread.

Nutrition per serve
Energy kJ (cals) 1760 (420)
Protein 27g
Total fat 19.8g
Saturated fat 4g
Fibre 3.6g
Carbohydrate 28g
Cholesterol 70mg
Sodium 485mg

Sweet Potato Patties

**Low kilojoule, low sodium, high fibre,
low–medium GI**

Preparation time: 15 minutes
Cooking time: 20 minutes
Serves: 2

Patties

250g (9oz) sweet potato, peeled and cut into large chunks
1 clove garlic, crushed
1 teaspoon garam masala
1 small/½ cup (60g/2¼oz) diced zucchini (courgette)
½ cup (60g/2¼oz) diced red onion
¼ cup (50g/1¾oz) drained and rinsed canned red
    kidney beans
1 tablespoon wholemeal plain (all-purpose) flour
1 tablespoon canola oil
2 tablespoons low-fat cottage cheese

Salad

1 cup torn mesclun
½ cup (75g/2½oz) halved cherry tomatoes
¼ cup (50g/1¾oz) drained and rinsed canned red
    kidney beans
½ cup (60g/2¼oz) diced zucchini (courgette)
2 teaspoons balsamic vinegar
1 x 25g (1oz) piece whole wheat flatbread (lavash)

To make the patties, place the sweet potato in a saucepan and cover with cold water. Cover, bring to the boil on high heat, reduce heat and cook for 5 minutes or until the potato is tender. Drain well, cool and mash. Add the garlic, garam masala, zucchini, onion and kidney beans to the mashed potato and mix well. Shape into four even patties. (The mixture should be easy to handle, if it is too soft, mix in a little wholemeal flour.) Place the flour into a plastic bag, add the patties one at a time and shake until coated with flour. Heat the oil in a large non-stick frying pan over a medium heat and cook the patties until golden on each side and cooked through, 10–12 minutes. To make the salad, combine the mesclun, tomatoes, kidney beans, zucchini and vinegar. Cut the flat bread into 2.5cm/1-inch squares and stir through the salad just before serving. Serve the patties drizzled with cottage cheese and with the salad on the side.

Nutrition per serve

Energy kJ (cals) 1280 (305)
Protein 12g
Total fat 10.4g
Saturated fat 2g
Fibre 9g
Carbohydrate 41g
Cholesterol 3mg
Sodium 297mg

Spicy Pork Noodles

Medium GI

Have all the ingredients prepared before starting to cook this recipe. It is delicious served hot or is suitable to be refrigerated and enjoyed the following day. If you like more heat and herbs, serve sliced chilli Thai basil and a wedge of lime on the side.

Preparation time: 15 minutes
Cooking time: 10 minutes
Serves: 2

60g/2¼oz vermicelli rice noodles, dry
3 teaspoons hoi sin sauce
1 teaspoon salt-reduced soy sauce
1½ tablespoons honey
1½ teaspoons rice wine vinegar
½ teaspoon Chinese five spice powder
1 tablespoon peanut oil
100g/3½oz sliced pork fillet
1 cup (150g/5½oz) diced red capsicum (pepper)
¾ cup (150g/5½oz) diced celery
1 cup (60g/2¼oz) sliced spring onions (scallions)

Bring 1 litre (1¾ pints) of water to the boil in a large pot. Add the noodles and cook for 3–5 minutes. Drain and rinse under cold water. Mix together the hoi sin sauce, soy, honey, vinegar and five spice. Heat the oil in a wok over a high heat and cook the pork until golden, 3–4 minutes. Add the capsicum, celery and spring onions and stir-fry for 2–3 minutes. Add the hoi sin sauce mixture and stir for 1–2 minutes. Stir in the drained noodles and cook until hot.

Cook's tip

To cook the pork until golden brown, have the pan and oil really hot before adding the pork and leave it to cook for about a minute or two before turning or stirring. If the pork has browned well it will be easy to move around the pan.

Nutrition per serve

Energy kJ (cals) 1963 (470)
Protein 18g
Total fat 11.7g
Saturated fat 2.1g
Fibre 4.3g
Carbohydrate 73g
Cholesterol 48mg
Sodium 377mg

Herbed Lamb Couscous

Low sodium, high fibre, low GI

Couscous is traditionally served as an accompaniment to tagines, however it is a very versatile ingredient and makes a great grain base for salads and complete meals. This recipe can be served hot or at room temperature.

Preparation time: 15 minutes
Cooking time: 15 minutes
Serves: 2

Couscous

2 teaspoons extra virgin olive oil
1 medium cup (125g/4½oz) sliced onion
1 clove garlic, crushed
100g/3½oz thinly sliced lamb loin eye
½ cup (75g/2½oz) frozen peas
¼ cup (60ml/2fl oz) salt-reduced vegetable stock
¼ cup (60ml/2fl oz) water
½ cup (100g/3½oz) couscous
1 tablespoon shredded mint leaves
½ cup (75g/2½oz) quartered grape tomatoes
⅓ cup (60g/2¼oz) canned drained chickpeas

Dressing

1 teaspoon extra virgin olive oil
1 teaspoon white wine vinegar
½ teaspoon brown sugar
½ teaspoon finely chopped rosemary

To make the couscous, heat oil in a non-stick frying pan over a medium heat. Add the onion and garlic and cook until golden, 3–4 minutes. Add the lamb and stir for 2–3 minutes. Add peas and stir occasionally until the peas are cooked, 2–3 minutes. Meanwhile, bring the stock and water to the boil and slowly pour in the couscous, remove from the heat, cover and let stand for 2–3 minutes before stirring with a fork to separate the grains. To make the dressing, combine the oil, vinegar, sugar and rosemary and stir well. Place the couscous in a large bowl, stir in the lamb mixture, mint, tomatoes, chickpeas and dressing.

Nutrition per serve
Energy kJ (cals) 1607 (384)
Protein 22g
Total fat 9.8g
Saturated fat 1.9g
Fibre 6g
Carbohydrate 51g
Cholesterol 33mg
Sodium 225mg

Chicken and Corn Frittata

Low kilojoule, low sodium, low–medium GI

Preparation time: 15 minutes
Cooking time: 10 minutes
Baking time: 25 minutes
Serves: 2

3 teaspoons canola oil
100g/3½oz sliced chicken breast fillet
1 cup (80g/2¾oz) sliced leek (white part only)
1 teaspoon sweet smoked paprika
2 x 50g/1¾oz eggs (omega-3 enriched)
¼ cup (75g/2½oz) creamed corn
1 teaspoon wholemeal plain (all-purpose) flour
2 teaspoons chopped chives
2 tablespoons (50g/1¾oz) creamed corn, extra

Salad
3 cups torn baby cos lettuce
1 cup (100g/3½oz) finely sliced red capsicum (pepper)
3 teaspoons vinaigrette dressing

Preheat oven to moderate 180°C (350°F/Gas Mark 4) and grease and line the base of 2 x 10cm (4 inch) diameter ovenproof dishes with ovenproof baking paper.

Heat oil in a non-stick frying pan over a high heat and brown the chicken, 2–3 minutes. Reduce heat and stir in the leek and cook for 3–4 minutes or until the chicken is cooked and the leek is soft. Stir in the paprika and cook for a further 1 minute. Divide mixture between the two prepared dishes. Beat the eggs lightly and mix in the corn, flour and chives and pour evenly over the chicken. Bake for 20–25 minutes or until golden and set. Cool for a few minutes and then turn out of the dishes, remove the baking paper and place on warmed serving plates. Serve with the extra creamed corn and salad.

Nutrition note

This is a good example of a recipe that is higher in fat and cholesterol but still low in saturated fat. If you're watching your weight, kilojoules are the most important thing to limit and the kilojoules in this recipe are low.

Nutrition per serve
Energy kJ (cals) 1390 (332)
Protein 19g
Total fat 21.8g
Saturated fat 3.9g
Fibre 4.7g
Carbohydrate 16g
Cholesterol 190mg
Sodium 297mg

Tofu, Spinach and Satay Rice

High fibre, low–medium GI

This recipe uses a commercial satay sauce that adds great flavour—check the nutrition label when purchasing the sauce and choose the lowest in sodium and saturated fat. Try substituting the rice with barley or chickpeas for variety.

Preparation time: 10 minutes
Cooking time: 35 minutes
Serves: 2

⅓ cup (70g/2½oz) brown rice
⅔ cup (170ml/5½fl oz) water
2 tablespoons raw peanuts
3 teaspoons peanut oil
1½ cups (125g/4½oz) brown onion wedges
1 cup (125g/4½oz) sliced carrot
2 cups tightly packed torn silverbeet or spinach leaves
¼ cup (60ml/2fl oz) satay simmer sauce
300g/10½oz well-drained and cubed soft silken tofu
1 long (30g/1oz) medium heat red chilli, sliced

Place the rice and water in a saucepan over a medium heat and bring to the boil, stir occasionally. Reduce heat, cover and simmer for 25–30 minutes. Remove from the heat and stand, covered, for 5–10 minutes before using. Heat a non-stick frying pan over a medium/low heat and dry fry the peanuts for 1–2 minutes and set aside. Heat the oil in the same pan and cook the onions until golden, 2–3 minutes. Add the carrot and cook for 1–2 minutes. Add the silverbeet and cook until the leaves are just wilted, 1–2 minutes.

Stir the satay sauce and vegetables through the rice and mix well. Divide the rice between two bowls and top with the tofu, peanuts and chilli.

Cook's tip

A simmer sauce is used as a recipe ingredient, typically in stir-fries, and is lower in sodium and saturated fat than a condiment (eg, ketchup) style sauce. You could also use a smaller quantity (2–3 teaspoons) of a more concentrated satay recipe base (paste).

Nutrition per serve
Energy kJ (cals) 1673 (400)
Protein 19g
Total fat 17.8g
Saturated fat 3.6g
Fibre 6.6g
Carbohydrate 41g
Cholesterol 1.6mg
Sodium 396mg

Chicken, Cheese, Cashew and Salad Wrap

Low sodium, high fibre

The delicious herb and cashew mixture in this recipe is made with heart-healthy oils and is full of flavour. It makes a great spread on any meat, salmon or tuna sandwich and would be perfect dolloped on lean barbecued meats or seafood.

Preparation time: 10 minutes
Cooking time: 10 minutes
Serves: 2

1 tablespoon chopped dill
1 tablespoon chopped chives
2 tablespoons (20g/¾oz) natural cashews, chopped
1 tablespoon (7g/¼oz) very finely grated parmesan cheese
3 teaspoons extra virgin olive oil
250g/9oz bunch green asparagus, trimmed
Canola oil cooking spray
100g/3½oz chicken breast fillet
2 cups baby lettuce leaves (mesclun)
2 x 75g/2½oz tomatoes, quartered
2 wholemeal flat breads (eg, lavash)
2 tablespoons (40g/1½oz) extra light cream cheese
   (5 per cent fat)

Place the dill, chives, cashews, parmesan and olive oil in a small bowl and mix well. Set aside to allow the flavours to develop. Steam or microwave the asparagus. Allow to cool. Heat a non-stick pan over a medium heat and spray with oil and cook the chicken, 6–8 minutes or until cooked, turning once. Wrap in foil to rest and cool. Place the salad leaves, tomatoes, asparagus and half the dill, chive, cashew and parmesan mixture in a bowl and mix well. Slice the chicken thinly. Spread the breads with cream cheese. Spread the remaining dill, chive, cashew and parmesan mixture over half of each bread with the chicken and roll up tightly. Cut the wraps into three or four pieces. Serve the wraps with the salad.

Nutrition per serve

Energy kJ (cals) 1661 (395)
Protein 26g
Total fat 18.8g
Saturated fat 4.3g
Fibre 6.4g
Carbohydrate 30g
Cholesterol 50mg
Sodium 269mg

Whip It Up Light Meals

Puréed Lentil and Vegetable Soup

For some added texture, add canned drained chickpeas or white beans after the soup has been puréed and before reheating. Heat 1 tablespoon sunflower oil in a saucepan and add 1 tablespoon Indian spice blend and stir for a few seconds. Add ½ cup chopped onion and stir until the onion is coated. Add ½ cup chopped parsnip, 1 cup diced pumpkin, ½ cup red lentils and about 2½ cups of water to cover the vegetables and lentils. Cover and bring to the boil. Reduce heat and cook, stirring occasionally, for about 30 minutes or until the lentils are tender. Puree the soup, reheat and stir through ½ cup diced fresh tomatoes and serve topped with low-fat plain (natural) yoghurt and sprinkled with lots of chopped coriander (cilantro) or parsley. Serve with warmed wholemeal pita bread. Serves 2

Stuffed Capsicum with Spiced Beans

This warm bean salad in a capsicum (pepper) cup makes a great light lunch followed by orange wedges or a bunch of grapes. Heat 2 teaspoons canola or peanut oil in a small saucepan, add 1 teaspoon garam masala and stir for 1 minute. Add ¾ cup drained canned four bean mix, ¾ cup canned diced (no added salt) tomatoes, cover and simmer on low heat for 10 minutes. Stir in ½ cup wholemeal or mixed grain breadcrumbs (look for the lowest sodium brand) and heat. Cut a capsicum (pepper) in half lengthways, remove the seeds and steam or microwave until tender. Fill each half of the capsicum with bean mixture and sprinkle with about a tablespoon of freshly chopped coriander (cilantro). Serves 2

Thai Lime Tofu and Noodle Salad

Chopped Thai basil or Vietnamese mint would be delicious mixed into this salad. Make a dressing of the juice and zest of 1 lime, 3 teaspoons sesame oil, ½ teaspoon fish sauce, ½ teaspoon each of minced chilli and ginger and 1 teaspoon sugar. Taste and adjust the flavour to your liking. Toss dressing through 1½ cups cooked rice noodles, ¾ cup fine capsicum strips, ¾ cup sliced green onions and ½ cup fine carrot sticks. Top with 200g (7oz) sliced tofu and 1 tablespoon finely chopped roasted peanuts. Serves 2

Beef and Bean Corn Tortilla Parcels

Corn tortillas (flat bread or lavash or wraps) are a perfect way to wrap up the Mexican spiced beef and beans into a neat parcel, and is also lower in sodium than many other breads. Heat 3 teaspoons canola oil, 1 tablespoon Mexican spice mix and ½ cup sliced onion and cook, stirring, for 1–2 minutes. Add 200g (7oz) lean mince and brown, 2–3 minutes. Add ½ cup drained canned kidney beans and 1–2 tablespoons water and cook, stirring occasionally, for about 3–5 minutes or until the mince is cooked. Spoon mixture into the centre of two tortillas and fold up like parcels. Serve with a salad of 1 cup diced tomato, ½ cup each of corn kernels and diced green capsicum tossed in a tablespoon smooth low-fat ricotta and a couple of tablespoons of chopped coriander (cilantro). Serves 2

Whip It Up Light Meals — Quickies

Red Cabbage, Almond and Orange Salad

This is a fresh crunchy salad that's high in fibre. Add a cup of chopped barbecued chicken with the skin removed and a wholegrain roll for a light meal, or enjoy on its own as a super-healthy snack (also delicious in a flat bread wrap with cottage cheese). Mix together 2 cups finely shredded red cabbage, ½ cup grated carrot, ¼ cup sliced celery and chopped chunks of a peeled orange (pith and seeds removed). Spray a non-stick pan with oil and lightly brown ¼ cup slivered almonds, cool and sprinkle over the salad to serve. Serves 2

Sardine, Chickpea, Sweet Potato, Spinach and Orange Salad

Combine 3 cups baby spinach leaves, 1 cup of cubed cooked sweet potato, 1 cup of drained, rinsed canned chickpeas, 1 cup sliced red capsicum (pepper) and the chopped flesh and juice of 2 oranges. Toss through 150g (5oz) drained sardines in springwater and serve with 4 slices dense grainy bread with 1 tablespoon cholesterol-lowering margarine. Serves 2

Egg, Rocket, Beetroot and Hazelnut Salad

Enjoy this salad as a light meal with a crusty grain roll or wholemeal bread (check the label to find the lowest in sodium). Boil 2 small eggs for 7 minutes, cool. Place 2 cups baby rocket leaves, about 8 canned, drained baby beetroots (quartered or halved depending on size) and 2 tablespoons halved roasted hazelnuts in a bowl. Mix 2 teaspoons extra light olive oil, ½ teaspoon each of balsamic vinegar, Dijon mustard and honey until smooth and toss through the rocket. Shell the eggs and quarter and fold through the salad. Serves 2

Tuna and Barley Salad

This is a great way to use up any leftover pearl barley. The barley adds a lovely nutty taste and great texture to this salad. Mix together 1 cup cooked cold pearl barley, 2 cups mixed salad leaves, a diced medium cucumber (seeds removed) and 2 diced medium tomatoes. Add a 185g (6½oz) can drained tuna in springwater chunks, 10 black olives and a dressing of 1 tablespoon canola or soy bean oil mayonnaise mixed with 2 teaspoons of lemon juice and chopped garlic to taste. Serves 2

Salmon and Butter Bean Salad with Bread

Mix 2 cups mixed salad leaves with 1 cup sliced capsicum (pepper), 1 cup snowpeas (mangetout) and 1 cup drained and rinsed canned butter beans. Top with 90g (3oz) drained canned salmon in springwater (with bones) and a squeeze of lemon juice. Serve with 4 slices dense grainy bread (look for the lowest in sodium) spread with 1 tablespoon cholesterol-lowering margarine. Serves 2

Grilled Beef, Lamb, Pork or Chicken Open Turkish

This is a delightful variation to a traditional burger. Choose the lowest sodium brand Turkish bread. Cut 100g (3½oz) lean beef, lamb, pork or chicken into two thin slices in half. Heat a little sunflower oil in a non-stick pan and cook meat as liked. Wrap in foil to rest. Cut a slice of wholemeal Turkish bread (approximately 10cm/4-inch square) in half lengthways and toast in the same pan. Top each toast with the cooked meat, ½ cup rocket leaves, 3 slices of tomato, 2 slices beetroot and about 2 teaspoons of the chutney or sauce of your choice. Serves 2

Fish Fill-all

This is great for filling baked potatoes, pita pockets, wraps, sandwiches and rolls. Makes 2 main meal serves or 4 light meal serves. Combine a 210g (7oz) can drained salmon in springwater (with bones), ¼ cup sweet corn kernels, 1 tablespoon finely diced Spanish (purple) onion, 2 teaspoons finely chopped dill or about ½ teaspoon dried dill, freshly ground black pepper and a blend of 1 tablespoon each of mayonnaise (choose brand lowest in sodium) and low-fat natural (plain) yoghurt.

Fish Fill-all Flat Bread Wrap

Spread 2 pieces of wholemeal flat bread or lavash with a half quantity of Fish Fill-all, 2 cups dark salad leaves and ½ cup mung bean sprouts. Roll up tightly and slice in half to eat. Serves 2

Chilli Bean Melt

Choose a chilli sauce to suit your taste. The filling would be great in taco shells with salad. Cut the tops of 2 wholegrain bread rolls and scoop out the bread from the centre (make bread crumbs out of the scooped out bread and tops and freeze to use later). Spread the inside of the rolls with 1 tablespoon cholesterol-lowering margarine. Mix together ½ cup each of diced green capsicum (pepper), 1 medium fresh tomato, 2 teaspoons chilli sauce and 1 cup drained and rinsed four bean mix. Spoon the bean mixture into the rolls and top each with 2 teaspoons grated reduced-fat, salt-reduced cheese. Grill until warmed through and the cheese melts. Serve sprinkled with chopped parsley. Serves 2

25: Mains

Creamy Mushroom and Beef Penne with Salad

Low sodium, high fibre, low GI

Preparation time: 15 minutes
Cooking time: 20 minutes
Serves: 2

1½ cups (125g/4½oz) wholemeal penne
1 tablespoon sunflower oil
200g/7oz piece lean beef (eye fillet)
1 cup (125g/4½oz) diced onion
1 clove garlic, crushed
¾ cup (125g/4½oz) diced carrot
2 x 90g/3oz flat mushrooms, diced
250g/9oz bunch broccolini or broccoli, trimmed, stems
    diced and florets reserved
1 cup (250ml/9fl oz) light evaporated milk (1.5 per cent fat)
2 teaspoons corn flour (starch), blended with 2 teaspoons
water

Mixed leaf salad
2 cups torn mixed salad leaves
2 x 40g (1½oz) tomatoes cut into quarters
3 teaspoons herb vinaigrette (see recipe page 230)

Bring 1¼ litres (2½ pints) of water to the boil in a large pot. Add the penne and continue to boil for approximately 9–11 minutes or until, when tasted, the penne is cooked as liked. Drain. Heat the oil in a non-stick frying pan over a medium heat. Add the beef to the pan and cook, 8–10 minutes, turning once, or until cooked as liked. Wrap in foil and rest in a warm place while preparing the sauce and vegetables—this makes it easier to slice. Add the onion and garlic to the pan and cook, stirring occasionally, until soft, 3–4 minutes. Add the carrot, mushrooms and broccolini stems and cook, stirring occasionally, until soft, 3–4 minutes. Stir in the evaporated milk and bring to the boil. Add the blended corn flour and stir until thickened. Stir in the drained pasta and reheat. Meanwhile, steam or microwave the broccolini florets, 2–3 minutes, and slice the beef finely across the grain. To make the salad, combine the leaves and tomato in a bowl and toss with the herb vinaigrette. Serve pasta topped with beef slices, any meat juices, broccolini and the salad.

Nutrition per serve
Energy kJ (cals) 2746 (656)
Protein 50g
Total fat 21.5g
Saturated fat 4.4g
Fibre 17g
Carbohydrate 65g
Cholesterol 74mg
Sodium 261mg

Spicy Lamb Risoni with Fennel, Olive and Zucchini Salad

Low sodium, high fibre, low GI

Preparation time: 15 minutes
Cooking time: 40 minutes
Serves: 2

1 tablespoon olive oil
1 clove garlic, crushed
1 cup (125g/4½oz) sliced brown onion
1½ teaspoons dried oregano
¾ teaspoon sweet smoked paprika
¾ teaspoon cumin
200g/7oz lean lamb cubes
1 cup (250ml/9fl oz) water
400g/14oz can whole peeled tomatoes (no added salt)
1 tablespoon lemon juice
1 teaspoon sugar
½ cup (100g/3½oz) risoni (orzo)
1 cup (100g/3½oz) drained canned borlotti beans
Chopped flat-leaf parsley

Salad

1 medium/1 cup (90g/3oz) finely sliced fennel bulb
2 tablespoons (30g/1oz) halved, pitted kalamata olives
1 cup (125g/4½oz) diced yellow zucchini (courgettes)
1 cup (125g/4½oz) diced green zucchini (courgettes)
1½ tablespoons orange juice

Heat the oil in a large saucepan over a medium heat. Add the garlic and onion and stir for 1–2 minutes until soft and transparent. Stir in the oregano, paprika and cumin and cook for 1 minute. Add the lamb and brown, stirring, for 2–3 minutes. Add the water, tomatoes, lemon juice and sugar and bring to the boil. Reduce the heat, cover and simmer gently for 20 minutes or until the lamb is tender. Stir in the risoni and cook, stirring occasionally for 8 minutes or until the risoni is cooked and the juices are almost absorbed. Add a little water if required. Stir in the borlotti beans and heat through. To make the salad, combine the fennel, olives and zucchini in a bowl and toss with the orange juice. Serve the lamb sprinkled with parsley. Enjoy with salad.

Nutrition per serve

Energy kJ (cals) 2394 (572)
Protein 37g
Total fat 17.5g
Saturated fat 4.5g
Fibre 10g
Carbohydrate 68g
Cholesterol 68mg
Sodium 232mg

Warm Beef Salad

High fibre, low GI

Preparation time: 10 minutes
Cooking time: 12 minutes
Resting time: 5–10 minutes
Serves: 2

Beef salad
2 teaspoons peanut oil
1 tablespoon raw peanuts
200g/7oz piece lean beef (eye fillet)
2 cups torn oak lettuce leaves
½ large (180g/6½oz) sliced red capsicum (pepper)
1 cup (150g/5½oz) sliced cucumber
1 cup (125g/4½oz) sliced red onion
1½ cups (125g/4½oz) mixed sprouts
2 small multigrain bread rolls

Lime, Sweet Chilli and Herb Dressing
Zest and juice of 1 lime
2 teaspoons white vinegar
1 teaspoon grated ginger
1 tablespoon sweet chilli sauce
½ teaspoon fish sauce
½ teaspoon salt-reduced soy sauce
1 teaspoon palm or brown sugar
2 teaspoons peanut oil
¼ cup tightly packed mint leaves
¼ cup tightly packed coriander (cilantro) leaves

Heat the oil in a non-stick frying pan over a medium heat and cook the peanuts for 1–2 minutes or until golden brown, set aside on paper towel to cool then chop roughly. Add the beef to the pan and cook, 8–10 minutes, turning once or until cooked as liked. Wrap in foil and rest in a warm place to allow the meat juices to settle. To make the dressing, place all the ingredients in a blender and purée until smooth or chop the mint and coriander finely and combine all the ingredients in a screw-top jar and shake well.

Slice the beef across the grain finely. Combine the lettuce leaves, capsicum, cucumber, onion and sprouts in a large bowl and toss well with the dressing. Top with beef slices, meat juices and the chopped peanuts and serve with the rolls.

Nutrition per serve
Energy kJ (cals) 1976 (472)
Protein 33g
Total fat 18.9g
Saturated fat 4.4g
Fibre 9g
Carbohydrate 41g
Cholesterol 67mg
Sodium 555mg

BBQ Chermoula Lamb and Burghul

High fibre

Chermoula is a dry, North African spice blend. You can buy it in most large supermarkets or specialty delis.

Preparation time: 20 minutes
Marinating time: 20 minutes
Cooking time: 25 minutes
Serves: 2

2 teaspoons chermoula spice mix
200g/7oz piece lean lamb (loin eye)
½ cup (90g/3oz) fine burghul (bulgar)
1 cup (250ml/9fl oz) boiling water
1 teaspoon chermoula spice, extra
2 cups (300g/10½oz) diced butternut pumpkin
½ cup (60g/2¼oz) sliced green beans
1 tablespoon sunflower oil
1 cup (125g/4½oz) sliced onion
2¼ cups (170g/6oz) sliced eggplant (aubergine)
Olive oil spray
½ cup (125g/4½fl oz) low-fat yoghurt
2 tablespoons chopped coriander (cilantro) leaves

Sprinkle the chermoula spice all over the lamb and press into the flesh; cover and refrigerate for 20 minutes. Meanwhile, place the burghul, boiling water and extra chermoula in a bowl and allow to stand for 15 minutes or until soft. Place the pumpkin in a small saucepan, just cover with water and cook, covered, until tender, 4–5 minutes, add the beans and cook for a further 1–2 minutes. Drain, reserving ¼ cup (60ml/2fl oz) of the cooking liquid. Heat oil in a non-stick pan over a medium heat and cook the onion for 1–2 minutes. Add the eggplant and stir occasionally, for 5 minutes or until cooked. Stir in the pumpkin, beans, reserved cooking liquid and burghul and cook, stirring, for 1–2 minutes. Keep warm. Spray a barbecue rackwith olive oil spray and cook the lamb as liked, turning once. Wrap in foil to rest in a warm place for 5 minutes then slice finely across the grain. Serve burghul topped with lamb, yoghurt and coriander.

Nutrition per serve

Energy kJ (cals) 2578 (616)
Protein 39g
Total fat 19g
Saturated fat 5.2g
Fibre 16g
Carbohydrate 71g
Cholesterol 71mg
Sodium 543mg

Herbie's Chermoula Spice Mix

Makes about $^1/_3$ cup.

If you want to blend your own chermoula, try Ian Hemphill of Herbie's Spices (www.herbies.com.au) favourite mix. You can also change the proportions and make it more like a salsa with the onion and fresh herbs forming the bulk of the mixture, which you then lightly spice. Simply combine all ingredients and use to dry marinate meat, chicken or a firm fleshed fish like tuna for about 20 minutes before cooking.

½ onion, finely chopped
1 teaspoon finely chopped fresh coriander (cilantro) leaves
2 teaspoons finely chopped fresh parsley
1 clove garlic, crushed
3 teaspoons ground cumin seed
2 teaspoons mild paprika
1 teaspoon turmeric
Pinch cayenne
Ground black pepper to taste

BBQ Chicken, Corn, Potato and Baby Beet Salad

Low sodium, high fibre, medium GI

Preparation time: 15 minutes
Cooking time: 20 minutes
Serves: 2

200g/7oz chicken breast fillet
2 x 200g/7oz corn cobs
3 teaspoons sunflower oil
300g/10½oz pink eye or desiree potatoes, scrubbed
⅓ cup (125g/4½oz) halved canned baby beets
2 cups baby salad leaves (mesclun)
½ cup (60g/2¼oz) sliced golden shallots or onion

Dressing
1 tablespoon white wine vinegar
2 teaspoons honey
½ teaspoon wholegrain mustard
½ teaspoon crushed garlic
2 teaspoons extra virgin olive oil

Slice the chicken breast horizontally through the centre into two even thinner fillets. Trim the corn and cut each cob into three even pieces. Heat a barbecue or griddle pan over a medium heat and brush the chicken and corn with oil. Place them on the barbecue and cook for 5–8 minutes, turning as required. Remove the chicken when cooked and wrap in foil and rest in a warm place. Cook the corn for a further 8–10 minutes or until cooked. Meanwhile, cook the potatoes, drain and cool and cut into large chunks. Combine dressing ingredients. Combine the baby beets, salad leaves, shallots and potatoes in a bowl and toss with half the dressing. Serve the chicken and corn drizzled with the remaining dressing and any chicken juices with the salad.

Cook's tip

Try roasting fresh beetroot, it's easy and the result is excellent. Trim a bunch of beetroot, wash and dry. Wrap beetroots individually in foil and place in a baking dish. Roast in a preheated moderate oven 180°C (350°F/Gas Mark 4) and roast for about 1 hour.

Nutrition per serve

Energy kJ (cals) 2449 (585)
Protein 35g
Total fat 20g
Saturated fat 3.3g
Fibre 15g
Carbohydrate 65g
Cholesterol 66mg
Sodium 322mg

Tandoori Chicken, Mint and Mango Salad

(see picture on page 116)

High fibre, low GI

The availability of tandoori pastes* on the market makes it easy to recreate authentic Indian flavours at home. You can choose from mild to hot.

* look for the brand lowest in sodium

Preparation time: 15 minutes
Marinating time: 30 minutes or overnight
Cooking time: 15 minutes
Serves: 2

200g/7oz chicken breast fillet
2 tablespoons low-fat natural (plain) yoghurt
1 tablespoon tandoori paste
3 teaspoons sunflower oil
2 small wholemeal pita breads

Yoghurt sauce

⅓ cup low-fat plain yoghurt
1 teaspoon tandoori paste, extra
2 teaspoons finely chopped mint
½ teaspoon crushed garlic
⅓ cup purée mango flesh

Salad

2 cups torn mixed salad leaves
2 x 150g/5½oz tomatoes, quartered
1 cup (150g/5½oz) sliced cucumber
½ cup torn mint leaves
⅔ cup chopped mango flesh

Slice the chicken breast horizontally through the centre into two even thinner fillets.

To make the marinade, mix the yoghurt and tandoori paste in a bowl until smooth and brush over the chicken pieces coating them thoroughly. Place the chicken on a flat dish, cover and refrigerate for 30 minutes.

Heat the oil in a non-stick pan over a medium/low heat and cook the chicken, 8–10 minutes or until cooked, turning once. Wrap in foil and rest in a warm place. To make the Yoghurt Sauce, mix the yoghurt, tandoori paste, mint, garlic and mango in a small bowl.

To make the salad, toss the lettuce, tomato, cucumber, mint and mango together in a bowl.

Serve the salad topped with chicken and any chicken juices and a dollop of sauce with a round wholemeal pita bread

Nutrition per serve

Energy kJ (cals) 2104 (502)
Protein 36g
Total fat 18g
Saturated fat 3g
Fibre 10g
Carbohydrate 46g
Cholesterol 69mg
Sodium 637m

Creamed Parmesan Barley and Cauliflower

Serve this recipe as part of the Roast Pork, Pears and Vegetables (recipe page 220) or serve it alone as a complete light meal, or a side to a barbecued grilled steak with a crisp garden salad.

1 cup (110g/3¾oz) pearl barley
1½ cups (150g/5½oz) small cauliflower florets
2 teaspoons cholesterol-lowering margarine
2 teaspoons wholemeal plain (all-purpose) flour
¾ cup (185ml/6fl oz) skim milk
1 tablespoon (15g/½oz) finely grated parmesan cheese

Place the barley and 1½ cups (375ml/13fl oz) water in a saucepan. Bring to the boil, stirring occasionally. Reduce heat and simmer gently for 35 minutes or until tender. Add a little extra water if needed. Place the cauliflower in a saucepan, cover with water and add a little skim milk. Bring to the boil, cover, reduce heat and cook until the cauliflower is just tender, 3–5 minutes. Drain. Meanwhile, place the spread, flour and milk in a small non-stick saucepan over a medium heat and stirring continuously (to avoid any lumps), bring the sauce to the boil. Reduce the heat and continue to stir for a further 2–3 minutes. Stir in the parmesan. Add the cauliflower and white sauce into the barley and stir over a low heat until hot.

Cook's tip

You can also make this recipe using brown rice if you prefer. Choose a medium grain rice.

Nutrition per serve

Energy kJ (cals) 1163 (278)
Protein 13g
Total fat 6.2g
Saturated fat 1.9g
Fibre 7.7g
Carbohydrate 43g
Cholesterol 8mg
Sodium 162mg

Steak with Grilled Vegetable Buckwheat

Low sodium, low GI

Preparation time: 15 minutes
Cooking time: 25 minutes
Serves: 2

1 x 200g/7oz red capsicum (pepper)
1 x 200g/7oz orange or yellow capsicum (pepper)
2 teaspoons sunflower oil
2 x 60g/2¼oz flat mushrooms, stems trimmed
2 x 100g/3½oz lean beef fillet or rump steaks
¼ cup (60ml/2fl oz) salt-reduced beef stock
¾ cup 200ml/7fl oz water
2 tablespoons (50g/1¾oz) tomato paste (no added salt)
½ cup (100g/3½oz) roasted or raw buckwheat
1 teaspoon sunflower oil, extra
2 teaspoons balsamic vinegar
2 tablespoons chopped dill
½ (90g/3oz) avocado, sliced

Cut each capsicum lengthways into four large slices, remove any white membrane and discard the seeds. To roast the capsicums, heat a grill (broiler) to medium–high heat and place the capsicums skin side up on the rack of the griller tray and brush lightly with a little of the oil. Grill, without turning, until the skin of the capsicum blackens, about 8–10 minutes. Remove capsicums and place in a freezer bag to sweat for 5–10 minutes. Place the mushrooms, stem side down, and the steaks on the griller rack and brush lightly with oil. Grill for 3–4 minutes on each side until the mushrooms are cooked and the steak cooked as liked. Wrap the steak in foil and rest in a warm place while preparing the buckwheat and vegetables. Blend the stock, water and tomato paste in a saucepan and bring to the boil, stir in the buckwheat and reduce heat to low. Simmer for 7–10 minutes, stirring occasionally, until the buckwheat is tender and the liquid is almost absorbed. Add extra liquid if needed. While the buckwheat is cooking, peel and slice the capsicums and chop the mushrooms. Stir into the cooked buckwheat and allow to heat through. Remove from the heat and gently stir in the extra oil, vinegar and dill. Slice the steak across the grain finely. Place half the buckwheat mixture on each plate and top with the beef slices and avocado.

Nutrition per serve
Energy kJ (cals) 2279 (544)
Protein 35g
Total fat 24g
Saturated fat 5.6g
Fibre 6.8g
Carbohydrate 47g
Cholesterol 67mg
Sodium 189mg

Chargrilled Salmon with Dill Risotto

Low sodium, excellent source of omega-3, high fibre, low–medium GI

It is worth spending the time to cook this risotto slowly. A risotto made with brown rice does not give the creaminess of a traditional recipe made with Arborio rice but the healthy heart benefits are great.

Preparation time: 10 minutes
Cooking time: 35 minutes
Serves: 2

½ cup (125ml/4fl oz) salt-reduced chicken stock
3 cups (750ml/1 pint 6fl oz) water
1 tablespoon extra virgin olive oil
1 cup (125g/4½oz) sliced onion
1 clove garlic, crushed
½ cup (100g/3½oz) brown rice, rinsed
1 tablespoon chopped dill
2 x 150g/5½oz skinless salmon fillets
250g/9oz bunch green asparagus, trimmed
Olive oil spray
8–16 (200g/7oz) baby carrots, scrubbed and trimmed
1 tablespoon aioli (see recipe page 231)

Place the stock and water in a saucepan, cover and bring to the boil. Reduce heat and leave to simmer. Heat the oil in a saucepan over a medium heat; add the onion and garlic and cook, stirring, for 2–3 minutes until the onion is soft. Add the rice and stir until rice grains are coated. Add a cup of stock and stir until the liquid is completely absorbed. Continue cooking the rice, adding only a cup of stock at a time, until the rice is tender, about 25–30 minutes. Add more liquid if required. Stir in the dill. Meanwhile, heat a griddle pan over a medium heat and spray with the oil. Place the fish on the griddle with the asparagus. Cook the fish for 5–8 minutes, turning once, and the asparagus for a further 2–5 minutes if needed, turning as required. Set aside, cover with foil and keep hot. Steam or microwave the carrots. Serve the risotto, topped with the fish, a dollop of aioli, carrots and asparagus.

Nutrition note
Using brown basmati rice will lower the GI.

Nutrition per serve
Energy kJ (cals) 2530 (605)
Protein 38g
Total fat 28g
Saturated fat 4.4g
Fibre 7.9g
Carbohydrate 50g
Cholesterol 78mg
Sodium 330mg

Mackerel Balls with Creamy Lemon Sauce

High fibre, excellent source of omega-3, low–medium GI

This is an excellent way of incorporating the goodness of whole grains with the great taste of heart healthy mackerel. The bread used in this recipe was made from wheat, kibbled whole rye and sesame seeds. The four bean mix that was combined with the fresh beans was a mix of red kidney, baby lima, garbanzo and great northern beans. Look for the lowest sodium content brand of bread and mayonnaise.

Preparation time: 15 minutes
Chilling time: 10 minutes
Cooking time: 15 minutes
Serves: 2

¼ cup (30g/1oz) traditional rolled oats
1 thick slice (45g/1½oz) mixed grain bread
2 x 125g/4½oz cans mackerel fillets in brine, drained
1 tablespoon (20g/¾oz) beaten egg
Stoneground wholemeal plain (all-purpose) flour for coating
350g/12oz sweet potato, peeled and cut into chunks
2 teaspoons chopped chives
1½ cups (180g/6½oz) trimmed and halved green beans
1 cup (150g/5½oz) drained and rinsed canned four bean mix
2 teaspoons canola oil

Sauce

3 teaspoons mayonnaise (soy/canola/sunflower oil based)
1½ tablespoons low-fat natural (plain) yoghurt
¼ teaspoon finely grated lemon zest
1½ teaspoons lemon juice

Place the oats and bread into a food processor and process until fine, 2–3 minutes. Add mackerel and egg and process until well combined, 2–3 minutes. Shape the mix into 12 walnut-sized balls and coat in flour. Place on a plate, cover with plastic wrap and chill in the refrigerator for 10 minutes. Steam or boil the sweet potato chunks for 8–10 minutes or until tender. Drain, mash (with a little skim milk if needed), stir in the chives and set aside, covered to keep warm or reheat just before serving. Steam or microwave the green beans, rinse in cold water and combine in a bowl with the four bean mix. Heat a non-stick frying pan over a medium heat and add the oil. When hot, cook the mackerel balls for 5 minutes or until golden all over. To make the sauce: Whisk all the ingredients together. Serve mackerel balls with potato and beans drizzled with the sauce.

Nutrition per serve
Energy kJ (cals) 2208 (528)
Protein 24g
Total fat 18.4g
Saturated fat 3.6g
Fibre 13g
Carbohydrate 66g
Cholesterol 67mg
Sodium 574mg

Snapper with Spinach and Orange Noodles

Great source of omega-3, high fibre, low sodium

Preparation time: 15 minutes
Cooking time: 15 minutes
Serves: 2

125g/4½oz noodles
2 x 45g/1½oz tomatoes, diced
⅔ cup (90g/3oz) diced cucumber
1 cup (185g/6½oz) sweet corn kernels
1 cup (30g/1oz) trimmed baby spinach leaves
1 x 300g/10½oz orange, halved
3 teaspoons walnut oil
½ teaspoon sugar
Olive oil spray
¼ cup (30g/1oz) walnut halves
2 x 150g/5½oz snapper fillets

Bring 2 litres (3½ pints) of water to the boil in a large pot. Add the noodles and continue to boil for approximately 8–10 minutes or until the noodles are cooked as liked. Drain and rinse. Combine tomatoes, cucumber, corn kernels and spinach leaves in a large bowl. Peel, remove seeds and dice one half of the orange and add to the salad bowl along with the drained noodles. Juice the remaining half of the orange. Combine the walnut oil, two teaspoons of the orange juice and the sugar and mix into the vegetables and noodles. Heat a non-stick pan over a medium heat and spray with oil. Add the walnuts and cook, stirring, 2–3 minutes—don't let them burn. Chop and set aside. Spray the pan with extra oil and increase the heat to medium–high. Add the fish, skin side down, and cook until golden, 3–4 minutes. Reduce heat; spray fish with a little oil, turn and cook until the flesh is white and flakes easily. Wrap in foil to keep warm. Add the remaining orange juice to the pan, bring to the boil and cook until reduced and slightly thickened.

Serve noodles topped with fish, drizzled with the orange juice and sprinkled with walnuts.

Nutrition note

Using soba noodles, spaghetti, fresh rice noodles or mung bean noodles will lower the GI.

Nutrition per serve

Energy kJ (cals) 2842 (679)

Protein 46g

Total fat 24g

Saturated fat 3.3g

Fibre 14g

Carbohydrate 70g

Cholesterol 92mg

Sodium 402mg

Spiced Tomato Spirals with Salad

Low kilojoule, low sodium, high fibre, low GI
The aromatic spices and ingredients in this pasta sauce combine like a melting pot of different cuisines.

Preparation time: 15 minutes
Cooking time: 40 minutes
Serves: 2

1 tablespoon canola oil
2 cloves garlic, crushed
1 cup (125g/4½oz) chopped onion
½ teaspoon sweet paprika
½ teaspoon ground cumin
¼ teaspoon cinnamon
400g/14oz can whole peeled tomatoes (no added salt)
1¼ cups (240g/8¾oz) drained and rinsed canned
   butter beans
½ cup (125ml/4fl oz) salt-reduced vegetable stock
¼ cup (60ml/2fl oz) water
1 tablespoon port or sherry
1 teaspoon brown sugar
1½ cups (125g/4½oz) wholemeal spiral pasta
2 tablespoons chopped coriander (cilantro)
4 lemon wedges

Salad
2 cups baby salad leaves (mesclun)
1 x (150g/5½oz) sliced yellow capsicum (pepper)
½ cup (60g/2¼oz) sliced carrot
3 teaspoons vinaigrette

Heat oil in a saucepan over a medium heat. Add the garlic and onion and cook, stirring, for 2–3 minutes. Stir in the paprika, cumin and cinnamon and stir for a further 1 minute. Add the tomatoes, butter beans, stock, water, port and sugar. Bring to the boil, stirring occasionally, reduce heat, cover and simmer for 30 minutes. Bring 1¼ litres (2½ pints) of water to the boil in a large pot. Add the spirals and continue to boil for approximately 9–11 minutes or until when tasted the spirals are cooked as liked. Drain. To make the salad, place the mesclun, capsicum and carrot in a large bowl and toss with the vinaigrette. Serve the spirals topped with the sauce, sprinkled with coriander, lemon and the salad.

Nutrition per serve
Energy kJ (cals) 1883 (450)
Protein 16g
Total fat 16.4g
Saturated fat 2.6g
Fibre 14.5g
Carbohydrate 57g
Cholesterol 0mg
Sodium 314mg

Roast Pork, Pears and Vegetables

Low sodium, high fibre, low GI

This recipe is a modern version of a classic roast pork and cauliflower cheese meal only much healthier and still with exceptional flavours. There are a few steps to making the complete meal but the succulence of the pork, the sweetness of the pear and creaminess of the barley and cauliflower make it worthwhile. It is a real treat!

Preparation time: 20 minutes
Cooking time: 45 minutes
Serves: 2

Olive oil spray
1 x 125g/4½oz onion, peeled and halved
1 (170g/6oz) beurre bosc pear, quartered and core removed
2 x 100g/3½oz) lean pork loin medallions
2 x 75g/2½oz tomatoes, halved lengthways
1 cup (150g/5½oz) frozen peas

Preheat oven to moderate 180°C (350°F/Gas Mark 4) and line a baking dish with baking paper and lightly spray with oil spray. Place the onion and pear in the dish and spray lightly with oil. Cook for 30 minutes. Add the pork and tomato and cook for a further 10 minutes or until cooked as liked. Wrap pork in foil to rest. Place the peas in a saucepan with a little water, bring to the boil and when bright green and cooked, drain. Serve the pork, tomato, onion, pear and peas with Creamed Parmesan Barley and Cauliflower (see page 209).

Nutrition per serve
(Pork and creamed parmesan barley)
Energy kJ (cals) 2198 (525)
Protein 42g
Total fat 10.3g
Saturated fat 3.3g
Fibre 16.9g
Carbohydrate 66g
Cholesterol 105mg
Sodium 259mg

Pork in Pomegranate with Couscous Salad

High fibre, low GI

Preparation time: 15 minutes
Cooking time: 35 minutes
Serves: 2

Oil spray
3 teaspoons (10g/⅓oz) pine nuts
2 x 100g/3½oz lean pork loin medallions
1 x 200g/7oz green apple, peeled and sliced
½ cup (125ml/4fl oz) salt-reduced chicken stock
½ cup (125ml/4fl oz) water
2 teaspoons pomegranate concentrated juice

Salad
½ cup (125ml/4fl oz) water
1½ tablespoons za'atar
½ cup (100g/3½oz) instant couscous
1 teaspoon cholesterol-lowering margarine
1 cup (125g/4½oz) finely diced zucchini (courgettes)
½ cup (60g/2¼oz) finely diced carrot
½ cup (60g/2¼oz) finely sliced red onion
⅔ cup (125g/4½oz) drained, rinsed canned kidney beans
1 tablespoon chopped flat-leaf parsley

Heat a non-stick frying pan over a medium/high heat and spray with oil. Add the pine nuts and cook, stirring, 1–2 minutes. Set aside. Spray the pan with a little more oil and add the pork. Brown on each side, 2–3 minutes, reduce heat and then cook as liked. Wrap in foil to rest. Add the apple to the pan and stir for 1–2 minutes, add the stock, water and pomegranate juice. Cover and simmer for 3–5 minutes until the apple is tender. Remove the lid and cook for a further 2–3 minutes. Add any pork juices and keep warm. To make the couscous, place the water and za'atar in a saucepan over a medium heat, cover and bring the water to the boil. Slowly pour in the couscous, remove from the heat, cover and stand for 2–3 minutes. Stir with a fork to separate the grains and mix in the cholesterol-lowering margarine. Stir in the zucchini, carrot, onion, kidney beans and parsley. Slice the pork and serve over the couscous with the apple sauce sprinkled with pine nuts.

Nutrition per serve
Energy kJ (cals) 2016 (482)
Protein 37g
Total fat 9.7g
Saturated fat 1.6g
Fibre 9g
Carbohydrate 61g
Cholesterol 95mg
Sodium 588mg

Green Curry, Water Chestnuts and Rice

High fibre

Preparation time: 15 minutes
Cooking time: 40 minutes
Serves: 2

½ cup (100g/3½oz) brown medium grain rice
1 cup (250ml)/9fl oz) water
2 teaspoons peanut oil
1 tablespoon green curry paste (look for the brand lowest in sodium)
1 cup (250ml/9fl oz) light coconut milk (6 per cent fat)
2 teaspoons brown sugar
½ teaspoon fish sauce
1 piece (150g/5½oz) pumpkin, peeled and diced
1 cup (125g/4½oz) sliced carrot
300g/10½oz firm tofu, cubed
150g/5½oz trimmed choy sum leaves
125g/4½oz drained sliced water chestnuts
Olive oil spray
½ cup (10g/⅓oz) amaranth breakfast cereal
1 kaffir leaf or the zest of 1 lime, finely shredded

Place the rice and water in a saucepan over a medium heat. Bring to the boil, stirring occasionally. Reduce heat, cover and simmer for 25–30 minutes. Remove from the heat and stand, covered, for 5–10 minutes before using. Heat the oil in a non-stick saucepan over a low heat and cook the curry paste for 1–2 minutes stirring until fragrant. Stir in the coconut milk, sugar, fish sauce, pumpkin and carrot. Bring to the boil, reduce heat and simmer for 10 minutes or until the vegetables are cooked, stirring occasionally. Stir in the tofu and heat through gently. Meanwhile, steam the choy sum leaves until just wilted, 2–3 minutes. Pat the water chestnuts dry on paper towel and heat a non-stick frying pan over a medium heat and spray with oil. Cook the chestnuts, stirring, for 5 minutes or until crisp and brown. Stir the amaranth through the cooked rice. Serve the rice topped with the curry, kaffir lime and water chestnut chips, with choy sum.

> ## Nutrition per serve
> Energy kJ (cals) 2653 (634)
> Protein 32g
> Total fat 24g
> Saturated fat 6.8g
> Fibre 11g
> Carbohydrate 73g
> Cholesterol 3mg
> Sodium 545mg

Whip It Up Mains

Cauliflower, Pea and Potato Curry

Enjoy this recipe with steamed brown rice and pappadums. Heat 1 tablespoon canola oil with 1 or 2 teaspoons curry powder, add 1 cubed potato and cook, stirring, for about 5 minutes. Add 3 cups cauliflower florets, 1 cup canned (no added salt) diced tomatoes and ½ cup water. Cover and simmer on low for 10 minutes, stirring occasionally to prevent sticking. Stir in a cup each of drained canned chickpeas and frozen peas and cook for 1–2 minutes until peas are cooked. Top with diced tomato, low-fat natural (plain) yoghurt and chopped coriander (cilantro). Serves 2

Chicken with Herb and Garlic Vegetable Pasta

Heat 1 teaspoon canola oil in a non-stick pan and cook 200g (7oz) lean chicken as liked. Wrap in foil to rest. Cook 80g (2¾oz) whole wheat pasta in a large pot of boiling water. Mix 1½ tablespoons cholesterol-lowering margarine, 1–2 tablespoons chopped fresh parsley, chives or dill and 1–2 teaspoons crushed garlic. Microwave or steam 1 cup each of carrot sticks, broccoli and cauliflower florets and stir into drained cooked hot pasta with 1 cup of finely shredded red cabbage and the herb and garlic mixture. Serve with the chicken. Serves 2

Chilli and Garlic Beef and Vegetable Stir-fry

Stir-fry 300g (11oz) lean beef strips, 1–2 teaspoons each of chopped garlic and chilli in 1 tablespoon hot canola oil for 2–3 minutes and set aside. Add ½ cup each sliced carrot, spring onions (scallions) and mushrooms to the pan and stir-fry for 2–3 minutes. Return the beef to the pan and add 1½ cups finely shredded Asian greens, 1 cup cooked soy beans and cook until hot. Stir in a few drops of sesame oil before serving sprinkled with chopped coriander. Serve with brown rice or noodles (optional). Serves 2

Lamb and Pumpkin Tagine

Enjoy the tastes of Morocco—this tagine could also be made with lean chicken or beef. Heat 1 tablespoon olive oil and brown 200g (7oz) cubed lean lamb leg chops, 3–4 minutes. Add 1 tablespoon of Moroccan spice blend, 1 teaspoon each of crushed garlic and ginger, a sliced medium onion and cook, stirring, for about 1 minute. Add 2 cups diced pumpkin (1cm/½-inch cubes) and water to just cover the meat. Cover and bring to the boil. Reduce heat and cook until the lamb is tender and the pumpkin is cooked, about 20 minutes. (If the sauce is too juicy, cook uncovered for a few minutes to reduce the liquid.) Stir in 1 teaspoon honey. Serve over couscous tossed in lemon zest and juice to taste with green beans and sprinkle with lots of chopped parsley and 2 teaspoons toasted flaked (slivered) almonds. Serves 2

Middle Eastern Chicken and Vegetable Skewers

Use this idea for beef or lamb and vegetable skewers or try rubbing the spice blend on trimmed lamb cutlets. Cube 200g (7oz) chicken breast fillet and rub it in 1–2 tablespoons of Middle Eastern spice blend and marinate for 30 minutes. Thread the chicken onto skewers that have been soaked in water for 30 minutes, alternating with cubed capsicum (peppers), mushrooms and zucchini (courgettes) and barbecue or grill (broil) until cooked as liked. Serve with a barbecued eggplant (aubergine), tomato and chickpea salad and with a tablespoon of low-fat natural (plain) yoghurt mixed with chopped mint. Serves 2

Marinated Tofu and Vegetable Kebabs

Great for the barbecue. Serve with rice salad or a green salad and fresh wholegrain bread. Marinate 200–250g (7–9oz) of hard tofu cubes in salt-reduced soy sauce and sweet chilli sauce. Thread onto skewers along with slices of capsicum (pepper), zucchini (courgette) and mushroom and barbecue or grill (broil) lightly on all sides. Serves 2

TVP Bolognese

Prepare TVP as per packet directions to make 200g (7oz) of TVP mince. Heat 1 tablespoon olive oil and cook 1 chopped onion and 1 teaspoon crushed garlic until soft, about 2–3 minutes. Add the drained TVP and 1½ cups no added salt canned crushed tomatoes, 1 tablespoon of no added salt tomato paste, 1 teaspoon of Italian herbs, cover and simmer for 10–15 minutes, stir occasionally. Toss in 1 cup cooked wholemeal pasta, heat and serve with a fresh garden salad. Serves 2

NOTE: TVP stands for Textured Vegetable Protein.

Whip It Up Mains—Quickies

Pumpkin, Bean, Sage and Walnut Penne

Enjoy this penne hot or cold with a green salad. Microwave or steam 2 cups diced butternut pumpkin until cooked and mix into 2 cups hot cooked whole wheat penne pasta with ½ cup drained and rinsed, canned kidney beans. Mix together 1 tablespoon olive oil, 1 teaspoon crushed garlic and 1 tablespoon torn sage and stir through the hot penne. Divide between two bowls and top each with 2 teaspoons low-fat natural (plain) yoghurt and two teaspoons chopped walnuts. Serves 2

Spicy Chinese Pork Noodles

For even spicier noodles serve some sliced fresh chillies on the side—a great way to achieve the desired heat level. Cook 90g (3oz) dried soba noodles according to the packet directions. Drain. Heat 3 teaspoons peanut oil and brown 100g (3½oz) lean pork strips, 2–3 minutes. Add 3–4 teaspoons Chinese five spice blend and stir for a few seconds. Add ½ cup sliced spring onions (scallions), 1 cup finely sliced carrot, 250g/9oz of sliced Chinese broccoli and about ½–1 cup water and stir-fry for 2–3 minutes or until the pork is cooked. Add the noodles and stir until hot. Stir in 1 teaspoon each of salt-reduced soy sauce and sesame oil. Serves 2

Teriyaki Beef and Barley Stir-fry

A tasty recipe to serve with crisp lettuce leaves—eat with or wrap in the lettuce like san choy bow. It's a great example of 'extending' meat with wholegrains—great for the body and the budget. Spray a hot pan with olive oil spray and stir-fry about ¾ cup sliced spring onions (scallions) (using the green part), and ½ cup sliced red capsicum (pepper) for about 1–2 minutes, set aside. Spray the pan again with oil and add 160g (5½oz) lean minced beef, browning well and stirring until cooked for about 5 minutes. Add 1 cup cooked barley, 3 teaspoons teriyaki sauce, the onions and capsicum and stir until hot. Serve sprinkled with ¼ cup diced cucumber and the cos lettuce leaves. Serves 2

Sesame Tofu and Vegetable Noodles

This noodle dish can also be served chilled as a salad. Heat 1 tablespoon canola oil and stir-fry 200g (7oz) cubed hard tofu until golden, set aside. Add 2 cups frozen stir-fry vegetables and stir-fry for about 2–3 minutes. Add 1½ tablespoons hoi sin sauce and about a tablespoon water and stir-fry for a minute. Stir in 1 cup fresh hokkien noodles and tofu and stir until hot. Serve sprinkled with 1 tablespoon toasted sesame seeds. Serves 2

TOFU TIP
Ensure you choose the right tofu for the dish. You need 'hard' or 'firm' tofu that can be sliced to add to stir-fries and soups. Silken tofu is best to blend/purée for desserts or dressings.

Whip It Up Sides, Sauces and Dressings

Broccoli and Green Bean Salad

Served either at room temperature or chilled this salad can be the perfect partner to turn barbecued meat, seafood or vegetables into a Mediterranean or Asian-style meal—try the different dressing suggestions. Add a noodle or brown rice salad to complete the meal. Steam or microwave 2 cups small broccoli florets and 1 cup sliced green beans until the colour has intensified yet, the vegetables are still crisp (al dente). Refresh and cool in cold water and drain. Combine with a clove of crushed garlic and a tablespoon of vinaigrette dressing or opt for an Asian flavour and toss in 1 tablespoon salt-reduced soy sauce or kecap manis and 1 tablespoon toasted sesame seeds. Serves 2 as a side salad

Apple and Pistachio Salad

A great side salad with a tomato and cos salad for grills, barbecues and cold meats. Fabulous in a grainy bread roll with lean beef and tomato. Combine 1 chopped green apple (skin on) with ½ cup sliced celery, 1½ tablespoons chopped pistachios and 1½ tablespoons canola and soy bean oil mayonnaise. Serves 2 as a side dish

Sweet Potato Wedges

Perfect for a snack or to serve with a quick roast or as a barbecue accompaniment. Preheat an oven to 200°C (400°F/Gas Mark 6). Blend 3 teaspoons extra light olive oil, ½ teaspoon ground sweet paprika and ¼ teaspoon ground cumin in a bowl. Add 2 cups peeled sweet potato wedges and mix to coat wedges. Spray a baking tray with olive oil and place wedges, in one layer, on the tray. Bake for 20 minutes or until cooked, turning once during cooking or cook in a disposable dish on a covered barbecue. Serves 2–4 as a side dish

Orange and Date Couscous

Serve as an accompaniment to Moroccan tagines and Indian curries or add some diced cooked chicken breast, baby spinach and extra orange juice and serve as a salad. Remove skin, pith and seeds from 1 orange and chop flesh. Bring ¾ cup water and chopped orange to the boil and stir in ¼ cup chopped dried or fresh dates. Remove from the heat. Stir in ¾ cup instant couscous, cover and stand for 2 minutes. Add a teaspoon of reduced-salt cholesterol-lowering margarine, fluff it up with a fork and stir in ¼ cup toasted chopped almonds. Serves 2 as a side dish

Ratatouille

This basic vegetable sauce is jam packed with colours and flavours and can be served as a topping with pasta, steamed vegetables, meats or toast, or added to a sandwich or roll for delicious Mediterranean flavour. Heat 1 tablespoon olive oil and cook 1 small sliced brown onion and a crushed clove of garlic until soft (about 5 minutes). Add half a diced small eggplant (aubergine) and cook until golden (2 minutes). Add 1 small sliced zucchini (courgette), 1 sliced small red capsicum (pepper) and stir for 2 minutes. Add 1 cup diced canned tomatoes, 1 teaspoon sugar and 1 tablespoon each of red wine vinegar and white wine. Stir well, cover and gently simmer for about 30 minutes. Serve immediately or refrigerate and use as required. Makes about 2 cups

Berry Sauce

Serve this sauce with lean grilled (broiled) or barbecued meats. Heat 2 teaspoons extra light olive oil and cook 1 sliced onion, 2–3 minutes. Add 1½ cups fresh or frozen berries and ¼ cup salt-reduced stock and ½ cup freshly squeezed orange juice. Add a dash of port or orange liqueur and simmer, until the berries are soft and the sauce has reduced. Stir while cooking. Makes about 2 cups

Reduced-Fat Cheese Sauce

Great over steamed vegetables or as the basis for a creamy pasta sauce—each serve contains 200mg calcium. Heat 3 teaspoons reduced-salt cholesterol-lowering margarine in a small non-stick pan. Add 3 teaspoons plain (all-purpose) flour and cook for 2 minutes while stirring. Remove from the heat and gradually add 1 cup skim milk (or soy milk) a little at a time, stirring constantly to avoid lumps. When all the milk has been added, place back onto a medium heat and stir until thickened. Add ½ cup of grated reduced-fat cheese and a pinch of nutmeg. Variations: Add 2 tablespoons of finely chopped parsley or dill, or the juice and zest of a lemon (off the heat to prevent curdling). Serves 4

Macadamia, Lemon and Caper Sauce

A tangy combination of flavours, which is perfect to serve with grilled, or barbecued fish or chicken, or over steamed green vegetables like asparagus. Heat a non-stick pan on a low heat and add 1 teaspoon canola oil. Add ¼ cup halved macadamia nuts and stir until golden about 1–2 minutes, remove nuts and drain on paper towel. Add a finely sliced onion to the pan and stir until transparent and soft about 3 minutes. Add 2 tablespoons lemon juice, 1 tablespoon water, ½ teaspoon grated lemon zest, 1 teaspoon rinsed and drained baby capers and the macadamias and stir until hot. Serves 2

Rocket and Almond Pesto

A peppery version of a traditional basil pesto. Serve a dollop on grilled fish, chicken or soup or toss through pasta. Place 2 cups baby rocket leaves, 1 tablespoon flaked (slivered) almonds, 1 teaspoon each of crushed garlic and grated parmesan cheese and 2 teaspoons olive oil in a small blender or food processor and blend until combined. Makes about 1/3 cup.

Vinaigrette

Place 1½ tablespoons extra virgin olive oil, 2 teaspoons lemon juice or white wine vinegar and ½ teaspoon wholegrain mustard in a screw-top jar. Shake to combine, taste and season with sugar and freshly ground black pepper. Add some freshly chopped or dried herbs, such as parsley, basil or dill for herb vinaigrette. Serves 2

Chilli and Lime Dressing

Place 2 teaspoons olive or peanut oil, 1 teaspoon sesame oil, ½ teaspoon salt-reduced soy sauce, 2 teaspoons sweet chilli sauce, 1 teaspoon lime juice and some freshly chopped herbs, such as Vietnamese mint, coriander (cilantro) or Thai basil in a screw-top jar. Shake to combine, taste and adjust flavour to suit. Serves 2

Citrus Dressing

Place 1 tablespoon freshly squeezed orange juice, 1 teaspoon freshly squeezed lemon or lime juice and 2 teaspoons olive or sunflower oil in a screw-top jar. Shake to combine, taste and adjust flavour to suit, adding a little sugar for sweetness if liked. Serves 2

Garlic Mayonnaise (Aioli)

If you struggle to eat enough vegetables, try them with a spoon of this delicious garlic mayonnaise (aioli) that combines healthy oils with the health-boosting effects of garlic. Mix 2 cloves crushed garlic and 1 teaspoon lemon juice into 1½ tablespoons canola or soy bean oil mayonnaise. Serves 2

All-purpose Italian Dressing

Place 3 teaspoons of extra-virgin olive oil, 2 teaspoons of balsamic vinegar, ½ clove crushed garlic and ½ teaspoon Italian herbs in a screw-top jar. Shake to combine, taste and adjust flavour to suit. Serves 2

Moroccan-style Dressing

Ideal to dollop on a couscous vegetable salad or a couscous made with toasted almonds and dates, served with a lamb tagine. Place 3 teaspoons soybean oil, 2 teaspoons apricot nectar, 2 teaspoons low-fat natural (plain) yoghurt and ¼ teaspoon Moroccan spice blend in a screw-top jar. Shake to combine, taste and adjust flavour to suit. Serves 2

Avocado Oil Dressing

Enjoy a little spooned over grilled fish or chicken and the remainder tossed into a mesclun, tomato and corn salad. Place 3 teaspoons avocado oil, 3 teaspoons lemon juice, a dash of Tabasco or chilli sauce and 2 teaspoons finely chopped dill in a screw-top jar. Shake to combine, taste and adjust flavour to suit. Serves 2

Mediterranean Barbecue Marinade

This is perfect for red meats such as beef, lamb, venison or kangaroo. Use this amount for 300g (11oz) raw meat. Combine 1½ tablespoons extra virgin olive oil, 1–2 teaspoons crushed garlic, 3 teaspoons lemon juice, 3 teaspoons finely chopped parsley and freshly ground black pepper. Pour over lean meat (trimmed of fat) in a sealed container and marinate in the fridge preferably overnight—allow 150g raw weight per person. Pan-fry or barbecue meat, discarding the marinade, and serve with an Italian style salad of mixed lettuce and marinated grilled vegetables in a little balsamic vinegar and chopped herbs. Serves 2

26: Desserts

Watermelon in Rosewater Syrup

Medium GI

This is one of those recipes where you can prepare everything in advance and chill; and assemble the dessert just before serving time. Rosewater gives the dish a fragrant perfume and flavour. You will find it available in many large supermarkets, in delis and in Middle Eastern produce stores.

Preparation time: 15 minutes
Cooking time: 5 minutes
Chilling time: 15 minutes (minimum)
Serves: 2

½ cup (125ml/4fl oz) water
2 tablespoons (40ml/1½fl oz) rosewater
1 teaspoon honey
1 teaspoon brown sugar
⅓ cup (80g/2¾oz) low-fat ricotta
1 teaspoon grated orange zest
1 tablespoon chopped toasted pistachios
2 teaspoons icing (confectioners') sugar, sifted
Dash of vanilla extract to taste
400g/14oz watermelon, chilled
1 tablespoon halved toasted pistachios

Place the water, rosewater, honey and brown sugar in a small saucepan and bring to the boil over a low heat, stirring occasionally. Continue cooking until the sauce has reduced by half. Remove from the heat and chill for at least 15 minutes. Mix together the ricotta, orange zest, pistachios, icing sugar and vanilla to taste until well combined. Chill until required. Cut the watermelon into wedges and remove any seeds.

Arrange into serving bowls and pour over the rosewater syrup. Serve with a dollop of the orange and pistachio ricotta on top and a scattering of the halved pistachios.

Cook's tip

To toast the pistachios, heat a non-stick pan over a medium/low heat and spray with olive oil spray. Add the 2 tablespoons whole pistachios and toast for about 2–3 minutes or until golden. Stir constantly for even toasting and to avoid burning. Cool. Chop half of the pistachios to add to the ricotta. Cut the remaining pistachios for scattering as the garnish.

Nutrition per serve

Energy kJ (cals) 744 (178)

Protein 7g

Total fat 8.8g

Saturated fat 2.9g

Fibre 1.9g

Carbohydrate 18g

Cholesterol 18mg

Sodium 84mg

Saucy Chocolate and Almond Puddings

High fibre, low GI

These little puddings have been developed to incorporate a little heart-friendly dark chocolate with the goodness of almonds into a really satisfying treat for the chocolate lover.

Preparation time: 15 minutes
Cooking time: 6 minutes
Standing time: 5 minutes
Serves: 2

2 tablespoons (20g/¾oz) self-raising (self-rising) wholemeal flour
3 teaspoons ground almonds (almond meal)
1 tablespoon (20g/¾oz) caster (superfine) sugar
1½ teaspoons cocoa powder, sifted
1 teaspoon cholesterol-lowering margarine
15g/½oz good quality dark chocolate, chopped
1½ tablespoons (30ml/1fl oz) skim milk
1 teaspoon vanilla extract
Extra cholesterol-lowering margarine for greasing
1 tablespoon brown sugar
2 teaspoons cocoa powder, extra
⅓ cup (80ml/2½oz) boiling water
1 cup (150g/5½oz) fresh raspberries

Place the flour, almonds, sugar and cocoa powder into a bowl and mix to combine. Place the margarine and chocolate into a microwave-safe bowl and microwave on medium 70 per cent power for 20–30 seconds. Mix to combine. Stir in the dry ingredients, milk and vanilla and mix well. Rub 2 x 200ml/7oz microwave-safe dishes or cups with the extra margarine and spoon the mixture evenly into the dishes. Sift together the sugar and extra cocoa and sprinkle evenly over each pudding. Carefully pour half the boiling water over each pudding and cover loosely with microwave-safe plastic wrap. Place dishes on baking paper and microwave on defrost (10 per cent power) for 3–5 minutes. The puddings will be cooked when the cake has risen to the top and has set. Stand puddings for about 5 minutes before serving with raspberries.

Cook's tip

Puddings can be baked in a moderate oven 180°C (350°F/ Gas Mark 4) uncovered for about 15 minutes.

Nutrition per serve
Energy kJ (cals) 913 (218)
Protein 5g
Total fat 8.3g
Saturated fat 2.5g
Fibre 5.7g
Carbohydrate 31mg
Cholesterol 1mg or less
Sodium 108mg

Kiwi, Strawberries and Almond Toffee

High fibre, low GI
Combining golden kiwi fruit with green kiwi fruit and the strawberries really makes this into a gold star dessert. It is high in vitamin C, antioxidants, fibre and flavour. The almond toffee is easy and quick to prepare and really adds a delightful sweet crunch.

Preparation time: 10 minutes
Cooking time: 5 minutes
Serves: 2

1 tablespoon (15g/½oz) flaked (slivered) almonds
3 teaspoons sugar
1 x 125g/4½oz green kiwi fruit, peeled and quartered
1 x 125g/4½oz golden kiwi fruit, peeled and quartered
250g (9oz) strawberries, hulled and halved
2 x 50g/1¾oz scoops low-fat ice cream

Heat a small non-stick pan over a medium heat and dry fry the almonds, stirring, for 2–3 minutes or until golden. Spread in a single layer in a 10cm/4-inch circle on a baking tray covered with foil. Add the sugar to the pan and stir until dissolved and turns light golden brown, 1–2 minutes. Pour toffee over the almonds and leave to set. Place the kiwi fruit and strawberries in serving bowls with the ice cream. Break the toffee in half and place on the top of the ice cream.

Nutrition per serve
Energy kJ (cals) 875 (209)
Protein 7.5g
Total fat 6g
Saturated fat 1.2g
Fibre 7.5g
Carbohydrate 31g
Cholesterol 5mg
Sodium 49mg

Anise-infused Rice Custard with Blood Orange

Medium GI

Preparation time: 10 minutes
Cooking time: 40 minutes
Chilling time: 30 minutes minimum
Serves: 2

1½ tablespoons (30g/1oz) medium grain brown rice
1 cup (250ml/9fl oz) water
1 teaspoon caster (superfine) sugar
½ teaspoon ground cardamom
2 whole dried star anise
1 (50g/1¾oz) egg yolk
1½ teaspoons caster sugar, extra
1 teaspoon corn flour (starch)
½ cup (125ml/4fl oz) skim milk
A dash of vanilla extract to taste
1 (300g/10½oz) blood orange or orange,
   peeled and segmented

Place the rice, water, sugar, cardamom and star anise in a small saucepan over a medium heat. Bring to the boil, stirring occasionally. Reduce heat, cover and simmer for 20–25 minutes until the rice is almost tender. Increase the heat, uncover, and boil for a further 5–10 minutes or until the rice is tender and the liquid is absorbed, stirring constantly—take care not to allow all the water to evaporate before the rice is cooked—add a little more water if needed. To make the custard, whisk the egg yolk in a small bowl with a fork and mix in the extra sugar. Set aside. Blend the corn flour with a little of the milk in a small saucepan. Stir in the remaining milk and heat over a medium/low heat, stirring constantly until hot—do not boil. Whisk the hot milk into the beaten egg and then pour the mixture back into the saucepan. Return to the heat and, stirring constantly to avoid any lumps, cook for about 1 minute or until the custard thickens and coats the back of a metal spoon—do not boil. Stir in the vanilla. Cover the surface of the custard with plastic wrap to prevent a skin forming and set aside. Remove the star anise from the rice and add the custard, mixing well to incorporate all the flavours. Spoon into two serving dishes and serve topped with the blood orange segments. In warm weather you might like to chill the custard before serving.

Cook's tip

A combination of citrus fruits segmented, such as lemon, lime and orange, would be suitable to serve with the rice custard or try with nectarine, peach, apricot or mango when they are in season.

Nutrition per serve

Energy kJ (cals) 723 (173)
Protein 6.4g
Total fat 3g
Saturated fat 0.9g
Fibre 1.5g
Carbohydrate 29g
Cholesterol 91mg
Sodium 41mg

Orange Trio: Salad, Liqueur Yoghurt and Shot

High fibre, low GI

This dessert is particularly good to serve warm in winter but can be enjoyed at any time chilled. The fruit salad keeps well in the refrigerator and can be reheated in the microwave. The shot is deliciously refreshing to sip while enjoying the dessert and makes a very special finish to a dinner. If you prefer the dessert without the liqueur see the cook's note.

Preparation time: 5 minutes
Cooking time: 15 minutes
Storage time: 3 days refrigerated
Serves: 2

100g/3½oz dried fruit salad mix (prunes, apples, pears, peaches, apricots)
1 x 170g/6oz navel orange, peeled and cut into 8 wedges and trimmed
2 cinnamon quills, broken
1 cup (250ml/9fl oz) water
2 tablespoons (40g/1½oz) low-fat vanilla yoghurt
1 teaspoon orange liqueur
½ cup (125ml/4fl oz) freshly squeezed orange juice
1 teaspoon orange liqueur, extra
½ teaspoon tiny mint leaves
2 sponge finges

Place the fruit salad, orange, cinnamon quills and water in a saucepan over a medium heat, cover and bring to the boil. Reduce the heat, and simmer for 10 minutes or until the fruit has plumped. Cool slightly. Mix together the yoghurt and liqueur and chill until required. Pour the orange juice and extra liqueur into shot glasses and add the mint, chill until required. Remove the cinnamon quills from the fruit salad and serve warm in bowls with a dollop of yoghurt and the shot and sponge finger on the side.

Cook's tip

Make this recipe alcohol-free by substituting the liqueur in the yoghurt with a little orange zest and a dash of honey to taste. Make the shot without the liqueur by adding orange zest with the mint to the juice.

> ## Nutrition per serve
> Energy kJ (cals) 926 (221)
> Protein 4.6g
> Total fat 0.9g
> Saturated fat 0.2g
> Fibre 6g
> Carbohydrate 47g
> Cholesterol 19mg
> Sodium 58mg

Scrunched Filo, Apples and Maple Glazed Nuts

High fibre, low–medium GI

There are numerous recipes for apple pies as it is one of the most popular desserts especially when it is home made. This recipe looks stunning and it really does taste as good as it looks!

Preparation time: 15 minutes
Cooking time: 40 minutes
Serves: 2

2 x 200g/7oz cooking apples
2 teaspoons salt-reduced cholesterol-lowering margarine
2 teaspoons 100 per cent pure maple syrup
2 teaspoons lemon juice
¼ cup (60ml/2fl oz) water
2 teaspoons 100 per cent pure maple syrup, extra
20g/¾oz (6 small) Brazil nuts
1 sheet commercial chilled filo pastry
A little icing (confectioners') sugar for sifting (¼–½ teaspoon)

Preheat oven to moderate 180°C (350°F/Gas Mark 4) and line a baking tray with baking paper. Peel, core and slice each apple into 12 wedges. Heat the margarine in a non-stick frying pan over a low heat and arrange the apples in the pan in a single layer. Pour over the maple syrup and lemon juice. Cook the apples, moving them around during cooking to cook evenly and turning only once, for 35 minutes or until golden and tender. Add a little water during cooking if needed. Place the water and extra maple syrup in a small non-stick pan over a medium heat and bring to the boil. Add the brazil nuts and continue to boil until the sauce has almost evaporated and the nuts are glazed, 2–3 minutes. Set aside. Cut the sheet of filo pastry in half and scrunch each half up roughly. Place on the prepared baking tray and sift a little icing sugar on to each pastry. Bake for 1–2 minutes or until the filo is light golden. Arrange the apple and Brazil nuts on serving plates with the filo on top.

Cook's tip

Golden delicious or delicious apples are perfect for this recipe but any cooking apples can be used.

Nutrition per serve

Energy kJ (cals) 997 (238)
Protein 2.7g
Total fat 10.5g
Saturated fat 2g
Fibre 4.4g
Carbohydrate 35g
Cholesterol 0mg
Sodium 67mg

Baked Stone Fruits and Berries

High fibre, low GI

This dessert can be popped into the oven while you are enjoying your main course and will be ready to serve when you are ready to enjoy it! The frozen berry mix we used in this dessert is high in antioxidants, containing bilberries, blackcurrants and wild blueberries.

Preparation time: 10 minutes
Cooking time: 20 minutes
Serves: 2

Oil spray
2 x 125g/4½oz yellow peaches, stone removed and sliced
2 x 100g/3½oz yellow nectarines, stone removed and sliced
1 cup (150g/5½oz) frozen berry mix
1–2 teaspoons finely grated lemon zest
2 teaspoons brown sugar
¼–½ teaspoon mixed spice
½ cup (125g/4½oz) low-fat yoghurt
1 teaspoon honey

Preheat oven to moderate 180°C (350°F/Gas Mark 4), and spray a flat ovenproof dish with oil. Arrange the peaches, nectarines and berries over the base of the dish. Sprinkle over the lemon zest, sugar and allspice. Cover the dish with foil and bake for 15 minutes. Remove foil and stir and continue to cook for a further 5 minutes. Serve warm topped with yoghurt and drizzled with honey

---

Nutrition per serve

Energy kJ (cals) 690 (165)

Protein 7g

Total fat 0.5g

Saturated fat 1g or less

Fibre 7.7g

Carbohydrate 32g

Cholesterol 3mg

Sodium 50mg

Whip It Up Desserts and Sweet Treats

Pears Poached in Red Wine

This is a great idea for enjoying the goodness of fruit with the bonus of red wine flavour and antioxidants, but without the alcohol (it is mostly evaporated during cooking). Simmer 2 medium pears, sliced in half lengthways, in ½ cup of red wine, ¼ cup of sugar, 3 cloves and 1 cinnamon stick for around 15 minutes in a covered saucepan, turning to ensure even coating. Serve with a heaped tablespoon of vanilla low-fat fromage frais (dairy dessert) and sprinkle with powdered cinnamon. Serves 2

Sweet Spiced Walnuts

* Kilojoule (calorie) alert!

These are much healthier than lollies, but go easy. This recipe is perfect for special occasions—be sure to share! Store in an airtight container in a cool, dark place. Beat an egg white with 1 tablespoon water. Add 1½ cups walnut halves and mix to coat, draining off any excess egg. Line a tray with baking paper and mix 1 teaspoon each of ground cinnamon and icing (confectioners') sugar together. Sieve a coating of the cinnamon mix on the baking paper and arrange a single layer of walnuts on the top. Sieve the remaining cinnamon mix on top and bake in a moderate oven 180°C (350°F/Gas Mark 4) until the coating has set and the nuts are warm (about 10–15 minutes; keep a watchful eye on them!). Allow to cool and store in an airtight container. Makes 6 serves

Chilli Chocolate Nuts

* Kilojoule (calorie) alert!

The idea of mixing chilli with chocolate is ancient. An exotic and interesting balance of sweet, smooth and hot. The heat from the chilli gives this chocolate extra benefits; antioxidants and it's harder to overeat! Roast, carefully, ½ cup of unsalted nuts under the grill (broil), such as almonds, cashews, peanuts or hazelnuts. Spread evenly on a sheet of baking paper, and add ¼ cup of puffed rice. Place 100g (3½oz) dark semi-sweet/high cocoa chocolate pieces in a ceramic dish and microwave for 1 minute, or until melted. Stir in 1 teaspoon chilli oil with a metal spoon and pour over the nuts and rice. Place any remaining nuts and rice on the top of the chocolate to ensure all are included. Allow to cool and set. Cut into 8 pieces. Makes 8 small serves

Whip It Up Desserts and Sweet Treats—Quickies

Grilled Banana with Cardamom and Walnuts

A perfect dessert to serve at barbecues. Make a syrup by heating ½ cup water, 1 teaspoon brown sugar and 1 teaspoon ground cardamom and stir until the sugar has dissolved. Simmer until the sauce has reduced by half. Barbecue or grill 2 bananas, cut in long slices, until browned. Serve each banana drizzled with syrup, a scoop of low-fat ice cream and sprinkled with a tablespoon of walnuts. Serves 2

Tropical Fruit Salad in Coconut

A great way to enjoy tropical fruits when they are in season—make ahead and chill well. Combine 1 cup each of drained canned or fresh lychees, mango and pineapple chunks. Mix through torn mint (about 1 tablespoon). Sweeten ¾ cup chilled light coconut milk with ½ teaspoon brown sugar and serve drizzled over the fruit. (Coconut flavoured evaporated skim milk can be substituted for coconut milk.) Serves 2

Berry Trifles

Try a combination of mixed berries in this trifle and use different flavoured jellies for variety. Layer evenly between two serving glasses: 2 Italian sponge fingers, broken into pieces, 1 cup berries, such as strawberries, raspberries or blueberries, ½ cup chopped raspberry jelly and 1 cup low-fat pouring custard. Top each with a few shavings of dark chocolate and serve with another sponge finger on the side. Serves 2

Apple and Prune Crumble

Crumbles are always popular and this topping is ideal for many fruit bases. Combine 1 cup cooked apple, 1 tablespoon finely chopped prunes and grated zest of ½ lemon. Spoon into individual serving dishes and top with ½ cup toasted muesli (granola) mixed with ¼ cup well drained low-fat ricotta cheese and 2 teaspoons brown sugar. Grill until golden about 1–2 minutes. Serves 2

Affogato

Prepare ¼–⅓ cup of strong black coffee (2 shots of espresso). Place a scoop of low-fat ice cream in the base of 2 short glasses or small cups and pour half the coffee over the top of each. Serve with a single Italian-style sponge finger biscuit. Serves 2

Light Tiramisu

This is a light twist on a rich Italian classic. Cut 4 Italian sponge fingers into pieces and place in the base of two parfait glasses. Pour 1½ tablespoons strong black coffee and 3–4 drops of rum essence over each. Top each with 2 tablespoons of low-fat coffee or chocolate yoghurt or dairy dessert and 2 tablespoons of low-fat ricotta cheese. Create a swirled effect by dipping and dragging the handle of a fork through the yoghurt and ricotta. Sprinkle with cocoa powder and garnish with fresh strawberries. Serves 2

Whip It Up Drinks

Quickies

Hearty Hot Chocolate

There's nothing like a cup of hot chocolate on a chilly evening. Combine 1¾ cups of skim milk or soy milk with ¼ cup of cocoa powder, 2 teaspoons of honey and 6 squares (25g/1oz) of dark bittersweet/high cocoa chocolate in a small saucepan. Heat gently until the chocolate is dissolved. Pour into 2 mugs, sprinkle with sifted cocoa powder and top with a marshmallow. You can make a mocha variation by adding 2 tablespoons of strong coffee. Serves 2

Iced Mocha

Prepare ⅓ cup of black coffee. Stir in 2 teaspoons of sugar and 2 tablespoons cocoa powder and allow to cool. Pour half the coffee mixture over ice into two tall glasses. Top up with 1 cup skim milk and stir well. Sprinkle with sifted cocoa powder and shavings of dark chocolate. Serves 2

Berry Spiders

Make delicious fresh or frozen berry 'spiders' for a refreshing snack or quick dessert. Pop two serving glasses into the freezer for a few minutes to chill. Into each glass, add ½ cup berries and a scoop of low-fat ice cream. Slowly pour diet ginger ale into each glass and enjoy. Serves 2

Sparkling Green Apple Iced Tea

This is a low-sugar, low-kilojoule drink with the goodness of apple and green tea antioxidants. Steep 2 green tea bags in 1 cup of hot water for 3–4 minutes and set aside to cool. Add 1 cup of unsweetened apple juice and 1 cup of diet lemonade (or soda water for a less sweet result). Serve in tall glasses over ice with a few apple slices and a sprig of fresh mint. Serves 2

DIY Chai Tea

This is a fantastic idea to prepare for afternoon tea on a weekend, or for when friends visit and you want something a bit special (simply double the amounts for 4 people). Serve in fancy china for the full ceremony. Place 1 cup of prepared strong black tea and 1 cup of skim milk in a saucepan with 1 cinnamon stick (or ¼ teaspoon powdered cinnamon), 1 clove, 1 piece of raw ginger (crushed to release the flavour), 2 cardamom pods (crushed), a pinch of nutmeg, ½ teaspoon vanilla essence and 1 tablespoon brown sugar. Simmer gently for 5 minutes. Pour into tea cups or short glasses through a strainer. Serves 2

Sangria Punch

This is a festive drink that's low in alcohol—1 standard drink per serve. The name sangria is derived from the Spanish word for blood, describing the colour from the red wine. Mix ¾ cup red wine, ½ cup chopped fresh fruits (orange, lemon, apple or pear), ½ cup diet lemonade or ginger ale and ½ cup pure fruit juice in a jug. Serve over ice in a fancy wine glass garnished with orange slices. Serves 2

Recipe Measures
We used Australian standard metric cup and spoon measures.

1 teaspoon = 5ml
1 tablespoon = 20ml/4 teaspoons (NZ, UK and American
    tablespoon = 15ml/3 teaspoons
1 cup = 250ml (9fl oz)

Part 4

Eating plan to beat cholesterol

27: Eating plan to beat cholesterol

So you're serious about getting your cholesterol down—great. We have an eating plan that's guaranteed to get you results. Studies show that if you follow these instructions, you can expect to lower your cholesterol by 20 per cent. Just adding 2g of plant sterols alone can get your cholesterol down 10 per cent. We've seen some people achieve 25–30 per cent reductions. To say they've been pleased is an understatement!

Prove it for yourself: visit your doctor for a cholesterol test, follow our plan for 3–4 weeks, and then have a repeat test.

The proof of eating to beat cholesterol will be in your numbers, and success has a habit of boosting your motivation to continue (as does feeling so much better). Losing a little excess weight will boost your result, but even if your weight stays the same this way of eating will lower your cholesterol, protect your heart and improve your health generally.

Think of eating to beat cholesterol as a checklist: the more boxes you tick, the better your result. Sure, there will be some days you don't tick as many boxes, or some strategies might be more challenging for you—the point is to know what the ideal diet looks like so you have something to aim for.

Remember, there are two steps to beat cholesterol:
STEP 1: Enjoy a heart-friendly diet.
STEP 2: Move more.

Here's how to do a heart-friendly diet. Remember don't worry if you can't do them all, just do as many as you can.

Your Eat to Beat Cholesterol 10 point plan

Top cholesterol-beaters
These foods are scientifically proven to lower cholesterol.
- Enjoy at least 30–45g/1–1½oz a day—6–8 teaspoons—of added healthy fats like vegetable oils and margarines, both polyunsaturated and monounsaturated.
- Of this 30–45g/1–1½oz of healthy oils, include 25g (5 teaspoons) a day of plant cholesterol-lowering margarine daily—enough to provide 2g plant sterols.
- Enjoy 1–2 handfuls (30–60g/1–2oz) of unsalted nuts most days.
- Include foods rich in soluble (or viscous) fibre daily such as oats, barley or psyllium-enriched cereals, eggplant (aubergine) and okra and/or take a soluble fibre supplement based on psyllium (isphagula), guar gum, inulin, wheat dextrin or methylcellulose.
- Include foods containing soy protein daily (optimal target 25g soy protein). Examples include tofu, tempeh, soy milk, soy-burgers, soy bread and breakfast cereal.

Top heart-friendly foods
These foods are known to protect your heart. They'll also look after your body in other ways, such as reducing your risk of diabetes.
- Enjoy fish in at least 2 meals a week, preferably oily fish such as salmon, sardines, mackerel and tuna.
- Include legumes (pulses) such as dried beans (eg, soy beans, kidney beans), chickpeas, or lentils in at least 2 meals a week (more is better).
- Eat at least 5 serves (5 handfuls) of vegetables daily—a variety of colours and types including green, red/purple/orange and white AND at least 2 serves (2 average sized pieces) of fruit daily—a variety of types including citrus, berries and other fruits like apples and pears.
- Ensure half your grain foods are wholegrain (at least 2 serves wholegrains daily): a serve is equal to 2 thin slices of bread; a bowl of wholegrain cereal or 1 cup wholewheat pasta).
- Include low GI foods at most meals. Examples include dense, grainy bread, pasta, barley, oats, sweetcorn, muesli (granola), porridge, most fruits, legumes, milk, yoghurt.

Healthy foods you need to eat
There are some foods you need to eat to obtain important nutrients, but it's important you choose the best ones.
- Low-fat milk and yoghurt (or suitable alternative)—aim for 2–3 serves a day. 1 serve is 1 cup of milk, 200g/7oz yoghurt, 40g/1½oz cheese. Choose reduced-fat cheese and limit to 2–3 times a week due to its high salt and saturated fat content.
- Lean meats or alternatives—aim for 1–2 serves a day. Trim the fat, buy lean cuts and remove skin from poultry. Other foods in this group are eggs, fish or meat alternatives such as legumes. You can eat 3–4 eggs a week.

How you can add flavour without salt
Boost natural food flavours with herbs and spices and reduce the amount of sodium (salt) you eat.

Choosing your optional extras
- If you choose to drink alcohol, limit to 1–2 drinks per day.
- If you drink tea and coffee, enjoy them in moderation: up to 3–4 cups of tea AND 2–3 instant coffees—or one strong coffee—daily.

Alcoholic drinks are fattening. Go for lower-kilojoule alcoholic drinks if you want to indulge without the bulge. Avoid sugary, creamy drinks and go for light beer, diet mixers and less alcohol.

Swap this	for this instead
275ml (9fl oz) bottle fruit flavour alco-pop	150ml (5fl oz) glass of sparkling wine 407kJ/97 cals
250ml (8½fl oz) Rum/vodka/scotch & cola 625kJ/149 cals	250ml (8½fl oz) Rum/vodka/scotch & diet cola 278kJ/66 cals
285ml (10fl oz) regular beer 430kJ/103 cals	285ml (10fl oz) light beer 294kJ/70 cals
150ml (5fl oz) Mudslide cocktail (with cream) 1489kJ/356 cals	230ml (8fl oz) coffee liqueur and skim milk 660kJ/158 cals

NOTE: these are average figures and individual products may vary

Getting your treats right

People often ask how often they can eat treats, also known as 'extra foods', 'fun foods', 'discretionary foods', 'empty calories' or 'sometimes foods'. The short answer is, less than you probably do right now. Dietary surveys show that we're eating too many extra foods and not enough 'core' foods that our bodies need. As well as adding saturated fat, trans fats and salt into the diet, they tend push out the nutritious foods we need to eat. They also tend to be high in kilojoules/calories most of us could do without.

Extra foods: eat these sometimes or in small amounts

Ice cream and frozen yoghurt

Biscuits, cookies

Cakes, muffins and slices

Chocolate, chocolate bars and confectionery

Soft/fizzy drinks (soda)

Potato/corn chips/crisps

If you can enjoy petite portions (such as 1 scoop of ice cream or 3 small squares of chocolate or 1 chocolate biscuit) you could probably get away with eating a treat most days.

If you struggle to limit the quantity of treats you eat, limit treats to once or twice a week. After talking with many people, a winning formula for treat-lovers is to not buy treats with the weekly groceries, but enjoy them occasionally at a cafe, restaurant or special outing.

If you are sedentary and do no regular exercise, you can't afford to eat too many treats.

If you are active and exercise regularly, you can get away with eating more treats without gaining weight but you still have to make sure you're eating the core foods your body needs.

How you can transform your diet

Transforming your diet and your health is often a matter of simple swaps and better choices of foods you already eat.

Foods I eat now	Cholesterol-beating heart friendly alternative
Sugary, low fibre breakfast cereal	High fibre, wholegrain low GI cereal
White bread	Whole wheat or mixed grain low GI bread
Whole milk	Low-fat milk
Butter	Cholesterol-lowering margarine
Cheese	Reduced-fat hard cheese or low-fat cottage or ricotta
Potatoes	Low GI potatoes such as carisma, nicola, new potatoes
White rice	Brown rice or lower GI basmati rice
Regular pasta	Whole wheat pasta
White crackers	Wholemeal or mixed grain crispbread
Hamburger (regular) mince (ground beef)	Premium lean mince
Regular ice cream	Low-fat ice cream
Chocolate or cream filled biscuits/cookies	Wholewheat biscuits
Confectionery	Mixed nuts and dried fruit

Putting it all together

The following menus show you how it all comes together. They include breakfast, lunch and dinner with some snack suggestions to keep you going in between. You really do need to eat three meals a day. Skipping meals sets the perfect trap for snack attacks on all the wrong foods. We have analysed them so you can see how they provide you with the optimal nutrient mix for cholesterol lowering and heart-protection.

You don't need to eat this exact menu every day, just aim for something similar in food types and amounts. We don't expect you'll score a perfect 10 every time, just aim to get as close as you can as often as possible for great cholesterol results and a healthy, happy heart.

Crunching the numbers:

Optimum daily nutrient targets for cholesterol lowering and a healthy heart

- Around 30 per cent of kilojoules/calories (kJ/cals) from fat—around 70g (2¾oz) in a typical diet.
- No more than 8 per cent kJ/cals (12–18g/day) from saturated fat—less than 20g/¾oz in a typical diet.
- 8–10 per cent of total kJ/cals from polyunsaturated fats—20–25g/¾oz in a typical diet.
- Polyunsaturated fat: Saturated fat ratio (P:S ratio) more than 1.
- Less than 200mg cholesterol.
- Less than 1600mg sodium.
- 28g fibre or more.

What is the P:S ratio?

For the best cholesterol lowering effect, there needs to be more polyunsaturated fats than saturated fats in your diet and this ratio is a measure of this. A diet with a P:S ratio more than 1 is ideal, and the higher the better. The well known Nurses' Health Study showed a direct association between a higher P:S ratio and lower cholesterol levels. Moreover, replacing saturated fat with polyunsaturated fat reduces the risk of cardiovascular disease.

Your energy needs

Energy (kilojoules) vary from person to person, however a typical daily kilojoule needs for adults is 9000 kilojoules (or 2000 calories).

You will need more if:

You are under 30 years of age
You are taller than average
You are heavy
You are very active

You will need less if:

You are over 50 years of age
You are shorter than average
You are slim
You are inactive
You want to lose weight

Example daily menu for cholesterol lowering— moderate in kilojoules (9000kJ /2000 cals)

This menu will suit you if you are average height and weight, less than 50 years of age and moderately active OR you're large and would like to lose weight.

Breakfast

1 cup wholegrain/high fibre cereal flakes + ½ cup muesli (granola) with
1 cup low-fat milk
1 cup fruit salad pieces
1 skim milk café latte

Lunch

2 slices wholemeal bread with 3 teaspoons cholesterol-lowering margarine
75g (3oz) drained sardines (in springwater)
3 cups mixed salad (with dark leaves, cooked kumara, chickpeas, red capsicum)
1 orange or 2 small mandarins
1 cup low-fat milk
OR see page 192 for Quickie recipe Sardine, Chickpea, Sweet Potato, Spinach and Orange Salad

Dinner

100g/3½oz (raw) lean meat (cooked in 2 teaspoons canola oil)
1 cup cooked pasta
2 cups mixed vegetables (carrot, broccoli, cauliflower, red cabbage)
3 teaspoons plant sterol enriched spread
1 small glass (100ml /3½ fl oz) red wine
Or see page 225 for Quickie recipe Chicken with Herb and Garlic Vegetable Pasta

Snacks/Dessert

15g/½oz almonds

1 apple or 2 nectarines

200g/7oz low-fat yoghurt

4 cups of tea (no sugar, or with sweetener)

Drinks: Ensure around 2 litres of fluid daily. Include plenty of water and up to 4 cups of tea and 1 espresso coffee (little or no sugar (or use sweetener), with a little reduced-fat milk).

On target nutrition information	
Kilojoules	9036
Calories	2158
Fat	65g (27%)
Polyunsaturated fat	19g (8% total kJ/cals)
Saturated fat	15g (6% total kJ/cals)
P:S ratio	1:3
Cholesterol	200mg
Sodium	1482mg
Fibre	50g

NOTE: A soluble fibre supplement containing psyllium (eg, Metamucil™) or wheat dextrin (eg, Benefiber™) will boost cholesterol lowering. Read pack directions for dosage recommendations.

Example daily menu for cholesterol lowering —low in kilojoules (6300kJ/1500 cals)

This menu will suit you if you are below average height, over 50 years of age and less active OR you'd like to lose weight.

Breakfast

1½ cups (50g/1¾oz) wholegrain/high fibre breakfast cereal flakes

1 cup reduced-fat, high calcium milk

1 cup strawberries (or other berries)

Lunch

2 slices mixed grain bread with barley with 4 teaspoons light cholesterol-lowering margarine

45g (1½oz) salmon in springwater, drained (2 slices)

1½ cups mixed salad (including 1 cup dark leaves such as baby spinach)

1 slice baked kumara (orange sweet potato)

(Flavour with lemon juice and zest, dill and parsley)

OR see page 166 for Quickie recipe Mixed Grain Lemon and Dill Salmon Salad Sandwiches)

Dinner

150g (5oz) lean beef

2 teaspoons canola oil

½ cup soy beans

1½ cups mixed vegetables including carrot and Chinese greens (or kale)

(Flavour with fresh garlic, chilli, spring onions (scallions), coriander (cilantro) and a few drops of sesame oil)

OR see page 225 for Quickie recipe Chilli and Garlic Beef and Vegetable Stir-fry

Snacks/dessert

15g/½oz almonds

1 cup fruit salad pieces

1½ cups raw vegetables—carrot, cherry tomato, capsicum (pepper)

200g/7oz low-fat yoghurt

See page 167 for Quickie recipe Indian Yoghurt Dip (Raita)

Drinks: Ensure around 2 litres (1¾ pints) of fluid daily. Include plenty of water and up to 4 cups of tea and 1 espresso coffee (little or no sugar (or use sweetener), with a little reduced-fat milk).

On target nutrition information	
Kilojoules	6276
Calories	1500
Fat	58g (34% total kJ/cals)
Polyunsaturated fat	16g (10% total kJ/cals)
Saturated fat	13g (8% total kJ/cals)
P:S ratio	1:2
Cholesterol	161mg
Sodium	1271mg
Fibre	38g

NOTE: A soluble fibre supplement containing psyllium (eg, Metamucil™) or wheat dextrin (eg, Benefiber™) will boost cholesterol lowering. Read pack directions for dosage recommendations.

Food on the go—work lunches

While most people agree that eating a healthy lunch is important, many people still skip it. 'Too busy' is the main catch-cry of lunch-skippers. But taking a bit of time to eat lunch is critical to maintaining health, controlling weight, boosting energy and concentration levels and simply feeling better overall.

Lunch doesn't need to be a big meal. But you need to choose a food from each group—grains, meat or fish, vegetables and fruit. Of course it's better to make your own lunch because then you know exactly what's in it, but life gets busy and buying your lunch is an inevitable part of modern living. Choose wisely and you can still keep your cholesterol down, look after your heart and keep your waistline in check.

Size matters

A big let-down for many take-out lunch options is the large portions.

- Keep your portions modest. Order smaller options.
- Try to ignore the voice in your head saying you need to finish everything on your plate. This wisdom was timely in the days of food scarcity but is a shortcut to obesity in this age of abundance.

What to look for

Priorities when choosing take-out lunches are to minimise saturated fat and kilojoules (calories) and maximise heart-friendly foods such as vegetables, fruit, whole grains, legumes, nuts and seeds and fish. Anything fried, in pastry or a creamy sauce, or covered in cheese is not a good option. Foods with wholegrain bread, rice, vegetables or salad, and beans are a better choice. Because of the increasing awareness about nutrition and health in the community there are healthier fast food choices becoming available.

Lunches to limit	Healthier lunches	Tips
Foccacia	Wholemeal salad roll	Include salmon for omega-3
Schnitzel sandwich	Chicken breast sandwich	Include plenty of salad
Creamy pasta (eg, carbonara)	Tomato-based pasta sauce	Sauce with vegetables (eg, primavera) or seafood (eg, marinara)
Meat pie/sausage roll	Filled potato with beans or creamed corn and tuna	Skip the cheese and sour cream
Tacos/nachos	Tortilla (eg, burrito) with bean filling	Skip the cheese and sour cream
Fish and chips	Grilled fish and salad	Add lemon juice and a little mayonnaise (good because it's made from healthy oils)
Burger with egg, bacon and cheese	Plain burger (lean is best) with salad or steak sandwich	Skip the bacon, egg and cheese
Indian creamy curry (with coconut)	Tandoori chicken (no skin)	With steamed rice and dahl (lentils)
Thai creamy curry	Stir-fry with vegetables and steamed rice	Seafood stir fry for omega-3 Tofu stir-fry for soy protein
Thai fried spring rolls/curry puffs	Thai beef and vegetable salad	Steamed rice on the side
Crêpe with cheesy filling	Wrap with salad	Include tuna or salmon for omega-3
Doner kebab	Falafel wrap chilli sauce and tabouli	Skip the cheese
Chips and gravy	Sushi rolls or sushi box	Include salmon or tuna for omega-3 Use very little (salty) soy sauce
Quiche (pastry)	Frittata and salad	Vegetable or salmon filling
Creamy soup	Minestrone soup	With wholemeal bread
Spring rolls (fried)	Rice paper rolls	Chilli dipping sauce
Pizza (meat)	Vegetable, bean or seafood	Thin crust is lower in kilojoules Skip the garlic bread
Fried chicken	BBQ chicken (no skin) or Chicken breast fillet burger	With wholemeal bread, corn and peas
Ice cream	Low-fat yoghurt	Small serving
Cake	Fruit salad	

Sodium alert

Take-out foods almost always contain too much salt. Help control this by saying no when asked if you want salt added to your food, as is typical in a sandwich shop for example.

Think about drinks

Water is the best drink, so get used to drinking it.

The kilojoules from sugary drinks can really add up (a 375ml (12½oz) can of soft drink contains up to 48 grams (1½oz) of sugar—that is 12 teaspoons). Stick to water or diet soft drinks to go with your lunch—or a cup of tea or coffee. Consider boosting your vitamins and antioxidants with a small mixed vegetable and fruit juice (try carrot, orange and ginger). Remember fruit juices contain just as many kilojoules (calories) as soft drinks (soda) so small is good, and including vegetable juice helps. For a sweet finish that's good for you, try a small flavoured low-fat milk, skim milkshake or smoothie.

How you can save kilojoules/calories with drink choices

Swap this	for this instead
Regular cola soft drink 375ml (12½oz) 694kJ/166 cals	Diet cola soft drink 375ml (12½oz) 8kJ /2 cals
Fruit juice 250ml (8½oz) 570kJ/136 cals	Half fruit juice, half water 250ml (8½oz) 285kJ/68 cals
Thickshake 440 ml (15oz) 2284 kJ/555 cals	Skim milk-shake 440ml (15oz) 1316kJ/315 cals
Large banana smoothie (low-fat) 650ml (22oz) 1900kJ/454 cals	Small banana smoothie (low-fat) 250ml (8½oz) 730 kJ/174 cals

NOTE: these are average figures and individual products may vary

Café society

Meeting for coffee has become common, and the choice of hot and cold drinks and sweet treats to go with them has exploded. Beware of highly sweetened regular-fat milk drinks with cream on top (hot or cold), and remember there is 10g/½oz of fat per cup of regular fat milk and close to zero in the same amount of skim milk. There are virtually no kilojoules in a cup of black tea or coffee with no sugar (or sweetener instead), and a dash of low-fat milk won't break the kilojoule budget. Resist the high fat cakes, slices biscuits, muffins and donuts on display (often over-sized). If you do decide to treat yourself, go for small portions. Biscotti, almond bread or scones (minus the butter and cream) are lighter café treats.

Eating out—restaurants and cafes

If you eat out occasionally as a special treat you can afford to order whatever takes your fancy and it won't make much difference to your health or your waistline.

However, if like many people eating out is a regular occurrence (several nights a week), the choices you make are more important.

10 tips for frequent diners

- Avoid arriving over-hungry—have a healthy snack such as a small handful of nuts or a low-fat milk or yoghurt to take the edge off your appetite and sharpen your resolve to eat well.
- Exercise portion caution. Restaurant portions are often too big for many of us, so order small. Try a starter size main and limit yourself to two modest courses.
- Ensure you order extra vegetables or salad—standard accompaniments are not usually enough.
- Alcoholic drinks are often larger than a standard drink—limit yourself to 1 or 2.
- Order some water and drink this to quench your thirst and to pace yourself between mouthfuls.
- Try to relax and eat slowly—make time for conversation and give your body time to register you have eaten.
- Skip the bread (unless it is wholegrain and then stop at one plain piece) and avoid butter (ask for unsaturated margarine spread instead). A little olive oil for dipping is fine.
- Avoid deep fried foods, pastry and rich sauces made with butter or cream.
- Ask staff how dishes are prepared and request no butter or cream—ask to have salad dressings on the side and you can serve yourself.
- If you have dessert, choose fruit or gelato, share a dessert, or skip straight to coffee/tea.

International cuisine eating tips

Eating out is often a multi-cultural experience. Choose options that are lower in saturated fat and salt and containing heart-friendly foods.

- Ordering a variety of dishes and sharing is a popular way to enjoy international cuisine but a good way to lose track of how much you've eaten. Serve yourself once only to avoid overeating.
- Order extra vegetables or salad, or make sure at least one dish is based on vegetables.
- Order starter-sized pasta and rice dishes when dining Italian.
- Remember that Asian cuisine is high in sodium.
- Indian food is traditionally cooked in ghee (clarified butter) and high in saturated fat.
- In Indian and Asian cuisines, vegetarian options may be lower in saturated fat as the cuts of meat can be higher in fat.

Italian

Dishes to limit	Healthier options
Garlic bread	Plain bread, bruschetta
Salami antipasto	Tuna/beef carpcaccio (raw, thinly sliced)
Lasagna/parmigiana	Grilled fish and vegetables
Cannelloni	Minestrone soup
Pizza/saltimbocca	Ravioli with tomato sauce
Pasta carbonara (creamy sauce)	Pasta Napolitana (tomato sauce)
Cheese/creamy risotto	Vegetable risotto
Tiramisu	Gelato or biscotti

Chinese

Dishes to limit	Healthier options
Dim sum, spring rolls, prawn toasts, prawn crackers (fried)	Satay sticks, chicken and corn soup, steamed dim sum
Pork and duck	Seafood, chicken and tofu dishes
Sweet and sour, honey, satay, plum sauces	Chilli, curry, braised, Szechwan, barbecue or stir-fry
Omelette, crispy skin chicken	Stir-fry chicken and almonds/cashews
Fried rice/noodles	Steamed rice
Sweet and sour fish	Steamed fish

Thai

Dishes to limit	Healthier options
Soups with coconut milk (eg, tom kha gai)	Hot and sour soups (eg, tom yum)
Spring rolls/curry puffs/money bags	Barbecued octopus, rice paper rolls
Chicken wings (fried)	Satay chicken or tofu sticks (go easy on the sauce), beef/chicken salad
Creamy curries (with coconut milk) eg, green, red massaman, Penang	Stir-fries with garlic, chilli, ginger, basil Dry curries
Fried rice/fried noodles (eg, pad thai, mee grob), coconut rice	Steamed rice
Duck	Seafood, chicken, tofu

Indian

Dishes to limit	Healthier options
Fried samosa, bhajia, pakora, bondas	Tandoori chicken, chicken tikka, fish tikka
Flavoured naan (eg, cheese filled), roti, poori, bhatura, parratha breads, pappadum	Plain naan, chapatti, wholemeal roti
Pilaf/pilau (fried rice)	Steamed rice
Pork	Lentil, chick pea, prawn, chicken, vegetable
Korma, passanda, masala sauces ('wet' curries)	Tandoori or madras, dry curries
Butter chicken, beef curry	Dahl (lentils), potato curry
Tandoori lamb	Tandoori chicken or fish
Lamb biryani	Rogan josh, madras, tikka with prawns, chicken or vegetables
Pork vindaloo	Chilli or pepper chicken

Lebanese

Dishes to limit	Healthier options
Starters in pastry (eg, sambusek, meat cigar/ladies fingers, fatayer)	Dips and Lebanese bread
Fried starters (mezza) eg, chicken wings (jawaneh)	Vine leaves, baked kibbi, stuffed cabbage leaves, broadbeans (foulia)
Sausage (eg, soujouk, makanek)	Tabouleh salad, fatouche salad, pilaf, pickled vegetables (kabeece), green beans in tomato sauce (loubyeh)
Lamb meat balls (eg, kafta)	Meat skewer (shish kebab, shawourma), skewers with prawn (mishwee) or grilled chicken (shishtawook)
Fried eggplant (aubergine), fried cauliflower	Grilled fish, lentil and rice pilaf (mjadra)
Sweet pastries (eg, baklava) and biscuits	Fruit, Turkish delight

Greek

Dishes to limit	Healthier options
Spinach and cheese triangles (spanakopita)	Greek salad, bread and dips, stuffed vine leaves (dolmades)
Egg and cheese pastry (tyropita)	Lima beans (gigandes)
Fried cheese (saganaki, haloumi)	Legumes (fassolia)
Fried whitebait	Grilled (broiled) prawns
Fried calamari	Chargrilled octopus
Meat or eggplant (aubergine) moussaka	Vegetable and meat skewers (souvlaki)
Pork sausage (loukaniko)	Chargrilled lamb, pork or chicken (tis skaras) broiled fish (plaki)
Stuffed eggplant (aubergine) in bechamel sauce (papoutsakia)	Stuffed vegetables (dolmos)
Sweet pastries (loukoumathes), biscuits (kourambiie) and cakes	Fruit or yoghurt or Turkish delight (loukoumi)

Further information

If you want to look into any topic in more detail, these will help you on your way.

Health

Heart health

Australia: www.heartfoundation.com.au
New Zealand: www.nhf.org.nz
USA: www.americanheart.org
UK: www.bhf.org.uk, www.heartuk.org.uk
Europe: www.ehnheart.org
Canada: www.heartandstroke.com

General health

Australia: Commonwealth Department of Health (Australia) www.health.gov.au
New Zealand: Ministry of Health www.moh.govt.nz/moh.nsf
USA: www.hhs.gov

Diabetes

Australia: www.diabetesaustralia.com.au
New Zealand: www.diabetes.org.nz
USA: www.diabetes.org
UK: www.diabetes.org.uk

Find a dietitian

Australia: Dietitians Association of Australia www.daa.asn.au
New Zealand: New Zealand Dietetic Association www.dietitians.org.nz
USA: www.eatright.org
UK: www.bda.uk.com

Nutrition and food

Coffee and caffeine: www.cosic.org
Dairy foods: www.dairyaustralia.com.au
Egg Nutrition Advisory Group www.enag.org.au
Food Standards Australia and New Zealand www.foodstandards.gov.au
Fruit and vegetables: New Zealand campaign for the promotion of vegetables and fruit for health www.5aday.co.nz/homepage.html
Australian vegetables and fruit promotion www.gofor2and5.com.au
Beef and lamb information and cooking tips www.themainmeal.com.au
Information on nuts and health (including recipes) www.nutsforhealth.com.au
Plant sterol-enriched spreads; recipes and information www.logicol.com.au/consumers/default.aspx; www.florapro-activ.com.au
Tea: www.tea.co.uk
Wholegrains: Go Grains www.glnc.org.au
Alcohol: Information site about alcohol from the Department of Health & Ageing www.alcohol.gov.au
Catherine Saxelby, Foodwatch: Expert nutrition advice and tips www.foodwatch.com.au
Nutrition Aust www.nutritionaustralia.org
Nutrition facts and analysis (U.S.A): www.nutritiondata.com/index.html (U.S.A)
Salt and health: www.saltmatters.org
USA food guide: www.mypyramid.gov

Dieting and weight loss

Dietitian, Australia: Dietitians Association of Australia www.daa.asn.au
Dietitian, New Zealand: New Zealand Dietetic Association www.dietitians.org.nz
Energy content of foods and online weight loss support: www.calorieking.com.au
Portion control and weight loss: www.weightwatchers.com.au
Portion sizes: This = that: a life-size photo guide to food serves, by Trudy Williams (2004). Publisher at Wesley Nutrition Centre, PO Box 383 Toowong Australia 4066; Ph +61 (7) 3870 8616 or visit www.foodtalk.com.au

Glycemic index

GI News (free e-newsletter): ginews.blogspot.com
Glycemic Index Database, plus information on GI and GL: www.glycemicindex.com
Glycemic Index Symbol Program: www.gisymbol.com.au

Eat to Beat Cholesterol is not just another diet or cookbook. The authors are very well qualified and have incorporated the most recent evidence about fats and nutrients into this book. It cuts through the clutter of information that can be found in the media. Nicole and Veronica present excellent tips for improving our diet, with easy and tempting recipes for meals that will fit into our busy lifestyles. Whether you have a cholesterol problem now or are interested in preventing heart disease there is something in this book for you.

Sandra Capra AM, PhD, FDAA
Professor of Nutrition and Dietetics
University of Queensland.

Chronic degenerative diseases such as heart disease, stroke and type 2 diabetes have arisen as a result of changes in our environment. Diet and exercise are the most important changes that have affected our health. Nicole Senior and Veronica Cuskelly understand the importance of motivating readers to restore a healthy eating and exercise pattern by providing positive messages and understandable advice. Their recommendations concerning diet are well researched and up to date. They provide insights into the nutritional basis for food selection. They also include important information about the quantities of food which helps readers to avoid the tendency that we all have to over-eat. *Eat to Beat Cholesterol* provides a logical progression from scientific reasons to individual menus and practical recipes. It provides a very useful resource for health conscious members of the public and those who need to deal with cardiovascular risk factors.

Dr David Sullivan,
physician and pathologist, Sydney

All over the world there are people who are living longer, happier and healthier lives than ever before. Everyone seems to agree that you should enjoy having a healthy life style and most of us are doing something about it.

Family history, we are told, has a lot to do with it. Today, it's not only a matter of inheritance; everyone can have a better life. Health, diet and fitness are part of today's way of thinking and we can take advantage of the many nutritionists and food writers who are dedicated to spreading the word about what we eat and why. Nicole Senior, a dietitian committed to good nutrition, and Veronica Cuskelly, an award-winning food writer, have put their clever heads together to share their beliefs, backed up by concrete knowledge that food is the best medicine, aware that when things go wrong there is an urgent cry for help... straight from the heart. For that is what this book is all about, you and your heart.

They get to the heart of the matter explaining the cholesterol connection with timely advice on avoiding heartbreak. The information is sound, easy to understand and best of all it is interesting to read—for me a real page turner, not usual in a book of this nature.

Congratulations all round.

Margaret Fulton OAM

Subject index

Recipe index

First published in 2007. Revised and updated edition published in 2012 by
New Holland Publishers Pty Ltd
London • Sydney • Cape Town • Auckland

The Chandlery Unit 114 50 Westminster Bridge Road London SE1 7QY
1/66 Gibbes Street Chatswood NSW 2067 Australia
Wembley Square First Floor Solan Road Gardens Cape Town 8001 South Africa
218 Lake Road Northcote Auckland New Zealand
www.newhollandpublishers.com

A record of this book is held at the National Library of Australia.

ICBN 9781742572727

Publisher: Fiona Schultz
Publishing director: Lliane Clarke
Designer: Greg Lamont, Tracy Loughlin, Stephanie Foti
Production director: Olga Dementiev
Printer: Toppan Leefung Printing Ltd (China)

10 9 8 7 6 5 4 3 2

Keep up with New Holland Publishers on Facebook and Twitter

http://www.facebook.com/NewHollandPublishers

US $19.99
UK £14.99